marie claire
COOKBOOK

marie claire
COOKBOOK

NIGEL SLATER

PAUL HAMLYN

FOR GLENDA BAILEY

The author would like to thank everyone at Marie Claire,
where most of the material for this book first appeared,
and especially the managing editor, Nancy Roberts.

This edition first published 1992
Paul Hamlyn is an imprint of Reed Consumer Books
Michelin House, 81 Fulham Road, London SW3 6RB
part of Reed International Books Limited

A catalogue record for this book is available from the
British Library

ISBN 0 600 57494 6

Produced by Mandarin Offset
Printed and bound in Malaysia

CONTENTS

INTRODUCTION

Marie Claire launched in Britain in the autumn of 1988. The magazine's food pages were instantly recognized as very different from the norm and light-years away from the fashionable 'pictures-on-plates' that proliferated throughout the restaurants, books and magazines of the time.

The food photography in Marie Claire reflects the philosophy behind the recipes: it is food we want to cook and eat – delicious to look at and simple to prepare. This is food that can be cooked by everyone, cooks and non-cooks alike, from easily accessible ingredients. It is food that excites by its flavour rather than leaving you speechless by its symmetry on the plate.

Marie Claire cooking is based on fresh produce and good quality basic ingredients. The recipes are designed to be prepared without fuss and the results are intended to be served without ceremony. Fresh fish, vegetables and fruit are treated simply, so that the ingredients can speak for themselves. Complicated procedures are not included because the results are rarely worth the trouble. By and large, simply-prepared food tastes better.

The recipes in Marie Claire are written with the intelligent non-cook in mind and are straightforward enough to be understood by those who have no knowledge of cookery whatsoever. The ideas are a mixture of the innovative and the classic, unusual enough to interest the experienced cook without intimidating those who are not.

This is a book of everyday cooking, so most of the dishes featured can be assembled in minutes rather than hours, although several longer recipes are included for the weekend cook. In keeping with healthy modern eating, the book contains a large number of recipes for pasta, fish, vegetables and fruit with somewhat less concentration on red meat. Bearing in mind that there is no such thing as unhealthy food, only an unhealthy diet, there are a good number of indulgent puddings and a smattering of home baking.

The recipes are not intended to be followed slavishly. Use each one as a springboard for your own ideas, adding to each recipe whatever takes your fancy, and dismissing ideas as you wish. If the recipes have a slightly relaxed feel to them then it is quite intentional, as I believe that a relaxed cook is a good cook, and following a set of rigid instructions takes the joy out of cooking. You are only making yourself something to eat, after all.

WORKING WITH MARIE CLAIRE

For years I had marvelled at the utterly beautiful, chic French magazine Marie Claire with its legendary photographs and I was very excited when I heard there was to be a British edition. From the moment I met the magazine's editor, Glenda Bailey, it was clear that Marie Claire's food was going to be very different from the usual women's magazine cookery features.

That Marie Claire's food pages have been such a success is due, I believe, to the extraordinary talent of everyone involved, in particular Marie Claire's managing editor Nancy Roberts and art director Suzanne Sykes, and the photographers whose work appears every month in the magazine. I would like to thank them all. I must thank Janice Anderson for her patience and for pulling together a somewhat chaotic pile of material into such a handsome book. I shall also take this opportunity to include here a personal thank you to Heather Love, Marie Claire's publisher and to Nicky Hughes, Amanda Evans and Jeanette Arnold and to acknowledge the enormous debt I owe to Jenny Greene and to the photographer Michael Boys.

THE PHOTOGRAPHS

A word about the photographs. From its first issue Marie Claire's food photography has been admired by its readers and a source of inspiration to others. The decision to abandon props, those traditional scene-setters, and the avoidance of styling and 'tweeking' the food to look good for the camera, led to a new distinctly natural style, and one that is instantly recognizable as 'Marie Claire'. In 1989 the magazine received the Glenfiddich Visual Award for its photography, the very first time that particular award had been presented.

For the most part the photographs have been taken by Jean-Louis Bloch-Laine in Paris, Kevin Summers in London and James Merrell on location. None of them is a specialist food photographer, who photographs plates of food day in, day out; in fact, far from it – each of them is involved in all manner of assignments, both editorial and advertising. It is their original artistic talent and the collective input of the team at Marie Claire that have made the magazine's food pages such a success, and, I believe, so unmistakably 'Marie Claire'.

Nigel Slater
London 1992

THE STORECUPBOARD

A sensibly stocked storecupboard is the key to effortless daily eating.
It can also provide inspiring alternatives for meals at a moment's notice.

Every storecupboard should contain a few essentials so that you don't have to start every meal from scratch and so that there is always something to fall back on when you haven't been shopping. A few thoughtfully chosen items will be much more use than cupboards full of spur-of-the-moment purchases.

Making a meal with odds and ends from the kitchen cupboard may start out as a rather desperate measure, but with imagination it can result in a delicious celebration of resourcefulness.

BASICS

Salt, sea salt (Maldon for preference) – The soft crystals of salt can be used both in cooking and at the table. Crush them between your fingers or use them in a salt mill.

Peppercorns – Black are the most often used, and should be ground as needed. Keep in a peppermill.

Oils – A couple of olive oils, a light fruity one for general use and a bottle of extra virgin oil for salad dressings and drizzling over vegetables.

LASTING QUALITIES

Dried or canned foods do not keep forever. Canned fish will keep well, even improve, for years, but, curiously, the same fish will only last for 12 months in tomato sauce, due, no doubt, to the acidity of the tomato. Most canned fruits and vegetables are fine for a year or so but never use the contents of a can that is rusty or has a blown appearance.

Expect dried fruits such as raisins and figs to deteriorate after a couple of months. Many stores now mark the packing date on their dried goods, but this doesn't account for the time spent in bulk storage prior to packing in smaller quantities.

A packet of shelled nuts can become stale after as little as a month. Likewise, oils pressed from nuts, especially hazelnut, walnut and pine nut should be used as quickly as possible after opening. Once broached, these last for weeks rather than months.

Opened bottles should be kept in the fridge; any resulting cloudiness in the oil will disappear at room temperature.

Infuriatingly, baking powders and bicarbonate of soda keep for little more than two months before loosing their potency. If you have some aging bicarb on your shelf it will be of more use in a little open pot in the fridge where it will absorb smells and help to keep the interior fresh.

Thickeners such as cornflour, gelatine and arrowroot are safe for up to a year; but flour, surprisingly, is not. Plain flour, which doesn't contain added raising agent will keep for six months, self-raising flour and the grain-enriched granary and wholemeal flours for about half that time.

Sweet foods, such as sugar, jam and treacle will keep for a year or more, but brown sugar and icing sugar may set solid after a month.

Rice, pasta and pulses, those staples of the kitchen cupboard, will come to no harm if left for a year, though I cannot say I have ever kept any such commodity for more than a few weeks. They will, of course, go stale more quickly if not kept in air-tight jars. The quaint and popular cork-topped green glass storage jars are not air-tight; rubber-sealed are better and also cheaper. Open packets encourage dry goods to absorb moisture and go stale.

HERBS AND SPICES

Spices can be a problem. Whole spices stored in an air-tight jar will keep for about six months; ground, however, their flavour and aroma will disappear much more quickly. If you grind your own spice for a recipe you can save any extra for about a fortnight in a small jar. Keep it out of the light, or in brown glass; many kitchen shops sell small ginger-beer-bottle coloured pots with screw caps just for this purpose.

Sniff spices to check their flavour; if they are not strongly scented, they will have lost their taste, too. After six months on the shelf you might just as well put sawdust in your curry.

Dried herbs on the twig such as rosemary, bay and thyme are useful to have around the kitchen. They will keep right the way through the winter if you hang them up in a brown paper bag to keep off any dust. If you buy them ready-crushed in jars, expect them to last no longer than a few months. Dried herbs are really only worth using for dishes that cook long enough to extract all their flavour. Herbs such as basil and dill are too delicate to buy dried.

SAUCES AND CUPBOARD SNACKS

Canned vegetables such as tomatoes, peas and sweetcorn make surprisingly fresh-tasting sauces. Add fresh herbs, including basil, to a tin of crushed tomatoes for an instant sauce for pasta or purée canned peas with yoghurt or fromage frais as an accompaniment for fish or fish cakes. Canned salmon or sardines make excellent fish cakes, since they have a strength of flavour that is missing from the more fiddly fresh fish versions.

Cupboards usually accumulate an assortment of beans, but often not enough to make a soup or hotpot from one variety alone. There is no reason why they should not be mixed in the same dish provided they take roughly the same time to soak and cook. Red kidney beans and black-eyed beans would work well, but large butter beans and diminutive mung beans would be a mismatch as it is impossible to cook the butter beans without the mung beans disintegrating.

Storecupboards can always be raided for snacks. Olives and anchovies, minced together, make a tangy spread for toast, and canned sweetcorn can easily be converted into crisp fritters. Oats and syrup produce favourite flapjacks in minutes.

SOUPS & SNACKS

Influenced by the street food of Europe, soups, sandwiches and
toasts make fast and satisfying snacks for impromptu eating.

Snacks may be fast food, but they are not care-less food. If it is to serve its purpose, a snack must be satisfying, freshly-made with first-class ingredients, easy to hold and to eat and – most important of all – quick to prepare.

SOUPS

A bowl of soup is one of the most welcoming foods imaginable. An unusual black bean and fresh coriander soup is a hearty soup for a winter evening, and very simple to make. Comforting yellow split pea soup always goes down well when the weather is inclement, as would a dark and interesting onion soup laced with champagne.

A favourite summer soup is the French soupe au pistou. It is almost enough for a main dish on a summer's day, thick with white beans and fragrant with freshly pounded basil leaves. Basil reappears in a gently flavoured melon soup that is the perfect thing for lunch in the garden.

SANDWICHES

A bowl of soup and a sandwich is one of the most sustaining meals, and one of the easiest to prepare. Classic sandwiches such as a French sandwich au jambon are difficult to beat, and the more elaborate croque-monsieur has stood the test of time and is as popular today as ever.

The best sandwiches are made with the freshest bread stuffed with first-rate ingredients and eaten as soon as they are made. Filled with classic or contemporary mixtures, sandwiches make the most impromptu and informal of all meals. The traditional sandwich loaf makes a neat-looking sandwich but offers nothing interesting in texture or flavour. Try sultana and walnut breads or granary or wholemeal loaves with whole seeds. Try a nut bread with coleslaw or goat's cheese and fruit bread with farmhouse cheeses such as Wensleydale or Caerphilly.

Olive bread has been making an appearance in the shops lately, and olive oil-rich focaccia. Both are ideal for holding layers of tomatoes and basil or as a base for an open sandwich spread with mascarpone cheese spiked with garlic.

It is only the British who insist on buttering their bread for sandwiches; in fact, butter clashes with such fillings as meat, eggs and cheese. Always use un-salted butter and season it yourself with freshly ground black pepper and salt, if you wish. Mash in chopped herbs, basil or marjoram for tomato sandwiches, and chopped dill for salmon or smoked fish. Try stirring in a little curry paste for chicken sandwiches and anchovy paste for sandwiches containing mushrooms or tuna.

Try lightly seasoned fromage frais or mascarpone cheese. Mash ricotta with snipped marjoram or oregano for cucumber sandwiches, and stir chopped gherkins into mayonnaise for club sandwiches and double deckers. Try savoury spreads such as pesto sauce for tomato sandwiches and tapenade for toasted mozzarella cheese.

Some sandwiches are more substantial than others; a French classic which is substantial enough for lunch is pan bagnat, the hollowed-out loaf filled with roasted peppers, sliced tomato and olives, that is sold everywhere in Provence.

We will probably never perfect the long crisp French baguette in Britain, but there are some passable attempts. Split and filled, they are enough for lunch and make ideal picnic food. It is the crust and not the bread that is the whole point of a baguette, so go for the thinnest and crispest you can find. They can also be toasted. Try them piled with goat's cheese and pickled cabbage for a piquant change from the more usual cheese and ham.

TOAST

The snack is an impromptu meal which can be made and eaten in minutes. Toast, hot and crisp and dripping with butter, is the simplest form of snack. It can be embellished to give bruschetta, the olive oil and garlic toast sometimes made with the addition of tomatoes. Other possible additions are anchovies, goat's cheeses, red pepper butter, and sun-dried tomatoes with a creamy herb cheese.

Try topping your toast with slices of aubergine and melted mozzarella or with scrambled eggs and grilled baby leeks.

Toast need not always be a savoury snack; try rounds cut from an Italian panettone, toasted, and topped with bananas and rum. Apples sliced thinly and dusted with icing sugar make a cheap and accessible topping for panettone, too, especially good when served with thick cream or yoghurt. Pain perdu, the ever-popular sweetened toast, is easy to make. Dip slices of bread into sweetened milk and beaten egg then fry in butter till golden and crisp.

PIZZA

With ready-made bases so widely available, the pizza is now easy to make at home. The classic pizza is the flat, open Pizza alla Napoletana. The round, crisp, savoury bread base is topped with tomato pulp, mozzarella and anchovies, with oregano and olive oil sprinkled over the top before baking. Olives, anchovies, tomatoes and salami feature strongly in Italian pizzas, but Californian pizza is more eclectic, piled high with any flavours that work well together. The base is usually thicker and a greater emphasis is made on onions, both red and golden, and char-grilled vegetables and herbs.

You can make your own pizza base at home in less than an hour. Adding olive oil helps the dough to brown, while rye flour adds character. If you use a stoneground flour you may need to add a little more liquid. Some pizzas need a layer of sauce between the base and the topping. This can be as simple as olive oil and finely chopped garlic, though a thick tomato sauce is traditional.

Put a baking sheet or quarry tile in the oven first to heat as it will help to give the pizza a crisp base. The pizza is cooked in about 20 minutes, when the outside rim and base are crisp and golden.

*Melon and
Basil Soup*

*page 11
Onion Soup
with
Champagne*

ONION SOUP WITH CHAMPAGNE

**455g/1lb onions, finely sliced
110g/4oz butter
dusting of flour
1 litre/1¾ pints stock or water
½ bottle of champagne
16 slices of French bread, toasted
110g/4oz Emmental cheese,
grated**

Place the onions and the butter in a
deep pan, cover with greaseproof
paper and a lid and soften over a low
heat for about half an hour. Stir occasionally so that the onions don't burn.
When they are golden, sprinkle over a
light dusting of flour, then stir and pour
over the stock and champagne. Simmer
gently for 20 minutes.

Preheat the oven to Gas Mark 5
(190°C, 375°F). Place a few slices of the
toasted French bread in an oven-proof
casserole and cover with some of the
onions from the soup and some of the
grated cheese.

Continue building up layers of bread,
onions and cheese. Pour over the liquid.
Place in the oven for 20 minutes until the
cheese topping is brown and crisp.
Serves 4

MELON AND BASIL SOUP

Ripe melons, with their heady scent, are
perfect for summer eating, simple to
prepare and sweetly refreshing. In
Lynda Brown's book *The Cook's Garden* (Century, 1990), they are made into
this soup, peppered with basil leaves.

**15g/½oz basil leaves,
stripped from their stalks
½tsp sugar
1 small, ripe melon
about 140-240ml/5-8fl oz mineral
water
about 140ml/¼ pint Greek
yoghurt, or plain yoghurt and
cream mixed
2-4tbsp sweet rich wine
(optional)**

Chop, then pound the basil to a sludgy
paste with the sugar in a pestle and mortar. Process the basil mixture, melon
flesh and any juice squeezed from the
skins in a blender until smooth, adding
water and yoghurt until the taste and
consistency seem right. Chill thoroughly.
Add the wine (if using), just enough to
sharpen slightly.
Enough for 4.

● Take the cold soup to a picnic in a
Thermos flask.
● Serve it in cups, or hollow out the
melon shells to use as bowls.
● Try this recipe with orange-fleshed
Charentais or Canteloupe varieties of
melon.

FISH SOUP

This soup is so simple that you can take
the ingredients with you on a picnic and
cook them in the open. At this time of
year look out for baby red mullet from
Cornwall and the Mediterranean, clams,
cockles and the tiny, sweet mussels that
are imported. Get the fishmonger to gut
and scale the fish, and buy cleaned mussels as this is not a job you will want to
do in a grassy meadow.

**1kg/2lb fish and shellfish, to
include half clams or cleaned
mussels
3tbsp olive oil
1 onion, finely chopped
2 cloves garlic, peeled and
crushed
455g/1lb tomatoes, roughly
chopped
a glass of dry white wine
salt and freshly ground pepper
a handful of fresh tarragon,
chervil or parsley**

Place the clams or mussels in a little
water in a large saucepan and cook
briefly over a high heat until the shells
open. Remove from the heat. Strain,
leaving any grit at the bottom of the pan,
and reserve the broth. Remove most of
the shellfish from their shells with your
thumbs.

Rinse the pan and pour in the olive oil.
Add the onion and cook until it softens a
little, then add the garlic and tomatoes
and cook for 10 minutes. Pour in the
wine and the reserved shellfish broth
and season with salt and pepper. Chop
and add the fresh herbs. Put in the seafood – add small fish and fillets first and
cook for about 5 minutes, then the shellfish, which will take no more than a
couple more minutes. Eat hot with
bread toasted in the embers of the
picnic fire.
Serves 4.

Fish Soup

SOUPE AU PISTOU

One of the pleasures of summer cooking is using fresh basil to make pistou. This aromatic paste with pine kernels, garlic and olive oil is the Provençal version of Italian pesto and can be made with or without Parmesan cheese. The herb's sweet, peppery flavour and heady aroma is released as you stir the pistou into the broth.

FOR THE PISTOU:
3 cloves garlic
4 stems of fresh basil
2tbsp pine nuts
2tbsp grated Parmesan cheese
2tbsp olive oil
FOR THE BROTH:
olive oil
I leek
I large potato
110g/4oz dried haricot or flageolet beans soaked overnight and simmered until tender for about 1½ hours
1.7 litres/3 pints water
salt and freshly ground pepper
230g/8oz green beans
2 courgettes
110g/4oz shelled broad beans
tomato
parsley

To make the pistou, crush the peeled garlic cloves in a mortar or food processor. Add the fresh basil leaves and the pine nuts and pound or process until you have a thick paste. Stir in the Parmesan, then slowly stir in the olive oil.

For the broth, pour a little olive oil in a thick-bottomed saucepan. Add the cleaned and chopped leek and leave it to soften on a low heat. Meanwhile, scrub the potato, cut it into 1 mm/½ inch cubes and add to the pan. Turn the heat up and throw in the cooked haricot beans and the 1.7 litres/3 pints water. Season with a little salt and simmer, covered with a lid, for 10 minutes.

Soupe au Pistou

Snap the green beans into four pieces. Chop the courgettes into small dice, and add with the green beans and broad beans to the pan. Skin and chop the tomato, add to the broth and simmer for 10 minutes. Season with salt and pepper, and add a handful of chopped parsley. Ladle the soup into bowls and stir a tablespoon of pistou into each one. Serves 4.

PIGEON BROTH WITH POT BARLEY

A simple, warming soup that's thickened by barley.

Itbsp dripping or groundnut oil
2 or more pigeon carcasses, including legs
I onion, quartered but unskinned
I stalk celery, chopped
2 carrots, chopped
a few parsley stalks
6tbsp pot or pearl barley
salt and freshly ground pepper

Heat the dripping or oil in a heavy pot. Add the carcasses and legs and leave them to brown, stirring and turning the bones so that they do not burn. Add the onion, celery and carrots, allowing them to brown a little. Pour off any excess oil and add enough water to cover the bones. Add the parsley. Bring to the boil, reduce the heat and allow to simmer for 45 minutes.

Remove from the heat, strain the stock through a colander and return to the pan with the barley. Simmer gently for 45 minutes to an hour, topping up with more water or stock if necessary. Pearl barley will cook more quickly than pot barley because it has had its outer (nutritious) husk removed. Season to taste with salt and pepper. Serve steaming hot with wholemeal bread.
Serves 2-4.

BLACK BEAN AND CORIANDER SOUP

A huge pot of steaming soup, served late on in the proceedings at a party, is always very welcome. Try a hot, pungent broth thick with black beans and onions and serve with hunks of dark rye bread. For large numbers multiply the recipe accordingly, but ease up on the chillies.

255g/9oz black beans, soaked overnight
2 small onions, diced
2 cloves garlic, finely chopped
I fresh chilli, finely chopped
450g/16oz can tomatoes, chopped, and their juice
salt
a handful of coriander leaves
6 tbsp grated cheese, such as farmhouse Cheddar or Cheshire

Put the beans in a large pot and cover with cold water. Bring to the boil, turn down the heat and simmer, with the onions, garlic and chilli, for about 15 minutes until the onions are tender. Pour in the tomatoes and their juice, add a little salt and simmer for about 1¼ hours.

Chop the coriander leaves and mix them with the grated cheese. Place in a bowl and sprinkle into the soup as it is served.
Serves 5 or 6.

*Artichoke
and Green
Olive Pizza*

YELLOW SPLIT PEA SOUP WITH CUMIN

Any dried peas or lentils, such as split green peas or red or brown lentils, make homely winter soups. Add more cumin to this recipe if you wish.

**280g/10oz yellow split peas
1tbsp groundnut oil
1 onion, roughly chopped
2 cloves garlic
1 bay leaf
2tsp cumin seeds, ground
or 2tsp ground cumin
2 stalks of celery
1 carrot
parsley stalks, if available
salt and freshly ground pepper
juice of half a lemon**

Wash the split peas in a sieve under cold running water. Heat the oil in a heavy-based saucepan and add the chopped onion. Fry the onion until it starts to soften, about 5 minutes, then crush the garlic and add it to the pan. Throw in the bay leaf and cumin. Cook over medium heat for 3 minutes until the garlic is cooked and spice absorbed.

Add the split peas and 4 pints of water. Chop the celery and carrot roughly and add to the soup with the parsley stalks if you have some. Season with salt and bring to the boil. Turn the heat down and simmer for about 45 minutes, by which time the peas should be very soft; if not, continue simmering until they are.

Remove the soup from the heat, liquidize in a blender or a food processor, or push through a sieve with a wooden spoon. Season with ground pepper and more salt if needed. This is one occasion where you may need to be generous with the salt. Add the lemon juice and return the puréed soup to the pan, leaving it to simmer for a further 5-10 minutes, then serve hot. Serves 4.

ARTICHOKE AND GREEN OLIVE PIZZA

To my taste, this is the finest pizza of all. For each 30cm/12in pizza you need about 455g/1lb artichokes in oil. Buy them by weight from Italian grocers and delicatessens, who often sell them from a large bowl.

FOR THE BASE:
**3tbsp warm water
2tsp (1 × 7g sachet) dried yeast
3tbsp rye flour
115ml/4fl oz warm water
1 tbsp milk
2tbsp olive oil
½tsp salt
230g/8oz plain flour**
FOR THE TOPPING:
**1 kg/2lb artichokes in oil
lemon juice
green olives
grated Parmesan cheese
chopped leaf parsley, to serve**

For the base, mix the 3tbsp warm water with the yeast and rye flour in a large bowl. Leave in a warm place for about 15 minutes, until it starts to bubble. Stir in the rest of the ingredients. Mix well and form into a ball. Add a little more water or flour if necesssary to make a firm dough. Knead the dough on a floured surface until it is soft and springy to the touch. How long this takes depends on the type of flour you use and the way you knead.

Put the dough in a lightly oiled bowl, cover, and leave in a warm place to rise. When doubled in size, after about 30 minutes, punch the dough down and leave to rise again. The dough makes two large bases (or four small ones). Cut the dough in half and press each piece out to a round 30cm/12in in diameter.

Add a little lemon juice to the artichoke oil, then use some of it to brush the pizza base. Cut the artichokes and their stems in half and lay them on the base. Dot with green olives and dust with grated Parmesan.

Pizza needs a hot oven, Gas Mark 7 (220°C, 425°F). Put a baking sheet or quarry tile in the oven first to heat as it will help to give the pizza a crisp base. The pizza is cooked in about 20 minutes, when the outside rim and base are crisp and golden. It will become hard if it is allowed to brown.

Scatter chopped parsley over the baked pizza before serving.
Makes 2 30cm/12in pizzas (enough for 4 servings).

● *Croûtons.* Melt plenty of butter in a frying pan, add a handful of garlic cloves and cook them gently in the butter till soft. Lift them out with a draining spoon, then fry 1cm/½in cubes of white bread in the garlic-scented butter. When they are golden, drain them on kitchen paper.

● *French Bread Croûtes.* Slice a loaf of French bread into 2cm/¾in rounds. Leave to dry out in a moderate oven (160°C,

325°F, Gas Mark 3) till crisp – about 30 minutes. Drop the croûtes into the soup as you serve it.

● *Focaccia.* Make a version of the Italian bread by brushing a round of pizza dough or a bought base with olive oil, scattering with coarse salt and, if you like, chopped rosemary. Bake until golden and crisp. Break into pieces and serve with the hot soup.

● *Grilled Croûtes.* Top croûtes with grated cheese and grill till golden. Try Cheddar, Gruyère, or a soft blue cheese. Or spread with olive paste and Parmesan cheese, and grill till hot.

● *Pitta Toasts.* Split a pitta bread completely in half. Toast it in a hot oven, inside uppermost. When crisp, brush over a little olive oil, scatter with oregano and grate cheese and return to the oven till melted.

CALIFORNIAN PIZZA

Use your imagination to create harmonious mixtures, in the Californian style. Using the pizza base – which may be home-made (see Artichoke and Green Olive Pizza, page 17) or purchased, perhaps from your local Italian delicatessan – spread it thickly with:

● Tomato sauce, then sun-dried, plum, cherry and pear tomatoes.
● Sautéed red onions with garlic and thyme.
● Pesto, goats' cheese and pine nuts.
● Grilled peppers, aubergines and courgettes with olive paste from a jar and sliced mozzarella.
● Caramelized onions topped with anchovies, capers and black olives.
   Bake in a hot oven Gas Mark 7 (220°C, 425°F), as for Artichoke and Green Olive Pizza.

TOASTED BAGELS WITH GRILLED ONIONS AND GOATS' CHEESE

4 large onions
salt and freshly ground pepper
the leaves from 4 sprigs of thyme
4tbsp olive oil
4 bagels
4 slices of goats' cheese

Peel the onions and cut them into slices about 1cm/½in thick. Heat the grill to medium. Lay the onions on the grill pan, season with salt, pepper and thyme and brush generously with oil. Place them under the grill and cook for about 8 minutes on each side until soft and golden.
   Toast the bagels. Heap on the onions and any juices from the grill pan. Lay a slice of goats' cheese on each onion bagel and flash under the grill for 2 minutes until the cheese starts to melt. Serves 4.

TAPENADE CROSTINI

Tapenade, the salty spread from Provence, is a good stand-by to have in the fridge. Use it on crisp French bread as a snack, or on small pieces of toast with pre-dinner drinks.

60g/2oz anchovy fillets
85g/3oz black olives, stoned
Itbsp capers, drained
Itsp French mustard
Itbsp brandy
olive oil
freshly ground pepper
8 slices of French bread

Rinse the anchovies in water, pat dry, then mash with the olives and capers until smooth. This is quickest done in a food processor; a pestle and mortar is the alternative. Turn the mixture into a small basin; stir in the mustard and the brandy. Pour in 2tbsp of olive oil in a continuous trickle while beating with a wire whisk, as if you were making mayonnaise. Season with a little pepper only; no salt is necessary because of the anchovies. Place in a screw-topped jar in the fridge until needed.
   Sprinkle a little olive oil straight from the bottle over the slices of bread. Toast them under a hot grill until golden, then spread with some of the tapenade and eat hot.
Serves 2 as a snack.

PIZZA BASICS

The base
● The best are crisp and chewy.
● Check out your local Italian grocer for supplies of freshly baked pizza bases. Some supermarkets now stock them, too.
● Buy them lightly smeared with tomato sauce, ready and waiting for your own toppings.
● Vacuum-packed pizza bases are fine, providing a savoury base on which to pile your own ingredients.
● They store well, so keep a few in the cupboard for a fast supper.
● Alternatively, make your own pizza base in half an hour.

The recipe
3tbsp warm water
2tsp (1×7g sachet) dried yeast
3tbsp rye flour
115ml/4fl oz warm water
Itbsp milk
2tbsp olive oil
½tspn salt
230g/8oz plain flour

Mix the 3tbsp water with the yeast and rye flour in a large bowl. Leave in a warm place 15 minutes. Stir in the rest of the ingredients. Mix well and form into a ball. Add more water if necessary to make a firm dough. Knead the dough till soft and springy. Leave to rise in a bowl in a warm place. When

doubled in size (30 minutes), pinch the dough down and leave it to rise again. Cut in half, press each into 2×30cm/12in bases.

The cheese
● Mozzarella is the traditional pizza cheese. The finest is *mozzarella di bufala*, made from buffalo's milk.
● Italian mozzarella has the best flavour. It should taste mild and milky and be very moist.
● Top with tomato sauce, garlic butter, salami, anchovies, olives, oregano, mushrooms.
● Bake pizza in a hot oven (220°C, 425°F, Gas Mark 7) for about 20 minutes.

Californian Pizza

PISSALADIERE

Pissaladière is a Provençal tart, which in its purest form has onions, anchovies and olives on a base of bread dough. Smarter versions include tomatoes, either sliced or puréed, and chopped herbs. Add cheese and you have a pizza. I like it best made with a shortcrust base.

FOR THE SHORTCRUST PASTRY:
230g/8oz plain flour
1tsp salt
170g/6oz cold butter, cut into chunks
FOR THE TOPPING:
2tbsp olive oil
8 medium onions, sliced
2 garlic cloves, sliced
4 tomatoes, skinned, seeded and chopped
freshly ground black pepper
1 small tin anchovies, rinsed
12 black olives, stoned

First, make the shortcrust pastry: put the flour in a large mixing bowl with the salt and add the butter. Rub the flour and the butter together with your fingertips until the mixture resembles fine breadcrumbs. If you have a food processor, you can do this in seconds. Sprinkle water over the mixture and stir until the dough starts to stick. Form the dough into a ball with your hands, then leave it to rest, covered with grease-proof paper or foil, for 15 minutes in the fridge.

For the topping, heat the oil in a large saucepan over a medium heat, add the onions and garlic and cook for about 20 minutes, until the onions turn golden. Stir in the tomatoes, turn up the heat and allow to bubble until almost all of the liquid has evaporated. Season with the pepper.

Preheat the oven to Gas Mark 6 (200°C, 400°F). Roll out the shortcrust pastry to a rough rectangle about 25 × 30cm/10 × 12 in. Spread the onion mixture on the pastry, then place the anchovies and the olives on top. Bake in the oven for 40 minutes. Eat hot. Serves 6.

MUSHROOM ROLLS

Once you have heated the oven, this snack takes about ten minutes to prepare. Don't miss out the lemon juice as it is important for the flavour.

4 white or brown rolls
60g/2oz butter
1 small onion, chopped
280g/10oz mushrooms, sliced
230ml/8fl oz double cream
squeeze of lemon juice
salt and freshly ground pepper

Preheat the oven to Gas Mark 6 (200°C, 400°F). Slice the tops from each of the rolls with a bread knife. Melt the butter in a small pan and brush a little of it inside the rolls and on the lids. Put them in the oven for about 7-10 minutes, until crisp. Meanwhile, fry the onion in the butter until soft, then add the mushrooms and cook until they start to soften. Pour in the double cream and allow to bubble for a couple of minutes until the mixture thickens. Season with the lemon juice and the salt and pepper.

Remove the rolls from the oven and spoon in the creamed mushroom filling. Cover with the roll lids.
Serves 2.

TARTINE AU CHEVRE CHAUD

Preheat the grill. Cut 6 rounds from a baguette and brush a tablespoon of olive oil over both sides of the bread. Lay the slices on a grill pan and grill until golden. Turn the bread over and place a slice of goats' cheese on the untoasted side. Place under the hot grill until the cheese is bubbling. Serve hot.
Enough for 2.

New ideas
- Spread a little pesto from a jar on the bread before adding the cheese.
- Smooth a teaspoon of anchovy paste over the bread, or a spoonful of sharp fruity chutney (gooseberry is particularly good), then cover with the cheese.
- Serve with a salad of crisp salad leaves, such as frisé or red batavia.
- Cut rounds of bread from a wholemeal or sourdough loaf with a biscuit cutter (or the top of a jam jar and a sharp knife) to use instead of the baguette for an added savoury note.
- Spread some chilli purée on buttered wholewheat bread, then add slices of Cheddar cheese, chopped fresh coriander and a sliced tomato. Add a second slice of buttered bread and grill or pan-fry in a little butter until golden.

Pissaladière

Basic Toast

BRUSCHETTA WITH AUBERGINE AND MOZZARELLA

Use any farmhouse loaf for this – wheatmeal bread is good, as are any of the open-textured Italian breads. Any fresh herbs would be interesting perhaps, but chopped parsley with coriander or basil would be particularly good.

I medium aubergine
salt
4 thick slices of bread
I clove garlic
2tbsp virgin olive oil
2 balls of mozzarella cheese
2tbsp roughly chopped fresh herbs

Cut the aubergine into 12 thin slices. Place in a colander in the sink, splash over a little water and sprinkle with salt. Leave for at least half an hour or longer if possible. Salting aubergines is not strictly necessary, although it does prevent the slices soaking up too much oil.

Toast the bread until light golden in colour under a preheated grill. Peel the garlic clove and cut in half. Rub the cut sides of the clove over the slices of toast, then sprinkle with half of the oil.

Cut each mozzarella ball into 8 slices. The cheese should be quite soft, so the slices will be rough in shape. Rinse the aubergines if you have salted them and place 3 slices on each toast, alternating with 3 slices of cheese. Cut the remaining 4 slices of cheese into small pieces and scatter over the toasts.

Mix the remaining olive oil with the chopped herbs and brush over the aubergine and cheese.

Place under a hot grill and cook for 5-7 minutes, until the cheese is melted and golden. Serve hot.
Serves 4 as a snack, or 2 as a main meal with salad.

BASIC TOAST

There are two main types of toast. The first is what I call 'hotel toast', which is thin, crisp and cold (and with which we are not concerned here). There is an art to making the second: thick, hot toast that's crisp outside and soft in the middle – the sort that dribbles butter down your fingers.

Take a loaf that is a few days old but not stale. Two-day-old bread is easier to slice and, once toasted, will keep crisp when the butter is spread. Cut thick slices – anything up to 1cm/½in – and place under a preheated grill. It is important that the bread cooks quickly to achieve a crisp outside and soft centre without drying out. Toasters are fine but may not take thick slices; they also tend to make the toast drier than when grilled.

The toast is done when it is dark golden on both sides; I like it when the edges catch and burn a little, but that is a matter of taste. Spread with butter and eat while hot.

BRUSCHETTA

This is, an Italian garlic toast. Use as a savoury base or as an alternative to garlic bread.

4 slices of bread
I clove garlic
4tbsp virgin olive oil
coarse sea salt

Toast the bread on both sides under a preheated grill until golden. Peel the garlic and cut in half. Rub the cut sides of the clove over the toasted bread.

Dribble the olive oil over the garlic toasts, season with the salt, and serve while hot.
Makes 4 rounds.

Bruschetta with Aubergine and Mozzarella

CROQUE-MONSIEUR

There are as many different versions of this savoury as there are French cheeses. This is the simplest.

Butter 2 slices of brown or white bread and lay a thick slice of Gruyère cheese on one. Lay a large slice of ham on top of the cheese and cover with the other slice of bread. Melt a knob of butter in a frying pan and sauté the sandwich for a couple of minutes on each side, until the bread is golden and the cheese melted. Alternatively, place the sandwich under a preheated grill.

New Ideas
● Spread mustard on the bread before you butter it.
● Add a little crushed garlic to the pan before you fry.
● Substitute a good mature Cheddar for the Gruyère.
● Work left-over pieces of cheese to a paste with a little butter and spread on the bread.
● For a smarter starter cut the bread into rounds with a large biscuit cutter.

ANCHOVY TOASTS

You can either make an anchovy paste with olive oil or an anchovy butter using unsalted butter.

Rinse a tin of anchovy fillets under cold running water. Then mash the fillets with a fork in a small bowl, or use a pestle and mortar, until they become a rough purée. Add a teaspoon of brandy if you have some. Work the purée and a squeeze of lemon juice into 110g/4oz softened butter, mix well and add a grind of black pepper.

Roll the mixture into a sausage shape, wrap in greaseproof paper and refrigerate until you need it. Toast a slice of bread until golden and spread with some of the anchovy butter. This butter keeps well in the freezer.

Pan Bagnat

BRUSCHETTA ALLA POMODORO

This is the classic Italian garlic toast topped with fresh tomatoes.

4 slices white crusty bread
1 clove garlic
2tbsp olive oil
salt and freshly ground pepper
4 ripe tomatoes, roughly chopped

Toast the bread on both sides under a hot grill. Cut the garlic clove in half and rub it over one side of the toasted bread. Dribble over the olive oil and season with salt and pepper. Spoon the tomatoes over and eat while the toast is still hot.
Makes 4.

MUSHROOM CROSTINI

Medium-sized brown cap mushrooms are best for this.

60g/2oz butter
1 clove garlic, peeled and crushed
455g/1lb mushrooms, sliced
1tbsp chopped parsley
salt and freshly ground pepper
12 slices of French bread, 5mm/¼ inch thick

Melt the butter in a small pan. Add the crushed garlic and cook gently until the butter is slightly scented. Don't let the garlic brown, as this would turn it bitter.

Turn up the heat and add the mushrooms. Cook for 5 minutes, then stir in the chopped parsley and season with the salt and pepper.

While the mushrooms are cooking, toast the French bread under a preheated grill. Spoon the cooked mushrooms on to the warm toast and serve immediately.
Serves 4.

PAN BAGNAT

Pan Bagnat is to Provence what the pasty is to Cornwall. It originated as an easily transported parcel of local ingredients taken to work in the fields. Pan Bagnat consists of tomatoes, peppers and anchovies wrapped in an olive-oil drenched loaf, left for a few hours for the flavours to blend. Made in the morning it will be ready for lunch, and is a good way of using up a day-old loaf.

One round flat loaf or a French baguette
115ml/4fl oz virgin olive oil
4tbsp wine vinegar
salt and freshly ground pepper
1 clove garlic, peeled and crushed
2 large tomatoes, thinly sliced
1 medium-sized onion
1 red pepper, seeded and cut into thin strips
12 anchovy fillets
12 black olives (stoned)

Slice the loaf in half horizontally. Sprinkle the oil, vinegar, salt, pepper and garlic on the cut sides. Arrange the tomatoes, onion, pepper, anchovies and olives on one half of the loaf. Place the other half on top and wrap in foil or a clean cloth. Place a weight (such as a bread board) on top and leave for at least 2 hours.

Cut into slices, like a cake.
Serves 2-4.

SUN-DRIED TOMATOES WITH PINE NUTS AND PARSLEY

4tbsp pine nuts, toasted
Itbsp oil from the tomato jar
I clove garlic, very finely chopped
Itbsp chopped parsley
8 halves of sun-dried tomato drained of their oil

Mix the pine nuts with the oil, garlic and parsley. Lay the tomatoes flat in a shallow dish, divide the stuffing between them and serve straight away.

• You'll find sun-dried tomatoes in Italian delicatessens and speciality food shops. Those from branches of Culpeper are particularly good.
• If using dried tomatoes that have not been stored in oil, soak them in cold water for two hours to plump them, then add a tablespoon of olive oil.

Red Pepper and Parsley Toasts

SUN-DRIED TOMATO CROSTINI WITH HERB CREAM CHEESE

These are good for serving with drinks or as a starter.

230g/8oz soft cheese, such as fromage blanc
4tbsp chopped tarragon, parsley and/or basil
salt and freshly ground pepper
12 slices of French bread, 5mm/¼ inch thick
8 sun-dried tomatoes in oil
2tbsp grated Parmesan cheese

Put the soft cheese into a bowl, stir in the chopped herbs and season with the salt and pepper. Leave in the fridge until needed.

Place the French bread slices on the grill pan and brush with oil from the tomato jar. Toast under a hot grill until golden.

Cut each tomato into four strips. Scatter over the toasts, then spoon the herb cream cheese on top. Sprinkle with the Parmesan cheese and return the toasts to the grill. Serve them as soon as they start to bubble with a few crisp salad leaves.
Serves 4.

RED PEPPER AND PARSLEY TOASTS

The best flavour for this spicy butter is achieved by grilling fresh peppers, turning them until they blacken, and then peeling off the skin. It takes ages but is worth it. Otherwise you can speed matters up by using canned red peppers.

I small red chilli, fresh or dried
small handful of fresh parsley
I small can red peppers, drained, or I red pepper, skinned
90g/3oz butter
salt
I French stick sliced into thick rounds

Cut the chilli in half, remove the seeds and the white inner membrane and chop it finely to a purée. If using a dried chilli, crush it to a powder. Chop the parsley finely. Chop the pepper into small pieces until it is almost a purée. In a small basin, cream the butter until soft with a wooden spoon. Stir in the chopped chilli, parsley and pepper. Season with a little salt.

Toast the bread on a barbecue or under a grill and while it is still hot, spread each piece generously with the pepper and parsley butter.
Serves 6.

Sun-dried Tomatoes with Pine Nuts and Parsley

FOCACCIA TOASTS WITH GRILLED LEEKS AND CREAMED EGGS

Use any bread for this – a country-style wheatmeal loaf would be just as good as an olive oil bread such as focaccia. Baby leeks are sweet and delicate in flavour, but spring onions are good cooked this way too. Use crème fraiche or double cream if you prefer a richer taste.

12 baby leeks or spring onions
olive oil for brushing
2 pieces of focaccia bread
30g/1oz butter
4 eggs
salt and freshly ground pepper
2tbsp fromage frais, crème fraiche or double cream

Trim the roots from the leeks or spring onions and place in a grill pan. Brush with olive oil and sprinkle with a little salt. Grill until they are a dark golden brown, turning once. While they are grilling, toast the focaccia bread.

Melt the butter in a small pan over a low heat. Beat the eggs gently with a fork and add the salt and pepper. Pour the eggs into the pan and turn up the heat slightly.

Beat the eggs with a small wire whisk while they are cooking, until they are creamy, slightly runny and almost scrambled – if you cook them for too long they will become dry. Stir in the fromage frais, crème fraiche or double cream.

Lift the grilled leeks on to the toasted focaccia and pour over any remaining olive oil. Spoon the creamed eggs on top of the leeks and serve hot.
Serves 2 as a snack.

BEANS ON TOAST

455g/1lb spicy pork sausages
½tbsp tomato purée
397g/14oz can beans – haricot, flageolet or borlotti
397g/14oz can tomatoes
salt and freshly ground pepper
4 slices of wholemeal bread

Cut the sausages into large pieces, about 2.5cm/1in long. Put them in a heavy bottomed saucepan and fry over a high heat until the cut ends are sealed and the skins are browned. Turn the heat down to medium. Add the tomato purée and cook, stirring, for 2 minutes.

Pour the drained beans and tomatoes into the pan and season with a little salt and a good grinding of black pepper. If you have dried oregano, sprinkle some of this too. Pour in half a can of water and simmer for 15-20 minutes, until the sauce has thickened. If after 20 minutes the sauce is not thick, turn up the heat to reduce it.

Toast the wholemeal bread under a preheated grill, then spoon the beans on top and serve.
Serves 4 as a snack, or 2 as a main meal.

APPLE CROUTES

Traditionally, fruit croûtes are made with generously buttered bread. If you use a sweet bread, such as brioche or panettone, you will find the butter unnecessary and the toast will not become soggy. This is a good way to use brioche that has gone slightly dry. Pears are a good alternative topping – use ripe ones, which take no longer to cook than apples.

4 slices of brioche or panettone, 1cm/½ inch thick
4 small apples (Cox's if possible)
2tbsp cognac
2tbsp pine nuts or raisins, or both
icing sugar to dust

Peel the apples if you wish and slice them thinly. Put them in a small basin and sprinkle over the cognac. Set aside for half an hour, or longer – they will come to no harm if left overnight.

Preheat the grill to very hot. Lay the slices of brioche or panettone on the grill pan, removed from the grill.

Place the apple slices, overlapping, on the bread. Sprinkle on the pine nuts and/or raisins. Dust each toast generously with icing sugar and place under the grill. Cook for 7-10 minutes, until the sugar has caramelized and the apples are golden. Serve hot.
Serves 4.

Apple Croûtes

PAIN PERDU WITH HONEY

You can serve pain perdu with honey as an alternative to sugar, with a spoonful of apple purée or as an accompaniment to poached fruit.

4 slices of brioche or white bread
I egg
140ml/¼ pint milk
2tbsp vanilla sugar
butter for frying
honey to serve

Remove the crusts from the bread and cut it into triangles. Beat the egg in a small basin.

Sweeten the milk with the vanilla sugar. Melt enough butter in a shallow pan to cover the base, and heat until it starts to sizzle.

Dip the bread first into the vanilla-scented milk and then into the egg. Place it gently in the hot butter and fry on both sides until crisp and golden.

Remove the bread from the pan and sprinkle each piece with sugar or dribble with honey.
Serves 4.

HOT BANANA PANETTONE

This pudding takes about 10 minutes to make. Avoid the temptation to butter the toast or sprinkle sugar over the fruit; it just isn't necessary. Try it with thick slices of brioche instead of panettone, if you prefer. You can sprinkle a few drops of rum over, just before the bread is grilled. Serve with live, natural yoghurt – cream would be far too rich.

4 slices of panettone, at least
Icm/½ inch thick
2 bananas
juice of half an orange
yoghurt to serve

Preheat the grill until it is very hot. Put the slices of panettone on the grill pan. Slice the bananas into pieces as thick as 10p coins and lay them, slightly overlapping, on top of the panettone.

Squeeze over the orange juice and place the panettone under the grill, until the banana starts to turn golden brown. Serve hot, with yoghurt.
Serves 4.

SANDWICH AU JAMBON

Cut a long crusty baguette or French stick into 4 equal pieces. Cut each piece lengthways through the middle and almost down to the bottom crust. Ease open and spread generously with an unsalted butter. Fill with thickly cut slices of country ham.

New ideas

● Use thinly sliced Parma or Bayonne ham.
● Add sliced mushrooms, about 3 medium ones per sandwich, which you have fried in a little butter and seasoned with a teaspoon of chopped fresh chives.
● Substitute salami for the ham and add sliced tomatoes with a little French dressing and a teaspoon of shredded fresh basil leaves.
● Cut thick ham into strips and sauté in a frying pan. Add enough soured cream to bind the strips, and scatter with chopped fresh herbs. Spoon into the baguette and eat while still warm.

SANDWICH AUX CRUDITES

Split a baguette as above and fill with one or more of the following:
● Chunks of cucumber stirred into thick soured cream with finely chopped *cornichons* (gherkins)
● Tomatoes, sliced and drizzled with French dressing
● Grated carrots and raisins dressed with a little vinaigrette and seasoned with lemon juice, poppy seeds or toasted cumin seeds
● Shredded carrots dressed with orange juice and fresh, chopped mint
● Peeled and sliced fresh figs laid alongside slices of goats' cheese.

THE   WORLD'S   GREAT   SANDWICHES

● *The B.L.T:* the famous American sandwich layers crisp bacon, lettuce and tomato with plenty of mayonnaise.
● *Pastrami on rye:* thin slices of warm pastrami heaped on rye bread. A reasonable attempt can be made with cold pastrami from an Italian or Jewish deli.
● *Frankfurter Sandwich:* a fairground tradition of a soft roll stuffed with a boiled sausage, smothered in ketchup. Mustard should be added in a line along the frankfurter.

● *Croque-monsieur:* the classic French cheese and ham sandwich, toasted or pan-fried in butter. Must be eaten hot while the cheese still oozes.
● *Cucumber Sandwich:* quintessential English tea fare, made with thin slices of white bread and peeled, thinly sliced cucumber, then cut into triangles. Only the unrefined would forget to remove the crusts.

● *Club Sandwich:* authentic versions are single decker only and consist of layered lettuce, mayonnaise, sliced chicken breast, tomato and crisp bacon sandwiched between toast.

Baguettes filled with Cheese and Herb Pâté (left) and Bayonne Ham and Mushrooms (right)

TAPAS

Tapas are the bite-sized, savoury snacks served with drinks in Spanish bars. Now, in Britain, the tapas bar has become a rival to the wine bar.

In Spain, where tapas provide the necessary nibble between lunch and a late supper, there can be as many as 60 varieties. In simple bars and *tascas*, the offering may be more modest: a few marinated olives, some local goats' cheese, or a slice of serrano ham.

Tapas travel well from bar counter to kitchen table. Crunchy croquettes filled with hot cheese, juicy snails in a garlic and herb butter and chilli-spiced aubergines make tempting first courses,

Olives Stuffed with Pimentos and Almonds

Peeled Prawns Fried with Garlic, Salt and Chilli

snacks or party food. Charred, spiced chicken with red peppers, grilled giant prawns with garlic, and pale green broad beans with chunks of ham can be eaten in larger portions as main courses.

Seafood, particularly shellfish, is a strong feature of a traditional tapas selection.

As simple as a plate of glistening olives or as substantial as grilled paprika-rich sliced *chorizo* sausage, tapas are to share with friends and to eat with the fingers or, at most, a fork.

Basic tapas

• Almonds warmed in a pan and sprinkled with freshly ground sea salt or tossed in a little paprika and served while still warm
• Sliced *chorizo* sausage
• Mountain ham, or *jamón serrano*, thinly sliced and served with bread
• Green olives stuffed with pieces of pimento, anchovies or almonds.

Simple tapas recipes

• Fried black pudding, served hot on bread
• Grilled sardines served with lemon
• Cold cooked prawns served with mayonnaise
• Home-made potato salad with strips of red pepper and blanched green beans
• Hot baked mushrooms with melted garlic butter
• Rings of squid dusted with flour, dipped in beaten egg and fried in hot oil
• Tinned line-caught tuna marinated in olive oil, wine vinegar and chopped onion, and served scattered with capers and finely chopped parsley
• Thick French fries, generously salted and served with home-made tomato sauce or, in more unorthodox style, with garlic mayonnaise
• Tapas served in traditional style – as a lid on a glass of wine. Roll up thinly sliced serrano ham and place on small pieces of country bread.

More adventurous recipes

Crush 455g/1lb green olives lightly with a rolling pin or cut two slits in each one. Pour them into a large kilner jar and sprinkle in 1tbsp coriander seeds. Add 1 sliced orange, 4 sprigs of thyme and then top up the jar with olive oil. Keep the olive in the jar for a week before serving with lemon slices.

● For each person, fry 1 clove of garlic, sliced, and a little salt in 1tbsp olive oil for 1 minute. Add 1 crushed and seeded dried chilli and 110g/4oz peeled prawns. Serve when hot.

● Slices of *chorizo* sandwiched between discs of thin puff pastry and baked in a hot oven till the pastry is light and golden

Tiny Artichokes Boiled with Lemon Slices

Grilled Slices of Fresh Chorizo and Black Pudding, Garnished with Marjoram

Marinated Cooked Mussels

● Grill 5mm/¼in slices of fresh chorizo and black pudding until crisp on the outside but still soft in the middle. Serve on squares of country bread and scatter with fresh marjoram.

● Marinate 12 cooked mussels in 4tbsp olive oil, 1tbsp lemon juice, 1tbsp chopped tinned pimento, ½tbsp chopped onion and 1tbsp chopped Italian parsley. Season and refrigerate overnight. Replace mussels in their shells and serve with lemon wedges.

● Marinate prepared and shelled squid, octopus, scallops and mussels overnight in 2 parts lime juice to 1 part olive oil, and season with coriander seeds. Before serving add chopped tomatoes and red peppers, slices of lime and fresh parsley.

● Cut slits in 8 baby aubergines. Boil in salted water for 10 minutes. Store in a jar for 4 days in 8tbsp olive oil and 285ml/½ pint wine vinegar, with 2 dried chillies and 4 cloves of crushed garlic. Season with black pepper. (Use the marinade for dressing).

● Blanch 455g/1lb broad beans in boiling, salted water for 3-4 minutes. Peel if you have the patience. Fry 110g/4oz diced bacon in 1tbsp olive oil till crisp. Drain, then add the beans, some salt and pepper, and serve when sizzling.

● Boil tiny artichokes in salted water with lemon slices until tender. Drain and serve either warm or cold with a simple vinaigrette or virgin olive oil and plenty of lemon juice. Serve with lemon wedges.

FISH & SHELLFISH

Quick to cook, enticingly versatile and
nutritionally sound, fish and seafood have taken a leading
role in contemporary cooking.

What could be finer than a fresh fish, simply grilled? The most popular current flavours are perfectly suited to fish, whether it is the uncontrived tastes· of the Mediterranean, or the ·powerful and stimulating spice of Thai and South American cooking.

Grilling lends an unmistakable character to summer fish dishes while vivid, strong spices and fresh herbs awaken new flavours. Bright and eclectic – headstrong chillies, pungent green coriander and rich fruity olive oils are the new basics for today's fish cookery.

SUMMER FISH

Summer varieties, like red mullet, imported or Cornish-caught, cry out for the sun-baked flavours of anchovies, olives and capers, while rich, dark fish, such as sardines or swordfish, respond to ripe tomatoes or simple pan-frying with copious quantities of lemon. The only exceptions are sea trout or salmon, whose delicacy demands the soft tones of fennel, or a light mayonnaise with a little dill stirred in.

Look out for summer shellfish: huge prawns, spiky langoustines and plump crayfish. Langoustine, Dublin Bay prawn and scampi are different names for the same creature. So embarrassed have we become by the term scampi (now usually used to describe a pink, fishy pulp trapped inside a vivid orange coating at a pub lunch), that the alternative names have taken its place.

Crayfish, plump little freshwater crustaceans, are much more difficult to find, although the British farmed ones appear in the shops from July onwards. Don't confuse them with crawfish, which are like huge shiny lobsters, and are best boiled and served cold with mayonnaise.

If you can buy shellfish uncooked then grill them as they are; they won't even need a squeeze of lemon. In Britain, most are already cooked but you can

make up for their slight lack of *joie de vivre* with a rustic accompaniment of spring onions, garlic and breadcrumbs.

Raw fish can be transformed into a smart salad with nothing more than a lime or lemon juice-based marinade. Use haddock or any white fish, sliced thinly and left for an hour or more in a dressing of citrus juice, with thinly sliced red or spring onions and shredded peppers. Add olive oil and some shiny black olives if you wish, to produce a mexican-inspired ceviche.

WINTER FISH

In winter we have the joy of choosing from the wide array of shellfish too. Tightly closed clams, blue-black mussels and oysters are on offer from the autumn right through until late spring. Quick cooking is the best way to keep them tasting of the sea, either in steam and served with a herb broth or with cider.

Other fine fish for winter include mackerel and herring, shimmering silver and blue on the fishmonger's slab. Try either fish stuffed with coriander and anchovies. Special occasions may call for a little money to be spent; search out a fishmonger who stocks turbot, a wonderfully flavoursome, firm-textured fish. Try serving it steamed and accompanied by an orange butter sauce.

Storecupboard fish suppers include fishcakes made with sardines from a tin.

CHOOSING FISH

If you have a choice of fishmongers, go for the one whose fish are wet and scattered with crushed ice. Choose firm specimens with glassy stares, bright colours and shining scales (fish that is, not fishmongers). Fish should smell not 'fishy' but of seaweed and salt. If you pass a fishmonger with a queue outside, then join it; there has to be good reason for such popularity.

Never be put off fish because you don't like cleaning it. Any fishmonger worth his salt will do it for you very quickly, and all you'll have to do is give it a quick once over at home.

Most important of all, be open-minded when you go shopping and, rather than sticking to a preconceived idea, choose the fish that looks best and construct your meal around it – most recipes here can be adapted for other, similar fish.

Offer halved lemons, or better still limes, tied up in muslin to stop the pips escaping, in place of the ubiquitous lemon wedges for fish.

Grilled Crayfish with Lime and Coriander

page 34 Oatmeal Fish Cakes (recipe, page 39)

page 35 Steamed Mussels with Tarragon Broth

GRILLED PRAWNS

Grilled spiced prawns are among the best things I have eaten in India, and in this recipe they need only an hour to marinate.

455g/1lb shelled prawns
115ml/4fl oz plain yoghurt
1 medium onion, finely chopped
2 red chilli peppers, chopped
2 cloves garlic, chopped
½tsp chilli powder
juice of 1 lime
salt and freshly ground pepper

Slit the prawns down the back and remove the dark vein. Process the other ingredients into a thick paste and pour it over the prawns. Leave to marinate for at least an hour.

Remove the prawns from the paste and place under a hot grill, cooking for a couple of minutes on each side.

Serve with chapatis and a spiced tomato dish like Tamatar Bhugia (see page 80).

Serves 4.

GRILLED CRAYFISH WITH LIME AND CORIANDER

You can use either crayfish, langoustines or large prawns for this recipe. Most shellfish of this kind is bought ready cooked, but buy it fresh if you can; it will not alter the cooking time.

2tbsp olive oil
8 spring onions, finely chopped
2 cloves garlic
4tbsp fresh white breadcrumbs
8 sprigs coriander
juice of 2 limes
8 crayfish or langoustines

Heat the oil in a pan over a medium heat and throw in the onions. Crush the garlic and add with the breadcrumbs. Cook for 3 minutes. Tear the leaves from the coriander and stir into the mixture, cooking for a further minute. Remove from the heat and stir in the lime juice.

With a heavy knife, cut the crayfish or langoustines in half down their length. Wash them thoroughly. Place each half, shell side down, on a grill pan. Spoon some of the herb mixture on top of each shellfish. Place under the grill and cook for 6 minutes or less, until the breadcrumbs have lightly browned. Serve immediately.

Serves 2 as a starter; double the amounts to make a main course.

GRILLED LANGOUSTINES

Buy uncooked langoustines (Dublin Bay prawns) for this as precooked ones will toughen and lose their sweetness grilled in this way. A main dish will need about eight per person.

With a heavy knife, cut each langoustine in half through the middle from head to tail. Rinse under running water.

Place on a grill pan, shell side down. Grill without oil, salt or pepper, for 4-5 minutes. Serve immediately, with a little salad of mâche, dressed with lemon.

STEAMED MUSSELS WITH TARRAGON BROTH

Quick and simple, these mussels are served with their cooking liquor as a fragrant broth.

900g/2lb mussels
½ bottle dry white wine
a few peppercorns, lightly crushed
bunch of tarragon (about 12 stalks)
1tbsp each, chopped parsley and tarragon

Scrub all the mussels thoroughly. Hold each one firmly, pull hard at the small 'beard' and discard, along with any mussels that float rather than sink, any with damaged shells or any that are not firmly closed. Place them in a steamer basket.

Pour the white wine into the base of a steamer, and add the peppercorns and tarragon; cover and bring to the boil. Place the steamer basket containing the mussels over the simmering wine, cover with a tight-fitting lid and steam the mussels for 4-5 minutes.

Remove the mussels to a large, warmed dish, leaving any still closed a minute or so longer in the steamer until they open. Scatter with the chopped parsley and tarragon.

Strain the tarragon-scented liquor through a fine sieve on to the mussels, then serve.

Serves 2 as a main course.

Grilled Prawns with Tamatar Bhugia (recipe, page 80)

MOULES AU CIDRE

This recipe is adapted from a recipe in *Le Creuset's French Country Kitchen* (£14.99, Ebury Press), a book of traditional recipes from the makers of the famous French cookware.

2kg/4lb cleaned assorted mussels
large whelks and small clams
4 shallots, skinned and chopped
a few parsley stalks
1 sprig fresh thyme
1 bay leaf
a few black peppercorns
285ml/½ pint dry cider
140ml/¼ pint double cream
1tbsp chopped parsley

Put the mussels into a sink of cold water and discard any that float or have broken shells. Pull off the beards with the help of a small, sharp knife. Put the shallots into a large, heavy-based casserole with the herbs, peppercorns and cider. Bring slowly to the boil, then cover and simmer gently for 5 minutes. Add the mussels, whelks and clams and cover. Cook quickly, shaking the pan constantly, until all the mussels have opened – this will take only a matter of minutes. Strain the cooking liquor into a saucepan. Cover the casserole and keep warm.

Boil the liquor rapidly until reduced to just under 140ml/¼ pint. Stir in the cream and heat gently. Taste the seasoning and adjust if necessary. Pour the sauce over the mussels, sprinkle the chopped parsley over and serve the dish at once.
Serves 4.

Moules au Cidre

OATMEAL FISH CAKES

It was Margaret Costa who first reported that canned salmon makes excellent fish cakes. In fact, I think any canned fish is tastier than fresh for these; it also takes a lot less time. Tiny canned petits pois make an instant sauce with yoghurt; the sauce is also good with steamed or pan-fried fish. I coat the fish cakes in fine oatmeal if I have it, fresh breadcrumbs if not.

FOR THE FISH CAKES:
680g/1½lb potatoes
60g/2oz butter
freshly ground pepper
2 cans sardines, drained
juice of half a lemon
1 egg, beaten
fine oatmeal or breadcrumbs
flour for dusting
oil for frying
FOR THE SAUCE:
230g/8oz can petits pois
salt and white pepper
4tbsp thick natural yoghurt

Bring a pan of salted water to the boil. Peel the potatoes, cut them into even-sized pieces and place in the water. Simmer for 15-20 minutes. Drain and place in a large basin. Add the butter and a little pepper and mash with a potato masher. (Don't be tempted at this point to use a food processor or the potato will end up the consistency of wallpaper paste.)

Mash the sardines with a fork and stir into the mashed potato. Squeeze in lemon juice; set aside to cool for 10 minutes.

Place the beaten egg in a shallow bowl. Sprinkle the oatmeal or breadcrumbs on a flat plate; dust your hands with flour. Take a large scoop of the fish cake mix and gently roll it in your hands until it is round and flat, about 7.5 cm/3in in diameter. Carry on until all the mix-

ture has been used. You should have 8 fish cakes.

Dip the fish cakes in the beaten egg and lay them on the plate with the oatmeal. Roll the fish cakes in the oatmeal or breadcrumbs until covered. Set aside on a large plate.

Pour about 4 cm/1½ inches oil into a shallow pan. Heat until a square of bread sizzles in it. Fry fish cakes, four at a time, until golden, 3-4 minutes on each side, turning once.

While they are cooking, make the sauce. Empty the can of peas into a small saucepan with 2tbsp of their liquid. Add a little salt and pepper and simmer, covered, for 2 or 3 minutes, until heated through. Remove from the heat, stir in the yoghurt and either whizz in a food processor for a few seconds or push through a sieve. Eat while hot, with the pea sauce served separately.
Serves 4.

STEAMED TURBOT WITH ORANGE SAUCE

Christian Delteil's L'Arlequin restaurant in Battersea, south London, serves this turbot recipe – plainly cooked with a rich but refreshing orange sauce. Use chilled butter for the sauce, otherwise it will melt and become oily rather than thick.

4 shallots
110g/4oz fennel, chopped
1 leek, sliced
small knob of fresh ginger, sliced
570ml/1 pint cold water
340g/12oz turbot
juice of 2 oranges
2 threads of saffron
1tsp cream
100g/3½oz cold butter, cut into cubes
salt and freshly ground pepper
orange segments and chervil, to garnish

Peel the shallots, slice two and chop the remaining two finely. Place the sliced shallots in a steamer base or saucepan, reserving the finely chopped ones. Add the fennel, leek and ginger. Pour in the cold water and bring to the boil. Set aside to infuse for 15 minutes.

Remove a ladleful (about 115ml/4fl oz) of the stock from the pot and reserve. Bring the pot of fennel stock back to the boil. Place the turbot on the steamer basket over the stock, cover and then steam for 10 minutes.

Place the reserved stock in a shallow pan with the finely chopped shallots and boil until the liquid has reduced to about one-third of its original volume. Pour in the orange juice and saffron. Reduce again over a high heat until there is approximately one-third left. Spoon in the cream and lower the heat. With a metal whisk, mix in a quarter of the chilled butter; the sauce will become opaque. Add the remaining butter in

three lots, whisking thoroughly each time. Season with salt and pepper.

Remove the fish from the steamer with a fish slice and divide between two plates. Spoon the sauce around the pieces of fish and garnish, if you wish, with a few orange segments and a sprig of fresh chervil.
Serves 2.

MACKEREL WITH ANCHOVIES AND CORIANDER

This method keeps the mackerel moist and juicy. If you prefer you can use parsley instead of the coriander. I serve this fish with plain boiled or mashed potatoes.

8 anchovy fillets
small handful of fresh coriander leaves, chopped
1tbsp seed mustard
freshly ground pepper
juice of half a lemon
2 small mackerel, cleaned

Mash together the anchovies, coriander leaves and mustard. Season with the pepper and lemon juice.

Remove the head from each mackerel and open the fish out flat. Remove all the bones and lay the mackerel skin-side down. Spread each with half the anchovy paste. Lay the mackerel in a steamer basket or on a large plate above a saucepan of boiling water. Cover and steam for 4-5 minutes. Remove with a fish slice and serve.
Serves 2.

BAKED FISH WITH FENNEL AND ROSEMARY

Any medium-sized whole fish is suitable for baking; bream, red snapper or sea bass are particularly good.

1 medium whole fish
2 large bulbs fennel
2 medium red onions
4 cloves garlic
1 lime or lemon
1tbsp fennel seeds (optional)
4 small sprigs rosemary
parsley
bay leaf
4tbsp olive oil
green peppercorns
salt and freshly ground pepper

Ask the fishmonger to scale and clean the fish for you. When you get it home, give it another thorough rinse in running cold water and check it is free from any loose scales. Preheat the oven to Gas Mark 5 (190°C, 375°F). Wash and thinly slice the fennel. Place the fish and fennel in a shallow baking dish or roasting tin. Peel and slice the onions and add to the dish.

With the flat blade of a knife, crush the garlic cloves and add them to the fennel and onions with a lime or lemon, peeled and finely sliced. Scatter over the fennel seeds, if you have them, and the sprigs of rosemary. A little parsley and a bay leaf would not go amiss either.

Pour over the olive oil and season with roughly ground pepper, green peppercorns and salt. Bake, covered, for 25 minutes, until the onion and fennel are tender.
Serves 2-3.

Baked Fish with Fennel and Rosemary

PAN-FRIED SKATE

When cooking fish, let clear, simple flavours shine through without the complication of sauces.

2 small wings skate
salt and freshly ground pepper
flour
butter for frying
small handful chopped parsley
lemon juice

Season the skate wings (or fillets of any white fish) with salt and pepper and dust with a little flour.

Heat the butter until it is foaming and hot, add the skate wings and cook until lightly browned. Turn them once and throw in the roughly chopped parsley and a squeeze of lemon juice.

Serve the skate wings with boiled, unpeeled potatoes.
Serves 2.

Salmon Tarragon Carpaccio

SALMON TARRAGON CARPACCIO

4 pieces of salmon cut from the
fillet, 60g/2oz each
I red onion, optional
juice of half a lemon
2tbsp virgin olive oil
2 sprigs tarragon (about 20 leaves)
2 tbsp chopped fresh herbs
salt and freshly ground pepper

Place a drop of the oil into a small clear plastic bag (the type that comes on a roll) and smooth your hand over the outside of the bag to spread the oil.

Slide one of the salmon pieces into the bag. Using a cleaver or a rolling pin, gently bat the fish out until it is about 18cm/7in in diameter and the thickness of a slice of smoked salmon. (Go carefully, or you'll shred it.) You can use two pieces of oiled greaseproof paper, but I

find it easier to see what I'm doing with a plastic bag. Repeat with the other fish pieces, removing them carefully from the bag or paper as they are very delicate. Lay on two chilled plates.

Finely chop the onion, mix with the lemon, remaining oil and all the herbs, finely chopped. Season and taste, adding more salt or pepper as necessary. Dribble the dressing over each plate.

Serve immediately, with tomato salad.
Serves 2 as a first course.

SPICED SALMON

A fast, easy fish dish, which can be done on the barbecue in summer.

2.5cm/I inch piece of fresh ginger
2 shallots, chopped
zest and juice of 2 limes
Itbsp five-spice powder
Itbsp soy sauce
sea salt
4 salmon escalopes

Heat the grill until very hot. Meanwhile, peel the ginger, put into the food processor with the onions. Whizz to a thick paste.

Add the lime zest and juice, five-spice powder and soy sauce to the paste, add salt to taste, and whizz briefly. Brush the salmon with the mixture.

Grill the salmon, turning over once, until evenly cooked.
Serves 4.

Pan-fried Skate

POACHED SALMON WITH FENNEL MAYONNAISE

Salmon is not too expensive by late spring. The novelty of the first wild salmon of the season has worn off, and the price has come down accordingly. I always buy the tailpiece, as my fishmonger usually gives a special price because of the higher ratio of bone to flesh. Salmon makes a good choice for a spring lunch or dinner – it's simple and straightforward but rather special.

I salmon tail piece
FOR THE MAYONNAISE:
Itbsp chopped fennel and its fronds
140ml/5fl oz mayonnaise

Wash the salmon tailpiece, removing any scales. Place the fish in a roasting tin with enough cold water to cover it. Salt the water, using about 15g/½oz to 2.3 litres/4 pints – there is no need to add bay leaves, lemon slices or other aromatics. Bring the water slowly to the boil, watching carefully, and as soon as the water is boiling, remove the roasting tin from the heat and cover it with a lid. Leave the salmon in the water to cool. I have always cooked small pieces of salmon in this way; when preparing a whole salmon, I let it boil for little more than a minute to the pound.

Meanwhile, make the fennel mayonnaise. Add the fennel to the mayonnaise. Leave in a cool place for the fennel to scent the mayonnaise.

Lift the cooled salmon out of its cooking liquor and drain before removing the skin carefully and serving cold with fennel mayonnaise.
Serves 2.

RED MULLET WITH GRILLED TOMATOES AND BLACK OLIVE BUTTER

8 small red mullet, scaled and cleaned
olive oil for brushing fish and tomatoes
FOR THE OLIVE BUTTER:
30g/Ioz anchovy fillets
60g/2oz stoned black olives
Itsp capers
Itsp lemon juice
Itsp mustard
Itsp brandy
2tbsp olive oil
freshly ground black pepper
110g/4oz softened butter

8 small, ripe tomatoes
8 sprigs thyme
salt and freshly ground pepper

Rub the red mullet with the olive oil and put on a grill pan. Set the grill to hot.

Using a blender, food processor or pestle and mortar, mix the anchovy fillets, black olives, capers, lemon juice, mustard and brandy to a smooth purée. Blend in the olive oil and season with the pepper. You will need no salt. Mix it in to the softened butter. Keep in the fridge.

Slice the tomatoes, brush with olive oil, sprinkle with the sprigs of thyme and season, then place them on the grill pan with the fish. Cook under the preheated grill for about 4 minutes on each side. It is not necessary to turn the tomatoes. Serve with dollops of the butter and crusty bread.
Serves 4.

BAKED RED MULLET WITH TOMATOES AND THYME

Sweet, crimson-red mullet from Cornwall, baked with tomatoes and herbs and drizzled with olive oil, is one of the simplest of summer meals. Tell your fishmonger you want fish for baking whole, and ask him to scale and clean it for you. Allow a whole small fish per person; if you buy larger fish, such as bream or grey mullet from the Mediterranean, you'll need to buy at least 230g/8oz per person.

2 red mullet
salt and freshly ground pepper
bay leaf
thyme
olive oil
½ lemon
4 tomatoes
white wine

Preheat the oven to Gas Mark 7 (220°C, 425°F). Wash the fish thoroughly, dry with kitchen paper, and rub inside and out with salt and pepper. Put a bay leaf and a sprig of thyme inside each fish, then place in a large, shallow dish. Dribble olive oil and squeeze half a lemon over both fish and bake in the oven for 10 minutes for large fish, 7 minutes for smaller ones.

Remove the fish from the oven and add the tomatoes cut in half. Season with salt and pepper and scatter with thyme, then pour over a large glass of white wine.

Cook for a further 15 minutes for large fish, 10 for smaller ones. Spoon the juices from the pan over the fish as you serve it.
Serves 2.

Baked Red Mullet with Tomatoes and Thyme

Haddock Ceviche

HADDOCK CEVICHE

**230g/8oz haddock, skinned
juice of 4 limes
I hot red chilli, chopped
I small red or Spanish onion,
sliced
I red pepper, halved, seeded and
thinly sliced
2tbsp olive oil
2tbsp stoned black olives
salt and freshly ground pepper
2 sprigs fresh coriander**

Slice the haddock into pieces, about as thin as a coin, and drop into a deep dish or bowl. Pour the lime juice over the fish, spoon over the chopped chillies, and put in the fridge for at least an hour. Place the sliced onion in a bowl with the red pepper, olive oil, olives and salt and pepper. Gently, so as not to break up the fish, stir the two mixtures together.

Scatter a few coriander leaves over and chill, covered, for a further half hour. Remove the ingredients with a draining spoon and divide between two large plates. Spoon some of the marinade over each plate and serve with leafy salad.
Serves 2 as a first course.

BASIL GARLIC MAYONNAISE

Using a pestle and mortar, crush a large clove of peeled garlic to a soft, smooth paste. Tear about 20 basil leaves into small pieces and mix into the crushed garlic then stir into 285ml/½ pint mayonnaise.

Leave the mayonnaise in the fridge, covered, for at least an hour for the aromatics to permeate.

Serve with grilled prawns, fried squid or use as a dip for raw fennel. It also makes a fine dressing for boiled, peeled new potatoes.

FRIED SQUID

Buy the squid ready cleaned and sliced into 5 mm/¼ inch rings by your fishmonger.

**4 tbsp plain flour
salt and freshly ground pepper
oil for deep frying
455g/1lb squid**

Sprinkle the flour on a large plate and season with salt and pepper. Heat a deep pan, half full of oil, until a square of bread turns golden when dropped in for a few seconds.

Dip the squid pieces in the seasoned flour and drop them, carefully, into the hot oil. Cook them, in 2 or 3 lots, for just 1 minute until they are golden. Drain them on kitchen paper, and serve while very hot with halves of lemon or a basil garlic mayonnaise (see recipe, right).
Serves 2.

SWORDFISH STEAKS WITH SUMMER TOMATO SALSA

If you see fresh swordfish, then snap it up. Most is found, ready cut into steaks, in the freezer cabinets of enterprising fishmongers, and is none the worse for that.

For the salsa, look out for large home-grown tomatoes which are very ripe but still firm. Meals rarely come simpler than this one.

2 large very ripe tomatoes
2 chopped spring onions
2 small fresh chillies
salt
1tbsp chopped fresh coriander
4 swordfish steaks
2tbsp olive oil
wedges of lime to serve

An hour before serving, skin the tomatoes by cutting a cross on the bottom of each with a sharp knife, dipping for a few seconds in boiling water then plunging them into cold water. Peel off the skins, cut the tomatoes in half and scoop out and discard the seeds.

Chop the tomatoes finely, and stir in the onions. Remove the seeds and chop the chillies very finely. Stir into the tomato and onion with the salt and chopped coriander. Leave for half an hour to allow the flavours of the salsa to combine, then brush the swordfish steaks with the oil and place them in a hot, preferably non-stick, frying pan to cook. This won't take long, only about 4 minutes on each side.

Serve the steaks with a little of the tomato salsa on the side, and with wedges of lime.
Serves 4 as a main course with salad.

KIPPER AND CUCUMBER PATE

This fish pâté recipe is based on a spread from Ambrose Heath's book *Good Sandwiches and Picnic Dishes*, published by Faber in 1948 and now, sadly, long out of print.

1 pair of kippers
½ small cucumber (about 110g/4oz)
squeeze of lemon juice
1 spring onion, finely chopped
freshly ground pepper
1tbsp fromage frais (optional)

Put the kippers in a large basin. Pour boiling water over and leave for three or four minutes. Lift out the kippers, drain and throw away the water.

Remove all the bones from the kippers, dropping the flesh into the basin. Grate the unpeeled cucumber into a small bowl, squeeze it to remove some of the water and stir into the kipper, mashing thoroughly with a fork. Add a squeeze or two of lemon juice and the chopped spring onion.

Season with the pepper for a fresh-tasting smoked fish pâté. If you prefer a creamy result, fold in the fromage frais. Chill in the fridge, then serve with wholemeal bread or a salad of mustard and cress.
Serves 2 as a starter or snack.

BEST TIMES FOR FISH AND SHELLFISH

Brill: all year, best January-March.
Carp: October-January.
Clams: all year.
Cockles: all year.
Cod: all year, best September-March.
Coley: best September-February.
Crab: available April-December, but best spring and early summer.
Crayfish: a little available all year.
Dover sole: at its best June-September.

Grey Mullet: July-February.
Haddock: all year, but best May-February.
Hake: best July-April.
Herring: June-February.
John Dory: at its best in the winter, January-March.
Langoustines: available all year.
Lemon Sole: best December-April.
Lobster: best April-September.
Mackerel: November-June, but available all year.

Monkfish: all year.
Mussels: September-March.
Oysters: September-April.
Prawns: May-November.
Red Mullet: June-September.
Salmon: all year, but best April-August.
Scallops: September-March, though available all year round.
Sea Trout: March-July.
Shrimps: all year, but best March-October.
Squid: May-October.
Turbot: August-February.

CHICKEN, GAME & OTHER MEATS

With our new interest in healthy eating, chicken and game are growing in popularity; traditional joints are assigned to special occasions.

Virtually everyone is eating less meat nowadays, with chicken and game more popular than ever. Our butchers and chain stores have responded by offering a more interesting selection of game and types and cuts of poultry than ever before.

CHICKEN

There are two main ways in which birds are reared for the table: free range and intensively farmed. A chicken labelled 'free range' is one that has had access to outdoors during daylight hours, but has had a warm dry place to sleep and escape from cold or wet weather.

Although food is provided, free-range birds are to some extent free to forage for at least some of their own food. As it is a bird's diet that helps make up the flavour of its meat, the supplement of herbs, seeds and grasses gives the meat its character. Birds fed entirely on a corn diet often have a yellow tinge to their flesh. Free-range birds' slower natural growth means that they are a little more expensive as they are generally kept longer before slaughter. Free-range birds are considered by almost everyone to have a finer flavour, more gamey and reminiscent of how chicken 'used to taste'.

Intensively reared birds are not permitted outdoor access and are fed a strictly controlled diet which will inevitably include ingredients to make them grow faster to increase profit. The birds are almost invariably blander in flavour. When buying chicken look for plump breasts and thighs. The heavier looking build of free-range birds is due to their breed, which is one more suited to an outdoor life. Gently press the bird's flesh to make sure it is firm and avoid any that has wet flesh. If the bird is wrapped in plastic, remove it as soon as you get home, cover the bird loosely with greaseproof paper and refrigerate it immediately.

Many people prefer to buy their chicken ready jointed. Although this is a convenient way to buy it, chicken, like all meat, tastes better when it has been cooked on the bone. I find nothing less appetising than the skinless chicken breasts available in supermarkets, since the skin, if cooked crisp, will also add flavour to the finished dish.

GAME BIRDS

Pheasant, partridge, pigeon and wild duck are some of our most popular autumn and winter meats. Fitting in with modern thinking about what we should eat, game birds are virtually fat- and additive-free and best when prepared simply and cooked quickly.

Once the food of the landed gentry and their grumpy gamekeepers, game is no longer tarred with the élitist image. From August onwards butchers, fishmongers and major chain stores will be displaying dressed and oven-ready game birds on their shelves. Hen and cock pheasants, sold singly or as a brace, grouse, wood pigeon, partridge and wild duck are all much more accessible than they were even two or three years ago, though it is worth noting that it is often the fishmonger rather than the butcher who holds the game licence in the high today.

The best birds are the young ones born last spring. Eat them early in the season rather than after Christmas when they may not be so tender. The unmistakable flavour of game, at once clean and rich, is improved and intensified by hanging the birds for several days, but those who prefer a milder flavour should look for farmed varieties and choose quail or pheasant that have been hung for just a short while only.

ROASTING MEATS

The best flavoured meat is that with a good marbling of fat, the thin lines of fat providing succulence. Look out for meat which has been traditionally reared, where the animals have had a 'free-range' existence – the meat has a much deeper richer flavour. Traditionally reared, organically fed meat is available from high quality butchers and a few chain stores.

Roast meats such as legs of lamb and loins of pork make succulent meals for special occasions. Try a leg of lamb spiked with rosemary and thyme and served with a herb jelly, or a roast pork loin with a spicy onion and raisin pickle.

Pork is particularly popular in Chinese cooking and can be included in a rich oyster hotpot. Leftover lamb works well in potato-topped pies such as one with leeks and parsley or a spicy Raj-style cottage pie. Offal can be put to good use in a crisp crusted pie with kidneys and capers.

page 49
*Cashew Nut
and Ginger
Chicken*

CASHEW NUT AND GINGER CHICKEN

Making a paste of onion, chilli, garlic and ginger is an orthodox way of setting the flavour of any dish of this type; adding cream isn't. Leave it out if you wish. You can use yoghurt instead, but add it at the end of the cooking time, and do not allow the sauce to boil.

**2tbsp groundnut oil
8 chicken pieces, breasts, thighs
or drumsticks
I onion
I small fresh chilli pepper
I piece fresh ginger, peeled and
grated
2 cloves garlic, peeled and
crushed
110g/4oz cashew nuts
2tsp ground coriander
2tsp ground turmeric
285ml/½ pint chicken stock or
water
2 large apples, cored and
chopped
4tbsp double cream**

Pour the oil into a heavy-based shallow pan and add 4 of the chicken pieces. Leave them to cook on a high heat until the skin turns crisp and golden; turn each piece once to cook the other side. Remove to a plate and repeat with the remaining chicken pieces.

While they are cooking, peel and coarsely chop the onion. Place it in a blender or food processor with the chilli pepper, fresh ginger, and garlic. Blend until a paste is formed, adding a tablespoon of water if the mixture becomes dry.

Add the paste to the pan in which you cooked the chicken and fry until it colours a little, about 3 minutes, stirring regularly. Add the cashews and spices and fry until the cashews are slightly toasted. Pour in the chicken stock or water and bring to the boil. Turn down

the heat, add the apples and cream and cook for 5 minutes before returning the chicken pieces to the pan. Simmer for 25 minutes, then serve hot with either brown rice or Chinese noodles.
Serves 4 as a main dish.

CHICKEN, MELON AND STEM GINGER SALAD

This is a delicately flavoured light salad, at its best eaten for lunch on a warm summer's day. Poaching is recommended for any chicken to be eaten cold, as it keeps it moist; but there is no reason why cold roast chicken could not be used instead.

**285ml/½pint chicken stock or
water
2 chicken breasts
Itbsp olive oil
Itbsp lemon juice
2 knobs stem ginger in syrup,
finely sliced
2tbsp syrup from the jar
an Ogen or Galia melon,
weighing approximately
680g/1½lb
salt and freshly ground pepper**

Place the chicken stock or water in a shallow pan and bring to the boil. Turn the heat down so that the water is barely moving, put in the chicken breasts, adding water to cover, and cook for 5-6 minutes. Remove the pan from the heat and allow the chicken breasts to cool in the stock to finish the cooking process.

Mix the olive oil, lemon juice, stem ginger and syrup in a basin. Cut the melon in half, scoop out the seeds and discard. With a teaspoon, or a melon-ball scoop, remove the flesh from the melon and add to the dressing. Do this over the dressing bowl so that the melon juice is not lost.

Remove the cooled chicken from the

poaching liquid, skin, and cut each breast into 10 pieces. Add with the salt and pepper to the melon and ginger dressing and leave the mixture in the refrigerator for half an hour.

Remove the chicken and melon pieces from the dressing with a draining spoon and divide them between 4 plates. Spoon a little dressing over each plate and serve with crisp lettuce leaves.
Serves 4 as a light lunch or starter.

GRILLED MARINATED CHICKEN

Grilled chicken is particularly good when marinated before cooking.

Preheat the grill to maximum. Remove the chicken pieces from the chosen marinade (see below) and place skin side down, on the grill pan. Baste lightly. Grill first at full heat for 3 minutes, then at moderate heat for another 6 minutes. Turn the chicken over and repeat until the skin is crisp and the flesh feels firm and springy.

Red Chilli, Garlic and Yoghurt Marinade

Mix together 2 peeled cloves garlic, I tbsp chopped fresh ginger, I tbsp ground cumin, ½tsp ground cardamom, ½tsp ground chilli, and 2tsp paprika in a liquidizer with 140ml/¼ pint natural yoghurt. When smooth, pour it over the chicken and leave for 3 hours.

Muscat Wine and Thyme Marinade

Dice a carrot, a small onion and a stick of celery, and cook in I tbsp of olive oil, until soft, with a few sprigs of thyme and 4 cloves of lightly crushed garlic. Pour in a half-bottle of golden muscat wine such as Essensia or Brown Brothers. The marinade is sufficient for 4 pieces of chicken. Leave the chicken to marinate in a cool place for 3 hours.

*Grilled
Marinated
Chicken*

COQ AU VIN

Thanks to the revival of Paris bistro cooking, we shall be seeing much more of this and other hearty stews.

FOR THE MARINADE:
570ml/I pint red wine
I onion, thinly sliced
I carrot, thinly sliced
I clove garlic, sliced
3tbsp olive oil
Itsp peppercorns
parsley, thyme and bay leaf
FOR THE CASSEROLE:
1.8kg/4lb chicken, jointed into 8 pieces
Itbsp oil
110g/4oz bacon, cut into cubes
110g/4oz button onions, peeled
110g/4oz mushrooms, quartered
flour for dusting
510ml/18fl oz stock
salt and freshly ground pepper
roughly chopped parsley, for sprinkling

Combine the marinade ingredients in a deep basin and add the chicken pieces. Cover and leave at room temperature to marinate for at least 4 hours.

Lift the chicken pieces from the marinade and dry them with kitchen paper. Put the marinade to one side. Heat the oil in a shallow pan and fry the bacon until well browned, then remove with a draining spoon and set aside. Place the chicken pieces, skin side down, in the hot oil and when golden brown, turn them over and brown the other side. Set aside with the bacon.

Fry the button onions in the hot oil, shaking the pan from time to time. Add the mushrooms, cook until they are golden and then remove both the mushrooms and the onions with a draining spoon and set them aside. Drain off most of the fat from the pan, leaving just a couple of tablespoonfuls for frying.

Remove the carrot and onion from the marinade and fry in the oil over a medium heat until soft but not browned. Dust over a little flour – the mixture will froth and bubble – then stir in the marinade and the stock and season with salt and pepper. Replace the chicken, bacon, onions and mushrooms and simmer over a medium heat for 45 minutes.

Check the seasoning, then remove the chicken with a draining spoon and place in a warm casserole. Turn the heat up under the pan and let the liquid simmer briskly for 3-4 minutes, until it starts to shine and has slightly thickened. Pour the sauce over the chicken and sprinkle with the parsley.
Serves 4.

CHICKEN LIVER AND SOURED CREAM SALAD

The soured cream dressing may also be served hot. Prepare the dressing first, heating it gently for 3 or 4 minutes without boiling, if you would like to serve it hot.

Itbsp oil or butter
455g/Ilb chicken livers
salt and freshly ground pepper
140ml/¼ pint double cream
Itbsp lemon juice
2tsp grain mustard
2 bunches watercress

Heat the oil or butter in a shallow pan until it starts to sizzle. Add the chicken livers, season with salt and pepper and leave for 2-3 minutes until they start to colour. It is important that they brown a little on the outside. Turn over and cook for I minute longer. The outsides will be brown and the insides still pink. Set aside in a covered, warmed dish.

Place the cream in a small basin and sour it by gently whisking in the lemon juice with a small hand whisk or fork. Stir in the mustard. Taste – you may wish to add more mustard. Season with salt and pepper.

Wash the watercress and divide it between 4 plates. Then place hot chicken livers on each plate. Spoon over the soured cream dressing.
Serves 4 as a starter, or 2 as a main course.

WAYS WITH CHICKEN

- Chicken is perhaps the most versatile meat of all; it has the added advantage of being extremely low in fat.
- Chicken steams very well – as the Chinese discovered long ago. Try steaming chicken pieces with lemon (putting lemon grass, root ginger, a small quartered onion and a few peppercorns in the steaming liquid in the bottom of the steamer). When cooked, serve the chicken with brown Basmati rice.

- When grilled, chicken becomes one of the most succulent of all foods, taking on a rich smokiness as the skin turns deep golden under the heat.
- Marinating chicken for several hours before cooking gives it a wonderfully rich flavour and extra succulence.
- Chicken livers are very good value, being amongst the cheapest meats available. Look for them in conveniently sized small tubs in the freezers of supermarkets and butchers.

- Properly thawed, chicken livers may be sautéed quickly in butter and are particularly suitable for scattering over a plate of salad leaves.

GRILLED CHICKEN WITH COCONUT AND CORIANDER

FOR THE MARINADE:
60g/2oz creamed coconut
4tbsp groundnut oil
1tsp chilli powder
2 cloves garlic, finely chopped
salt and freshly ground pepper
8 chicken thighs
FOR THE SAUCE:
60g/2oz creamed coconut
1 small onion, finely chopped
2tbsp groundnut oil
2 cloves garlic, finely sliced
2 fresh chillies, seeded and chopped
salt and freshly ground pepper
1tbsp chopped fresh coriander leaves

First make the coconut milk for the marinade, by dissolving the creamed coconut in 230ml/8fl oz boiling water. Then mix it with the oil, chilli and garlic, and season with salt and pepper. Lay the chicken in a shallow dish and pour the marinade over. Set aside in a cool place for a couple of hours, turning the chicken from time to time.

For the sauce, make the coconut milk in the same way as for the marinade. Fry the onion in the oil until soft, then add the garlic and cook for a minute or two longer. Stir in the chillies, fry briefly, then pour in the coconut milk and season with salt and pepper. Bring slowly to the boil, stirring continuously, and simmer gently for about 4 minutes, until the sauce thickens slightly. Stir in the chopped coriander.

Remove the chicken from the marinade, then grill on a barbecue over a medium heat (or cook under a domestic grill) until the juices run clear. Serve the chicken with some of the hot coconut sauce on the side.
Serves 4.

CHICKEN KEBABS WITH YELLOW SPLIT PEAS AND CASHEW NUTS

1.8kg/4lb free range chicken
115ml/4fl oz soy sauce
115ml/4fl oz saké
3tbsp dry sherry
2tbsp honey
1 clove garlic, crushed
bay-leaf, parsley and an onion for stock
black peppercorns and salt
230g/8oz dried yellow split peas
140g/5oz cashew nuts

Remove the meat from the chicken carcass and cut into pieces about 5cm/2in square. Small cubes may look neater but the meat dries out too quickly. Put the bones aside. Thread the chicken on to skewers and place them close together in a shallow-sided dish. In a small saucepan, mix the soy, saké and sherry with the honey and the crushed garlic, bring to the boil and pour over the chicken pieces. Leave to marinate for at least half an hour; it will come to no harm if covered and left overnight in the fridge.

Put the chicken bones in a large saucepan and cover with cold water. Add the bay-leaf, some parsley stalks if you have them and an unpeeled onion cut in half. Add half a dozen peppercorns, bring to the boil, lower the heat and simmer for about 20 minutes.

Drain the chicken stock and discard the bones. Pour the stock back into the saucepan, season with salt and add the yellow split peas, bring to the boil and cook for 25 minutes until tender but not mushy. They should have a nuttiness about them and retain some bite. Drain and leave to cool.

About 15 minutes before you are ready to cook the kebabs, place the cashews in a hot, non-stick frying pan and fry them over a high heat until they start to turn golden and the kitchen is

filled with a warm nutty smell. Alternatively, heat them in a pan with 1tbsp oil. Add the cooked split peas and season with salt and pepper. When heated through fully, place a lid on the pan and leave on the side of the cooker or the barbecue while you cook the kebabs.

Place the chicken kebabs under the grill or on the barbecue. Brush them with any spare marinade and cook for 6-7 minutes on each side until the outside is glossy and crisp. Serve hot, with the split peas and cashew nuts.
Serves 6.

Chicken Kebabs with Yellow Split Peas and Cashew Nuts

Roast
Pheasant

CHICKEN LIVERS WITH GRAPES AND WALNUT OIL

455g/1lb chicken livers
large knob of butter
2 handfuls red salad leaves
salt and freshly ground pepper
2tsp balsamic vinegar
1tbsp sherry or red wine
vinegar
2tbsp walnut oil
2tbsp olive oil
110g/4oz grapes, halved and
seeded if you wish

Gently rinse the chicken livers, removing any of the slightly greenish bitter parts. Dry them thoroughly with a paper towel.

Melt the butter in a frying pan and when it sizzles and lots of little bubbles appear, tip in the livers. Fry them, shaking occasionally (stirring would break the delicate flesh), for 2-3 minutes. Meanwhile, rinse and shake dry the salad leaves – radicchio, oak leaf, red batavia or what have you (avoid the fashionable but tasteless red lollo). Divide between 4 plates.

Dissolve the salt in the vinegars in a small basin and stir in the oils. Season with the pepper. Remove the livers from the pan with a draining spoon – they should be brown and slightly caramelized on the outside and pink within – and tip them over the leaves.

Pour the dressing into the pan with the grapes, let it heat through quickly without boiling and then spoon over the livers and leaves.

Serve with brown rice.
Serves 4 as a first course.

ROAST PHEASANT WITH MUSHROOM GRAVY

The flavour of young pheasant is akin to a free-range chicken; it only really becomes gamey when hung for a week or so. Look out for it from 1 October until 1 February. Follow tradition by roasting the younger birds and casseroling older ones. Pheasant is the most common of all game birds and one of the best to choose if you are planning a dish more elaborate than a simple roast. A pheasant is enough for two, and the hen birds are generally plumper.

about 6 vine leaves
4 rashers unsmoked bacon
1 pheasant
110g/4oz small mushrooms
1 glass red wine
salt and freshly ground pepper

Preheat the oven to Gas Mark 5 (190°C, 375°F). Wash and dry the vine leaves to cover the bird and retain moisture while cooking. Wrap the bacon and vine leaves over the breast and set the pheasant in a roasting tin. It makes little difference whether you put the bacon or the vine leaves over first. If you choose to put the vine leaves next to the breast and you are using preserved leaves, make sure you have soaked them thoroughly to remove the brine. Secure with string.

Roast the pheasant for 35 minutes, then snip the string and remove the bacon and leaves. Roast for a further 10 minutes, or 15 minutes if the bird is large, then lift the bird from the roasting tin and set on a warm plate. Place the roasting tin over a moderate heat and add the mushrooms. Pour in the red wine and allow to bubble while you scrape up every bit of crusty sediment from the tin with a wooden spatula. These concentrated juices and crispy bits are the heart of any sauce, so don't

leave them behind on the sides of the roasting tin.

Allow the gravy to simmer for 3-4 minutes, then season with the salt and pepper and pour into a sauceboat as an accompaniment to the pheasant.

Serve with an oak leaf lettuce salad. Serves 4.

Mushroom
Gravy

SAUTEED PARTRIDGE WITH SPICED DAMSONS

Partridge comes into season on 1 September and is good right until the New Year. It has been my Christmas roast for three years running and is a delicious alternative to turkey.

Faced with the choice of red- or grey-legged birds, go for the latter; they are generally considered to have a more delicate flavour.

Allow one bird per person and cover with a little fat before roasting in a hot oven. Make sure your bird comes complete with its liver; this is a delicacy and should be roasted inside the bird.

Partridge is even quicker to sauté than chicken and takes about 15 minutes to roast. Plums and berries seasoned with coriander and a spoonful of honey make a piquant accompaniment.

4 partridge
salt and freshly ground pepper
large knob of butter
1tbsp oil
280g/10oz damsons or small plums
230ml/8fl oz red wine
1 stick cinnamon
1tsp allspice berries
½tsp ground coriander
1tbsp honey

Cut the partridge in half lengthways with a large, sharp knife. Season the birds on both sides with the salt and pepper. Heat the butter and the oil in a sauté or heavy-bottomed frying pan. When it starts to bubble, add the partridge and sauté until golden on both sides.

Meanwhile, place the damsons or plums in a small saucepan with the wine, spices and honey, and bring slowly to the boil. Turn down the heat and simmer until the fruit is just starting to burst its skins, then remove from the heat and set aside. Lift the damsons from the pan

with a draining spoon, pour the spiced wine over the partridge and simmer gently for 15 minutes. Return the damsons to the partridge pan and simmer for a further 5 minutes.

Remove the partridge and the fruit with a draining spoon and place on a warm serving plate. Turn up the heat under the pan and reduce the wine until it starts to turn slightly syrupy; this will take 2-5 minutes depending on the quantity of juice from the fruit. Spoon the wine over the partridge.

Serve with chicory salad and bulgar wheat pilaff.
Serves 4.

WILD DUCK AND BAKED ORANGES

In season from 1 September to 31 January, wild duck leads an energetic life and is therefore leaner than the more fatty farmyard ducks available both fresh and frozen in the supermarket. Mallard is the most popular, although you will also come across widgeon and teal. Wild duck does not benefit from sweet accompaniments; it is far better to team it with grain, rice and grilled or pan-fried pears, or roast it with peeled and baked whole oranges.

60g/2oz wholewheat (from health food shops)
2 small onions, skinned and chopped
30g/1oz butter
60g/2oz long grain brown rice
1 bay leaf
60g/2oz wild rice
salt and freshly ground pepper
2 wild duck
1 orange, halved
knob of butter
4 oranges, peel and pith removed

Put the wholewheat into a sieve and wash the grains under cold running

water until the water runs clear. Soften the onion in the butter over a gentle heat. Add the wholewheat, the brown rice and the bay leaf and cover with water. Bring to the boil and simmer for 50-60 minutes, until the grains are plump and tender, then drain.

Rinse the wild rice. Bring 570ml/1 pint of water to the boil, salt it and add the wild rice. Cook over a gentle heat for 30 minutes, by which time the rice should still be a little chewy. Pour into a colander and set aside to drain.

Preheat the oven to Gas Mark 8 (230°C, 450°F). Season the duck, inside and out, with salt and pepper. Stuff the halved orange inside, add the walnut-sized knob of butter and put the duck in a roasting tin. Put the whole oranges round the bird, then roast in the oven for 15 minutes to 455g/1lb. The average mallard takes about half an hour.

Remove the duck from the roasting tin and set on a board to carve. Mix the grains and rices together and add to the tin. Return to the oven for 5 minutes to heat through and soak up the juices. Carve the duck and serve with the hot rice and baked oranges.

Serve with watercress salad.
Serves 4.

Wild Duck and Baked Oranges

FIVE-MINUTE PIGEON

Wood pigeon is in season all year but makes the best eating during summer and autumn. When buying, look for pigeons with light-coloured flesh, and avoid any very dark red ones as they may be bitter. At all costs avoid the reddy-brown cling-wrapped grenades at the bottom of your butcher's freezer; they are usually bitter and impregnable. Pigeon needs just a few minutes in the oven but is probably far better grilled. Use a little butter, sprinkled with a few juniper berries and lemon, to baste the grilled bird.

Pigeon breasts are the most prized cut of the bird (frankly, there's not a lot else). Use red leaves such as oak leaf lettuce, bitter radicchio and red batavia to make a base for the breasts and add a lemony thyme dressing.

breasts from 4 wood pigeons
I wine glass red wine
3tbsp olive oil
6 juniper berries, crushed
freshly ground pepper
leaves from 4 sprigs of thyme
4 handfuls red salad leaves, washed
I lemon, quartered

Put the pigeon breasts in a glass dish. Mix together the wine, oil, juniper berries, pepper and thyme to make a marinade and pour over the pigeon. Leave for an hour at least, longer if convenient.

Heat a dry cast-iron pan or thick-bottomed frying pan till very hot. Remove the pigeon breasts from the marinade and place them in the hot pan. Let them sizzle for a little longer than a minute. Turn them over and cook for a minute longer. The skin will be brown, the inside pink. If pink is not your colour, cook them for an extra minute on each side, but no longer or they will toughen. Remove the breasts and set aside, then pour 4 spoonfuls of the marinade into the pigeon pan. Turn the heat down slightly.

Scatter the salad leaves over 4 plates. Carve each pigeon into thick slices, divide them among the leaves and spoon over the dressing. Squeeze the lemon quarters over the pigeon before you eat it.
Serves 4.

POT-ROAST PIGEON, WHEAT AND MUSHROOM SALAD

Don't believe everything you read about pigeons being dry. Like all birds, the flesh will stay moist if it's not over-cooked. After 8 minutes of cooking, check to see if the bird is done as you like it: pierce the flesh with the point of a knife to see the juices run; the pinker they are, the more rare the bird will be. Substitute light olive oil for walnut if you prefer.

4tbsp groundnut oil
2 pigeons, dressed
I lemon
salt and freshly ground pepper
3 sprigs thyme
110g/4oz large brown cup mushrooms, roughly chopped
110g/4oz cracked or bulgar wheat
230ml/8fl oz water
2tbsp walnut oil

Preheat the oven to Gas Mark 7 (220°C, 425°F). In a heavy oven-proof pot, heat 1tbsp groundnut oil until it starts to sizzle and add the pigeons. Seal the birds in the oil, just browning a little on the breasts and back for a couple of minutes. Remove the pot from the heat, squeeze over the juice of half the lemon and season with salt and pepper. Add 2 of the sprigs of thyme and the mushrooms to the pot, reserving the remaining thyme and lemon for the dressing.

Cover the pot with a lid and place in the oven for 12-15 minutes. Remove from the oven, lift out the pigeons, leaving the mushrooms and juices behind, and place on a plate. Sprinkle the cracked wheat into the pot with the water (or the same amount of stock, if you have it) and stir to moisten. Return the pot to the oven, without the lid, and cook for 8-10 minutes until the liquid has evaporated. The wheat, flecked with mushroom pieces, should be moist but not wet.

While the wheat is cooking, cut slices from the breasts of the birds, reserving the bones for soup. Make the dressing in a small basin by mixing the juice from the remaining lemon half with the rest of the groundnut oil and the walnut oil. Pick off the leaves from the last sprig of thyme and add, with salt and pepper, to the dressing.

Remove the wheat from the oven, spoon on to a large plate or individual plates. Coat the pigeon slices with the lemon dressing and place on top of the wheat. Serve with any remaining dressing served separately.
Serves 4 as a starter, or 2 as a main course.

ROAST GROUSE

The season for grouse is from 12 August to 10 December. Roast the bird, plain and simple, with a generous knob of butter or a handful of raspberries or blueberries. At the end of the season, try a casserole or the superb Alastair Little dish, right.

**salt and freshly ground pepper
juice of ½ lemon
2 young grouse and their livers
4tbsp raspberries
8 rashers of unsmoked bacon
2tbsp cognac**

Preheat the oven to Gas Mark 7 (220°C, 425°F). In a small pot mix the salt, pepper and lemon juice together. Rub it all over and inside the birds. Reserve the livers for later. Spoon the berries inside the grouse and wrap the rashers of bacon around the birds, taking care to cover the breasts. Place the grouse in a roasting tin and roast in the preheated oven for 20 minutes. Remove the bacon and roast for a further 10 minutes. The juices should run pink.

Lift the birds from the roasting tin and set on a carving board. Skim off any excess fat from the juices, place the tin over a medium heat and pour in the cognac and a cupful of water. Mash the reserved livers with a fork and add to the tin. Leave the liquid to bubble gently for a minute or so, stirring and scraping up the crusty bits with a wooden spatula.

Pour the gravy into a sauceboat.

Serve with toasted breadcrumbs, redcurrant jelly, game chips, parsnip chips and bread sauce.
Serves 4.

ALASTAIR LITTLE'S GROUSE WITH LENTILS

This warming, autumnal dish is typical of the inspired but simple cooking to be found at Alastair Little's restaurant in Soho, London.

**1 stick celery
2 carrots, 1 finely diced, 1 chopped
1 leek, the white part finely diced and the green coarsely chopped
110g/4oz puy lentils
110g/4oz bacon, cut into 1cm/½ inch strips
2 young grouse
oil for sprinkling
salt and freshly ground pepper
1 bayleaf
2 glasses red wine
2tsp arrowroot or potato flour**

Preheat the oven to its hottest setting. Finely dice half the celery. Place it with the finely diced carrot, the white part of the leek, the lentils and bacon in a saucepan and pour in water to cover. Bring to the boil and simmer 30 minutes.

Place the grouse in a roasting tin – they should be a fairly tight fit – and sprinkle with a little oil and salt and pepper. Cover with butter papers and roast for 20 minutes, turning them over as often as you remember. When cooked, the breast will give slightly, becoming firmer as the birds approach overcooking. Remove from the oven and set aside for the juices to seal. After 5 minutes remove the legs and breasts with a sharp knife and keep to one side on a hot plate.

Coarsely chop up the remaining half of the celery and place in a deep frying pan with the chopped carrot, leek greens and bay leaf. Add the bones from the grouse and sauté over a high heat for 2 minutes. Add the wine and boil for 2 minutes, then turn down the heat and simmer gently for 15 minutes. Sieve, pressing hard with a wooden spoon to extract all the juices. There should be about 285ml/½ pint.

Slake the arrowroot or potato flour in a little water. Warm the sauce in a small pan and check the seasoning, adding salt or pepper if necessary. Add the arrowroot, stirring until it thickens a little.

Return the breasts and legs of grouse to the roasting tin, cover with butter papers and warm through in a low oven for 5 minutes. Place a mound of the lentil mixture in the middle of each plate, surround with the pieces of grouse and spoon the sauce over them.
Serves 2.

Among accompaniments traditionally served with game are glistening redcurrant and rowan jellies, golden brown toasted breadcrumbs and platefuls of rustling game chips. Less well-known ones include:

● *Creamed Parsley:* place 230g/8oz parsley in enough water to cover and simmer for 2-3 minutes. Drain the parsley then squeeze it dry with your hand and purée in a blender. Pour over 75ml/3fl oz double cream. Season, gently reheat and serve.

● *Parsnip Chips:* peel 1kg/2lb parsnips and cut lengthways into slices 5mm/¼in thick. Dry them thoroughly with kitchen paper – if they are wet they will cause the oil to bubble over. Fry them, half at a time, in a light oil in a deep saucepan for 4-5 minutes, until light brown.

ROAST LOIN OF PORK WITH ONION AND RAISIN PICKLE

Ask your butcher to bone the loin of pork and to roll and tie it up for you. With the current trend towards Continental butchering, more fat is being removed from joints, so make sure the butcher doesn't take off too much if you like crackling on your roast.

Pork is a rich meat, especially with this accompaniment, so I serve it with steamed or boiled potatoes and some lightly cooked spinach.

1.4kg/3lb loin of pork, boned, and tied
salt and freshly ground pepper
onion and raisin pickle (see recipe right)

Preheat the oven to Gas Mark 6 (200°C, 400°F). Season the outside of the pork with the salt and pepper. Place in a roasting tin and cook in the oven for 10 minutes. Turn the heat down to Gas Mark 4 (180°C, 350°F) and leave the pork to roast for 1½ hours, basting the meat with its own juices 3 or 4 times during cooking.

Thirty minutes before the pork is due to be ready, remove the roasting tin from the oven, baste the joint as before, and spoon the onion and raisin pickle round the meat. Return the tin to the oven for its final half hour. The pork is done if the juices run clear when a skewer is pushed into the meat; continue cooking if the juices are still slightly pink. Remove the tin to arrest the cooking process, turn off the oven and leave the door open a little to let out the worst of the heat; then return the tin to the switched-off oven for 15 minutes to allow the pork to rest. Slice quite thickly and serve with the pickle, spooning any pan juices over the slices of pork. Serves 4 with enough over for second helpings.

ONION AND RAISIN PICKLE

This pickle is a good partner for hot or cold roast pork, chicken or baked ham. Scented with orange, it is also well suited to grilled oily fish or trout.

20 shallots
1tbsp sunflower oil
2.5cm/1 Inch piece fresh ginger
1tbsp yellow mustard seeds
4tbsp raisins
1tbsp cider vinegar
2 oranges, Seville if possible
salt and freshly ground pepper

Peel the shallots and cut off the small root at the base. Place them in a shallow pan with the oil. Cook over a high heat for 5-6 minutes until the outsides of the onions start to colour. Peel the ginger with a small sharp knife and cut into matchstick-like shreds.

When the onions start to turn golden on the outside, add the yellow mustard seeds and stir them in. As they start to pop, add the ginger, raisins and cider vinegar.

Preheat the oven to Gas Mark 5 (190°C, 373°F).

While the mixture is heating, grate the rind from the oranges on the medium or coarse side of the grater. Stir into the onion mixture with a little salt and a generous grinding of black pepper, cover with a lid and place in the oven (or spoon it around the meat if you are serving it with the roast pork – see recipe below), for 30-35 minutes. Stir the pickle now and again, adding an extra tablespoon of cider vinegar if the mixture becomes dry or sticks to the bottom of the pan. Serve warm or cover and store in a cool place. The pickle will keep for several days in a screw-topped jar in the fridge.

POON'S CRISPY PORK AND OYSTER HOTPOT

One of the best of London's many Chinese restaurants is Poon's, where the house speciality is wind-dried duck, bacon and sausage, but it's well worth trying their delicious hotpots, sweet and sour crispy wontons and monks' vegetables, too.

455g/1lb belly pork
4 cloves garlic
2.5cm/1 inch piece fresh ginger
4 spring onions
2tbsp vegetable oil
8 bamboo shoots
140ml/¼ pint water or stock
1tbsp soy sauce
8 oysters
flour
1 egg
oil for frying
1tbsp cornflour
3tbsp water

Cut the belly pork into 2.5cm/1 inch pieces and grill until crisp.

Crush the garlic cloves, grate the ginger and chop the onions. Heat the oil in a frying pan or wok and add the garlic, ginger and onions. Fry, stirring continually for 2 minutes. Add the pork, bamboo shoots, water or stock and soy, and simmer for 4 minutes.

Meanwhile, shell the oysters, dust them with flour and dip them in the beaten egg. Fry the oysters in hot oil until crisp – about 1 minute.

Mix the cornflour and water, stir into the sauce, then add the fried oysters. Serves 2.

Poon's Crispy Pork and Oyster Hotpot

ROAST LEG OF LAMB WITH THYME, ROSEMARY AND HERB JELLY

1 leg of lamb, about 1.8kg/4lb
6 sprigs of rosemary
6 sprigs of thyme
a little oil
salt and freshly ground pepper
2 or more glasses of white wine
or water
4tbsp apple or herb jelly

If the lamb has been in the fridge re-move it an hour before roasting, to allow it to return to room temperature. Preheat the oven to Gas Mark 7 (220°C, 425°F). Place 2 sprigs of rosemary in a deep roasting tin.

Strip the leaves from the remaining rosemary and the thyme and scatter on a large plate or chopping board. Rub the leg of lamb with a little oil, then roll it in the herbs, so that they stick to the fat. Place the lamb on the rosemary in the roasting tin.

Roast the lamb for 15 minutes – the intense heat will make the fat translu-cent and stop any juices running out of the meat – then season the lamb with a grinding of salt and pepper.

Once the meat is sealed, reduce the oven temperature to Gas Mark 5 (190°C, 375°F). Roast the lamb for 12-15 minutes to the 455g/1lb if you like it dis-tinctly pink and 20 minutes to the 455g/1lb if you prefer it less so. Open the oven door every 20 minutes and baste the lamb by spooning the roasting juices over. This will keep the meat moist during cooking.

To test if the lamb is cooked, stick the point of a small, sharp knife or skewer into the meat: the juices should run clear and be slightly pink. Remove the meat from the oven and allow it to rest in a warm place for 20 minutes or so before carving it, to render it even more succu-lent and delicious.

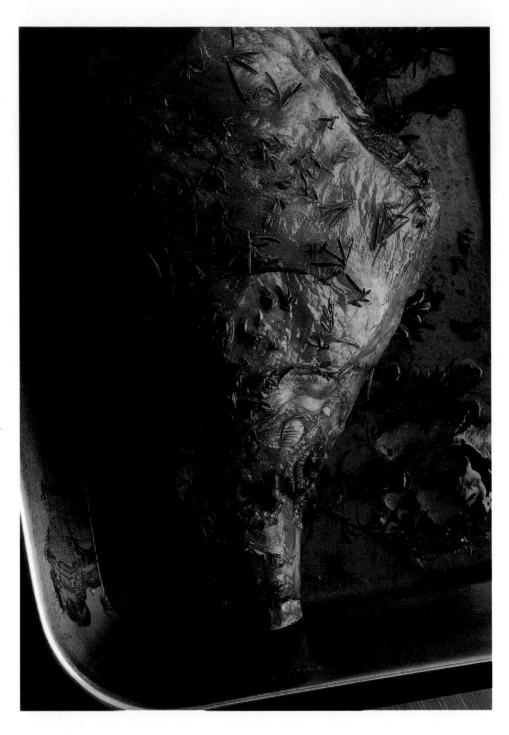

Just before carving, remove the lamb and the rosemary sprigs from the roast-ing tin and place the tin over a medium heat. Add the white wine or water and as it starts to sizzle, scrape up any cara-melized meat juices from the pan with a spoon and stir well. Allow to bubble for a few minutes, then add the apple or herb jelly, stirring until it is dissolved.

Season with a few more fresh herbs if you wish, then pour into a warm jug or sauce-boat.

Carve the roast lamb and pour over the sauce as you serve. Eat with Baked Broad Beans and New Potatoes (see page 71).

Serves 4-6, with enough over for second helpings.

Roast Leg of Lamb with Thyme, Rosemary and Herb Jelly

SPRING LAMB, LEEK AND PARSLEY PIE

Cold, pink roast lamb is exceedingly good, but on days when I have lamb left over from a joint I use it in a hot dish like this. The juices are unthickened so the pie is best served in bowls and eaten with a spoon.

340g/12oz left-over lamb with the bone
455g/1lb leeks
4 medium-sized onions, peeled
6 peppercorns
small handful of roughly chopped parsley
1tbsp chopped rosemary and thyme
455g/1lb old potatoes, peeled
salt and pepper

Place the stripped lamb bone in a large saucepan and cover with water. Add one of the leeks, sliced into fine rings, and one of the onions, halved. Season with the peppercorns and a stalk or two from the parsley. Bring to the boil and simmer gently for 45 minutes.

While the stock is simmering, cut the lamb into bite-sized pieces and lay in the base of a pie dish. Thinly slice the remaining leeks and onions and layer them on the meat. Scatter over the chopped parsley, rosemary and thyme.

Preheat the oven to Gas Mark 6 (200°C, 400°F). Slice the potatoes as thick as a 50p coin. Strain the stock, season it with the salt and pepper and return it to the pan. Blanch the potatoes in the stock for 4-5 minutes, then remove and layer on top of the vegetables and lamb. Carefully ladle over the stock and bake for 45 minutes, until the potato slices turn golden.

Serve hot, in warmed bowls, with crusty bread.

Serves 2 as a main course.

KIDNEYS WITH MUSTARD AND CAPERS IN A FILO PASTRY CRUST

This is lighter than a traditional meat pie, and much quicker to prepare. Instead of capers you could add 2tbsp of halved and seeded grapes.

1 medium onion
2tbsp olive oil
110g/4oz streaky bacon
85g/3oz brown mushrooms, quartered
340g/12oz lambs' kidneys
285ml/½ pint stock
1 wine glass red wine
2tbsp capers, drained
1tbsp dijon mustard
freshly ground pepper and salt
4 sheets filo pastry

Preheat the oven to Gas Mark 7 (220°C, 425°F). Peel the onion, chop finely and place in a shallow pan with 1tbsp oil, then cook over a gentle heat for about 10 minutes until the onion is translucent. Cut the bacon in to 2.5cm/1in pieces and add to the pan; turn up the heat and cook for 3-4 minutes. Add the mushrooms and stir well. Turn the heat down slightly; cover with a lid.

Cut the kidneys in half, remove the fine skin from around the kidney and cut away the sinew. Place the kidneys in a colander and rinse them under cold running water for 5 minutes; drain and add to the pan. Cook for 2 minutes before adding the stock, red wine, capers and mustard. Season with pepper and a little salt. Simmer for 4 minutes, then remove the meat and onion mixture from the pan with a draining spoon and place in a shallow 20.5-23cm/8-9in ovenproof dish.

Turn up the heat and let the sauce remaining in the pan bubble until it is reduced by half. Taste for seasoning and pour the sauce into the dish.

Place the four sheets of filo on top of each other and cut a circle of pastry 2.5cm/1in larger than the diameter of your dish. Brush each of these four large discs of pastry with some of the remaining oil and lay them on top of each other. Brush the edge of the dish with oil and place the pastry on top, pressing firmly down around the edge of the dish to seal.

Place on a baking sheet in the oven and bake for 12-15 minutes until the pastry is golden and crisp; serve with mashed potato and a green salad.
Serves 2 people as a main course.

GRAVY AND PAN JUICES

● *Thin Gravy:* when the roast is cooked remove from the roasting tin to a warm platter. Allow the juices in the tin to cool a little – the fat will rise to the top. Pour off the fat and return the tin to the heat. Pour in a glass or two of wine, scraping at the crusty deposits on the tin with a spatula. Reduce the liquid to a syrup over a high heat, then serve with the roast.

● *Thick Gravy:* pour off all but 3 tbsp fat from the roasting tin. Stir 3 tbsp flour into what is left and cook over a medium heat until thick, stirring continuously. Pour in 350ml/12fl oz stock or water, stirring till the gravy thickens. Season with salt and pepper and serve.

● *Cream Gravy:* remove the roast from the tin. Keep it warm. Tip off almost all of the fat from the roasting tin then stir in 2 tbsp flour. Slowly stir in 230ml/8fl oz milk or single cream, continuing to stir till it thickens. Season with salt and pepper and serve hot.

VEGETABLES

Vegetables are the stars of 1990s cooking. Their bold flavours
and simple treatments celebrate many eclectic influences.

The past few years have seen a dramatic change in our vegetable cookery. What was once an 'slso ran' on the side of the plate is now possibly the most imaginative part of the meal. Basic vegetables like the onion have been used for little more than flavouring a stew or a sauce for rabbit until recently. The onion now finds itself buttered and glistening alongside roast meats, stuffed with a savoury mixture of goat's cheese, sun-dried tomatoes and thyme or sliced and baked in a pastry shell.

Mushrooms are one of the most versatile of all vegetables. Try them sliced and sautéed in butter or piled into a filo pastry croustade and served as a main dish. Button, cup and large flat mushrooms are not the only ones; greengrocers now stock chewy shiitake or soft and velvety oyster mushrooms, too. Use such fancy mushrooms as you would the more usual varieties.

Vegetables associated with the Mediterranean are particularly popular right now. Aubergines, although best known stuffed, can be crisply fried and served with spiced yoghurt, or mashed and used to stuff crisp pastry parcels. Fennel, the aniseed-scented bulb, is also good when baked and stuffed. Try it with walnuts, flat-leaved parsley and lemon as a main dish. White vegetables such as fennel, celeriac and garlic can be whizzed into a fluffy purée as an accompaniment to fish or game.

New treatments for old favourites include baby broad beans baked with cream and new potatoes as an accompaniment for lamb, and parsnips sliced paper-thin, fried in butter and served with a spiced cream sauce. Broccoli, whose rock-hard brilliant green florets have become our most popular vegetable next to frozen peas, takes on a good deal more character when cooked slowly with olive oil and lemon juice and zest.

Grilling adds an aromatic smokiness to vegetables, particularly when grilled over wood. Most vegetables are suitable but aubergines and red peppers undergo a dramatic change when cooked over or

under direct heat, taking on a smoky sweetness. Shredded and mixed with onions and Mediterranean herbs, both can be served on a crisp pastry case for supper or a light lunch. Sweetcorn and mushrooms are fine grilling material, too, especially if you can track down sweetcorn still in its husk. It is important to baste any vegetable continually as it grills if it is to be truly succulent.

Choose your vegetables carefully, avoiding any bruised or damaged ones, and do not be shy about picking out the best or returning a second-rate one to the shop. Vegetables are best stored in a cool place, the salad drawer of the fridge being probably the most suitable place. Any vegetables wrapped in plastic, particularly potatoes, will benefit from being unwrapped and loosely packed in damp newspaper in the bottom of the fridge.

POTATOES

The potato has recently become the most chic of foods. Those in the know offer generous dollops of buttery mash or a creamy gratin, whilst chips, cooked crisp outside and fluffy within, are gracing the smartest menus.

Potatoes fall into two main types, depending on

the season, and are usually either 'earlies' or 'main crop'. I prefer to divide them by texture; 'waxy', which are suitable for salads and gratins, or 'floury', the best for baking, roasting and mashing.

The difference is easy to discover: floury King Edwards will crumble if you try to make a salad with them; attempt a bowl of mash with tiny new Jersey potatoes and you have glue. Good mashed potatoes are made with floury, dry King Edwards or Maris Pipers, which give a fluffy purée. Mash has undergone a transformation in recent years; once served only with sausages, it has become the most requested accompaniment in fashionable restaurants.

For best results you need to boil the potatoes in their skins so that they do not absorb too much water. Drain, then peel them – the skin slides off easily – and leave them in a warm place to dry out a little. Return the potatoes to the pan and add a generous knob of butter. Mash them with a fork or potato masher, then beat them with a wooden spoon to make them fluffy.

Creamy gratins are suddenly up front again. A good gratin is made by layering waxy potatoes with cream and cooking them slowly in the oven. The potato slices on top become crisp and golden, hiding a creamy centre. The best gratins are achieved by rubbing a garlic clove around the inside of a baking dish and buttering it generously, then adding sliced potatoes and cream. Others argue that cheese, particularly Gruyère, is essential. One innovation on this theme comes from Jacqueline Saulnier, till recently my counterpart on the French edition of *Marie Claire*, who layers her potatoes with chopped herbs and crème fraiche and serves the gratin cold, like a terrine.

Baked potatoes are a perennial favourite. Eat them straight from the oven, split open, and smothered with fridge-cold butter, or scoop out the flesh and pile it back into the skin with something fragrant and spicy, such as anchovy and olive paste from a jar, or piquant and creamy, like soft blue cheese.

ASPARAGUS

Allow eight spears per person as a first course. Untie the spears and wash them under running water to remove any grit. The skin towards the stalk ends of fat asparagus may be a little tough, so scrape it away with a potato peeler. The thinner the stem, the less likely it is to need peeling.

Tie the asparagus back into bundles, about twelve in each, using kitchen string. Tie them twice, loosely, once just under the spears and once near the stalk end. This will prevent them moving around and becoming damaged while cooking and make them easy to lift out of the water.

Put enough water in a deep pan to cover two-thirds of the stalks. Add salt and bring to the boil. Lower the bundles of asparagus, stalks first, into the boiling water, standing them upright and loosely packed. Form a piece of tin foil into a dome to cover the top of the pan. This method allows the stalks of the asparagus to cook in the boiling water while the tender tips steam under the dome.

Cook the asparagus for 10-15 minutes. Test them after 10 minutes: they should not resist the point of a sharp knife when inserted at their thickest part. Lift them out of the water and drain carefully on a clean, crumpled tea-towel.

Be confident – eat asparagus with your fingers and don't worry about butter dripping down your chin. I hate finger-bowls but I make sure I always have plenty of napkins – or kitchen paper – for mopping up.

Serve asparagus warm with melted butter, lemon butter or herb cream.

ONION TART

This simple savoury tart is idea as party food or for a light lunch. As the pastry mixture is quite short, allow it to rest in the fridge for at least 15 minutes; it will be easier to roll, and less likely to shrink during cooking. The pastry can be made up to three hours in advance and stored in the fridge, if wrapped in greaseproof paper.

FOR THE PASTRY:
340g/12oz plain flour
170g/6oz butter
2 egg yolks
approx. 2tbsp cold water
FOR THE FILLING:
12 medium onions (use the red variety if you prefer)
110g/4oz butter
2 egg yolks
salt and freshly ground pepper

Sieve the flour into a large bowl, cut the butter into small chunks and rub into the flour with your fingertips until the mixture resembles coarse breadcrumbs. Beat the egg yolks with a fork, then stir them into the flour and butter. Sprinkle over 2tbsp cold water, or more as necessary, to bring the pastry together. Form the pastry into a ball, wrap in greaseproof paper and leave in the refrigerator for 15-20 minutes.

Peel the onions, and slice each from sprout to root into four segments. Melt the butter in a heavy-based pan on a low heat, add the onions and cook, with a lid on, until golden and soft. This will take at least half an hour; stir now and again to stop the onions sticking to the base of the pan. When they are cooked, season with a little salt and black pepper.

Preheat the oven to Gas Mark 6 (200°C, 400°F). Remove the pastry from the fridge and roll out to fit a baking tray, 30 × 35cm/12 × 14in or 33 × 33cm/13 × 13in. Push the pastry into the corners with your finger tips; even if

it doesn't reach up the sides of the tray, the filling should not spill out. Rest the pastry-filled tray in a cool place for 10 minutes.

When the onion mixture has cooled a little, stir in the egg yolks, then spoon on to the pastry, spreading right up to the edges of the baking tray. Bake for 35 minutes (40 minutes if necessary) until the onions are golden brown and the pastry edges crisp.

Cut the tart into squares and serve warm.
Serves 6.

ROAST ONIONS

Delicious eaten on their own for supper on a cold night, roasted onions, with their rich golden colour and sweet, buttery flavour, also make a good accompaniment to cold roast meats or baked ham. Roast them alone or around a joint.

8 medium onions
110g/4oz butter
freshly ground pepper

Preheat the oven to Gas Mark 4 (180°C, 350°F). Peel the onions and slice off the roots. Bring a pan of water to the boil and drop in the onions. Simmer for 15 minutes. Remove the onions with a draining spoon, place in a shallow dish and add the butter, cut into chunks. Season with the pepper, and a little salt if you have used unsalted butter. Roast in the oven for 40-45 minutes, basting frequently with the butter.
Serves 4 as a side dish.

Onion Tart

BAKED STUFFED ONIONS WITH GOAT'S CHEESE, SUN-DRIED TOMATOES AND THYME

Onion hearts, softened in butter, make the basis for numerous types of stuffing. Scoop as much of the onion out as possible, leaving a shell just two or three layers thick. It should be strong enough to keep its shape while baking, but thin enough to cook right through.

**4 large onions, weighing about
280-340g/10-12oz each
4 sun-dried tomatoes (dry or in
oil from Italian delicatessens)
60g/2oz butter
leaves from 4 sprigs of thyme
110g/4oz goat's cheese
2 egg yolks
freshly ground pepper**

Peel the onions and slice off a quarter from the top of each, chop these roughly and then reserve in a bowl. Cut off the roots and, holding each onion flat on the chopping board, remove the centres with a teaspoon or melon-baller. Chop and add to the rest of the chopped onions.

Dry tomatoes should be covered with boiling water and left to swell a little while you prepare the rest of the stuffing. Those bottled in oil should simply be added later. Melt the butter in a heavy-based pan, add the chopped onion and cook on a gentle heat for 25 minutes until the onion is golden and transparent. Stir in the thyme and set aside to cool a little.

Bring a deep saucepan of water to the boil, drop in the hollowed-out onions and lower the heat to simmer for 10 minutes. Remove the onions with a spoon and turn upside down to drain.

Crumble the goat's cheese into the onion and thyme mixture; drain the tomatoes and slice into thin strips, then stir in with the egg yolks and pepper.

Place the onions in a shallow, oven-proof dish and spoon the stuffing into each one, filling them generously. Bake in a preheated oven at Gas Mark 4 (180°C, 350°F) for 40 minutes, basting occasionally.
Serves 4 as a starter or snack, 2 as a main course.

SWEET POTATO, BACON AND CHESTNUT PASTRIES

Chestnuts are at their best in November – the time when chestnut sellers set up their stands in the street – but as an alternative you can use shelled hazelnuts, roasted for 10 minutes.

**2 medium-sized sweet potatoes
12 whole chestnuts
2 rashers bacon
freshly ground pepper
30g/1oz melted butter, cooled
3 sheets filo pastry**

Preheat the oven to Gas Mark 6 (200°C, 400°F). Peel the sweet potatoes, cut them into thick slices and place in a steamer basket or in a colander, over a pan of boiling water. Cover and steam for 10-12 minutes until tender. When cooked, they will be bright orange and soft enough to mash with a fork. Turn them into a basin and mash until smooth.

With a sharp knife, make slits through the skin of the chestnuts, place on a baking sheet and roast for 25 minutes. Remove from the oven and peel, while still hot, using the point of a knife.

Meanwhile, cut the bacon into 2.5cm/1in strips and cook in a dry pan until brown and crisp. Remove from the pan and add to the mashed sweet potato. Chop the chestnuts and add to the mixture; season with freshly ground pepper.

Continue as for Spiced Aubergine Pastries with Yoghurt and Mint (see page 74), using butter to brush the filo. Makes 12.

(see page 74)

FLAVOURED BUTTERS FOR POTATOES

Serve thoroughly drained new potatoes, which have been boiled in salted water, with any of the following flavoured butters.

● *Tarragon and Lemon Butter:* to each 30g/1oz butter add 1 tspn chopped fresh tarragon and 1 tspn lemon juice. Season with a grind or two of black pepper and follow the method for Mint and Parsley Butter.

● *Mint and Parsley Butter:* mix 60g/2oz unsalted butter at room temperature with 1 tspn each chopped mint and parsley. Do not chop the parsley too finely, or it will be dry, with all the moisture and much of the flavour mashed into the chopping board. Mint, like many other herbs, can be placed in a thick glass tumbler and snipped with scissors, so preserving its flavour and scent. Roll the butter into a sausage shape in greaseproof paper and chill in the fridge till hard. Mint and Parsley Butter freezes well.

● *Butter Sauce:* put 3 tbsp white wine vinegar into a small pan with 2 tbsp water and about a dozen peppercorns. Boil hard and reduce to 2 tbsp. Leave to cool. Beat 3 egg yolks into the vinegar mixture and put into a bowl over hot, not boiling water. Add 170g/6oz melted butter, slowly in a steady stream, whisking all the time. The sauce will thicken to a coating consistency. Season carefully with salt and lemon juice.

*Baked
Stuffed
Onions with
Goat's
Cheese, Sun-
dried
Tomatoes
and Thyme*

TAGLIATELLE OF PARSNIPS AND CARROTS WITH SPICES AND CREAM

The subtle spicing in the sauce adds a nutty warmth to the parsnips and carrots. Use a vegetable peeler to pare long thin strips of root vegetables to resemble tagliatelle, or cut the vegetables into thin rounds if you prefer. Use the vegetables as a base for thin slices of cold roast beef or pork cut from a joint. It only takes a few minutes to grind the spices or you can use a ready-made spice mix such as garam masala.

20 green cardamom pods
1cm/½ inch piece cinnamon
½tsp black peppercorns
½tsp whole cloves or 2tsp
prepared spice mix such as
garam masala
2 large parsnips
1 large carrot
2tbsp light oil such as groundnut
1tsp cumin seed
140ml/¼ pint double cream
salt
cold roast beef or pork to serve

If grinding your own spice mixture, remove the green shells from the cardamom pods and place the small dark brown seeds in a spice mill or mortar.

Smash the cinnamon into flakes, add to the cardamom, followed by the peppercorns and cloves. Grind all four to a fine powder, either in the coffee or spice mill or with a pestle in a mortar.

Peel the parsnips and the carrot. Using the peeler or a mandolin cutter if you have one, pare off strips of carrot and parsnip the full length of the vegetables. As you peel off the strips, let them fall into a basin of cold water so that they curl up.

Heat 1tbsp of the groundnut oil in a heavy frying pan. Drain the root vegetables. Add half of the strips to the pan,

Tagliatelle of Parsnips and Carrots with Spices and Cream

allowing them to brown slightly and turning them once, gently, with a palette knife so they do not stick. Cook them for only 3 or 4 minutes, so that they retain their crispness; then remove to a warm basin as soon as they have coloured a little, while you fry the other half in the remaining oil. Set aside with the rest of the vegetables.

Add the cumin seeds to the pan and roast until they turn dark brown, taking care that the seeds do not burn; if they show signs of cooking too quickly, remove the pan from the heat. Add 2tsp of the spice mixture. Store any remaining spice in a sealed jar for use another day. Cook the spice mixture for 2 or 3 minutes.

Pour in the cream and stir to mix in the spices. Season with salt. Allow the cream to bubble gently for 2 minutes until it starts to thicken. Toss in the vegetable tagliatelle and leave for a minute to heat through. Divide the mixture between two warm plates and serve with thin slices of cold roast meat. Serves 2 as a main course.

BAKED BROAD BEANS AND NEW POTATOES

I have used this dish as a vegetarian main course served with a salad, and on other occasions have substituted canned butter beans for the broad beans.

340g/12oz new potatoes
1 clove garlic
170g/6oz shelled broad beans
285ml/½ pint double cream
salt and freshly ground pepper

Wash the potatoes, only scrubbing them with a vegetable brush if they need it. If the new potatoes are very small leave them whole; otherwise cut each one into two or three, so that they are the same size as the broad beans.

Slice the garlic finely and scatter it

over the base of a shallow pie or flan dish. Tip the potatoes and broad beans into the dish, pour over the cream and bake in the oven on the shelf under the roast.

The vegetable dish will take about 35 minutes to cook at Gas Mark 5 (190°C, 375°F), so put it on the lowest shelf in the oven about three-quarters of an hour before the roast is due to be served. It will come to no harm if it is kept waiting for a while.
Serves 4.

LONG-COOKED BROCCOLI

For a change from boiling broccoli and serving it crisp and bright green, try cooking it slowly with garlic and olive oil.

115ml/4fl oz extra virgin olive oil
4 cloves garlic, peeled and sliced
455g/1lb broccoli, cut into florets
juice of 1 lemon
freshly ground salt and pepper

Pour the olive oil into a casserole, place it over a gentle heat and add the sliced garlic. Heat gently until the garlic becomes fragrant (about 3 minutes on a low heat), add the broccoli florets, lemon juice and salt and pepper. Stir gently and pour in just enough water to cover the florets. Bring to the boil, turn down the heat and cover with a lid. Simmer gently for 45-50 minutes, then drain (saving the stock for soup). Serve warm.
Serves 2 as a side dish.

● Serve with grilled, baked or roast fish or poultry.
● Try adding a whole chilli, dried or fresh, to the pan. Test the broccoli as it cooks and remove the chilli when it has added enough heat.

LEEKS AND CHEVRE IN FILO PASTRY

These little pouches of cheese and vegetables look special, but couldn't be easier to make. I use any crumbly cheese, British goats' cheese or French chèvre. Greek feta is another possibility.

2 leeks, total weight 230g/8oz, trimmed and cleaned
Itsp sunflower oil
Itbsp toasted pine nuts
110g/4oz goats' cheese
salt and freshly ground pepper
4 sheets filo pastry
60g/2oz melted butter, cooled

Preheat the oven to Gas Mark 6 (200°C, 400°F). Slice the leeks crossways into thin shreds. Smear the bottom of a shallow pan with the oil; add the nuts. When they start to colour, add the leeks and cook slowly until they start to wilt. Drain off any liquid in the pan.

Crumble the goats' cheese into the leeks, mix thoroughly but gently and season with pepper, adding salt with care since goat's cheese can be salty. Set the mixture aside.

Lay the sheets of filo pastry on top of one another, then cut them in half lengthways to make 8 rectangular strips. Brush one strip of pastry with sunflower oil and place a second strip on top. Brush that too with sunflower oil. Spoon a quarter of the filling in the centre of each rectangle and gather the pastry up with both hands so that the filling is enclosed. Pinch the pastry firmly just above the filling and twist together, pressing the pastry together.

Continue with the other three parcels in a similar manner, then set on a baking tray. Bake for 10-20 minutes, until the pastry is well browned.
Serves 4 as a starter, 2 as a main dish.

BAKED FENNEL WITH WALNUTS, PARSLEY AND LEMON

6 bulbs of young fennel
110g/4oz fresh breadcrumbs
85g/3oz walnuts, chopped
a good handful of parsley, chopped
4 heaped tbsp grated Parmesan
rind and juice of I lemon
I clove garlic, finely chopped
salt and freshly ground pepper
Itsp fennel seeds
Itbsp olive oil

Bring a saucepan of salted water to the boil. Add a drop of wine vinegar or a squeeze of lemon to the water to stop the fennel discolouring. Remove the feathery fennel fronds and put to one side. Slice the fennel in half vertically and drop into the boiling water. Turn the heat down and simmer for 8-10 minutes until the point of a sharp knife goes into the fennel with ease.

Meanwhile, prepare the stuffing. Preheat the oven to Gas Mark 6 (200°C, 400°F). Place the breadcrumbs, walnuts, parsley, Parmesan, lemon and garlic in a mixing bowl. Add the salt and pepper, fennel seeds and fronds.

Drain the fennel, reserving the cooking liquid, and place flat side up in a shallow baking dish or roasting tin. Add 6 tablespoons of the cooking liquid to the stuffing and mix well. Place spoonfuls of stuffing on to the fennel until it is all used up. Drizzle the olive oil over and pour two fingers' depth of the cooking liquid into the bottom of the dish. Place in the oven and cook for 25-30 minutes until the stuffing is crisp on top.
Serves 6 as an accompaniment, 3 as a main dish with brown rice.

● Young fennel bulbs are best for this dish. Avoid the large bulbs with thick stalks and heavily ridged flesh as they are too fibrous.

FRIED AUBERGINE WITH SPICED YOGHURT

Spice creamy thick Greek-style yoghurt with Eastern flavours – coriander, garlic, ginger and cayenne – to accompany the bland taste of quick-fried aubergine.

3 small aubergines
6tbsp olive oil
2 cloves garlic, crushed with a little salt
2tsp grated fresh root ginger
½tsp cayenne pepper
salt and freshly ground pepper
230g/8oz thick yoghurt
Itbsp fresh coriander leaves, optional

Wipe the aubergines and slice them into rounds 5mm/¼ inch thick. If you have time, put them in a colander, sprinkle with salt and leave for 30 minutes to remove any bitterness there may be and to prevent the aubergines soaking up quite so much oil. Rinse and dry if you have salted them.

Pour the oil into a frying pan and when sizzling add half the aubergine slices. Fry, turning once, until they are brown on each side, adding more oil if they are thirsty. Remove with a slotted spoon and drain on a warm plate lined with kitchen roll. Keep them warm while you fry the rest.

Drain any excess oil from the pan leaving just a thin layer. Add the garlic and fry on a moderate heat for a minute (garlic burns easily). Add the ginger, cayenne and a little salt and pepper, stirring while you cook for I minute. Turn off the heat and stir in the yoghurt. Serve the fried aubergine slices on warm plates with the spiced yoghurt dressing on the side. Scatter with chopped coriander leaves if you wish.

Serve with a fish dish like grilled red mullet.
Serves 2.

Baked Fennel with Walnuts, Parsley and Lemon

SPICED AUBERGINE PASTRIES WITH YOGHURT AND MINT

These savoury pastries can be served as a first course or snack, with a cucumber or chick pea salad.

I large aubergine weighing about 455g/Ilb
salt and freshly ground pepper
I clove garlic
5tbsp olive oil
Itsp ground cumin
285ml/½ pint thick natural yoghurt
2 sheets filo pastry
2tsp sesame seeds
Itbsp chopped fresh mint

Preheat the oven to Gas Mark 6 (200°C, 400°F). Wipe the aubergine, cut in half lengthways and cut each lengthways again. Chop each quarter piece into slices, about as thick as a pound coin. Place the slices in a colander and sprinkle with salt. Leave 20 minutes to allow the bitter juices to run out, rinse quickly under the cold tap, then drain.

Peel the garlic clove, and crush it with a little salt, using the blade of a knife. In a small basin, mix 4tbsp of the oil with the ground cumin and the crushed garlic, and season with black pepper.

Line a grill pan with foil, cover with the aubergine slices, closely packed together but in one layer, and brush with the seasoned oil. Place under a hot grill for 5-7 minutes, until the slices start to turn golden brown. Remove from the foil with a fish slice or spatula and place in a mixing bowl. Add 4tbsp of the yoghurt and stir.

Lay the filo sheets on a board and cut each one into four strips lengthways. Brush one of the eight strips with some of the remaining olive oil and place 2tbsp of the aubergine and yoghurt stuffing near one end, about 2 inches in from the short side. Fold one corner of the short side over the stuffing to form a triangle at the end of the strip. Fold the triangle over and over again, along the length of the pastry strip to make a fat triangle package. Repeat with the other strips of pastry and the remaining aubergine stuffing. Place the parcels on a baking sheet, brush with oil and sprinkle with the sesame seeds. Bake the pastries in a preheated oven for 10-12 minutes until golden and crisp.

While the parcels are cooking, mix the remaining yoghurt with the chopped fresh mint and season with a little salt. Chill until required. Serve the aubergine pastries with the minted yoghurt on the side.

Makes 8, to serve 4 as a starter, 2 as a light meal.

MUSHROOM CROUSTADE

This recipe is much simpler than it appears.

I onion, coarsely chopped
4 small parsnips, or mixed parsnip and pumpkin
I large potato
4tbsp olive or walnut oil
salt and freshly ground pepper
455g/Ilb assorted mushrooms
Itbsp chopped parsley
4tbsp broken walnuts
2tbsp stock
3tbsp fromage frais or crème fraîche
85g/3oz butter
8 sheets filo pastry

Preheat the oven to Gas Mark 6 (200°C, 400°F). Peel and coarsely shred the onion, parsnip, pumpkin and the potato on the largest holes of a grater. Heat 2tbsp of the oil in a large shallow pan until it is hot but not smoking and add the grated vegetables. Season with the salt and pepper.

Sauté the vegetables until the shreds start to turn golden. Stir to stop them sticking, adding a little more oil if necessary. Remove from the pan with a draining spoon and place in a large pudding bowl. Scrape the pan clean but do not wash it. Add the remaining 2tbsp of oil, then sauté the mushrooms until they start to give up their juices. This will take about 5-7 minutes (wild mushrooms take a short time, the flat field mushrooms and brown cap longer).

Remove the mushrooms from the pan with the draining spoon and add to the root vegetables with the chopped parsley. Add the walnuts and the stock to the hot pan to deglaze it. Scrape the bottom of the pan to dislodge any crisp deposits and pour the mixture over the root vegetables and mushrooms. Stir in the fromage frais, or crème fraîche. Check for seasoning as you mix gently, then set aside.

Melt 30g/Ioz butter in a small pan and allow to cool, but not set. Place 8 sheets of filo pastry on the board and cut in half lengthways, so that you have 16 long pieces. Brush 8 of the pieces with butter and place the other 8 on top, to make 8 double-thick slices of pastry.

Butter a 25cm/10in round pie dish or shallow baking tin. Place the first double piece of filo in the dish with one end at the centre of the dish, leaving most of the pastry hanging over the edge. Lay the other strips of pastry in the dish in the same way, each one at a slight angle, so that they radiate from the centre to cover completely the bottom of the dish. Spoon on the mushroom and root filling and then, starting with the last piece you positioned, fold each strip back over the mushrooms toward the middle of the dish so the strips overlap to cover the filling. Twist the end of each piece of pastry to form a scroll.

Sprinkle over any remaining butter and bake for 25 minutes. Serve hot with extra crème fraîche, if you wish. Serves 4 as a main dish.

Mushroom Croustade

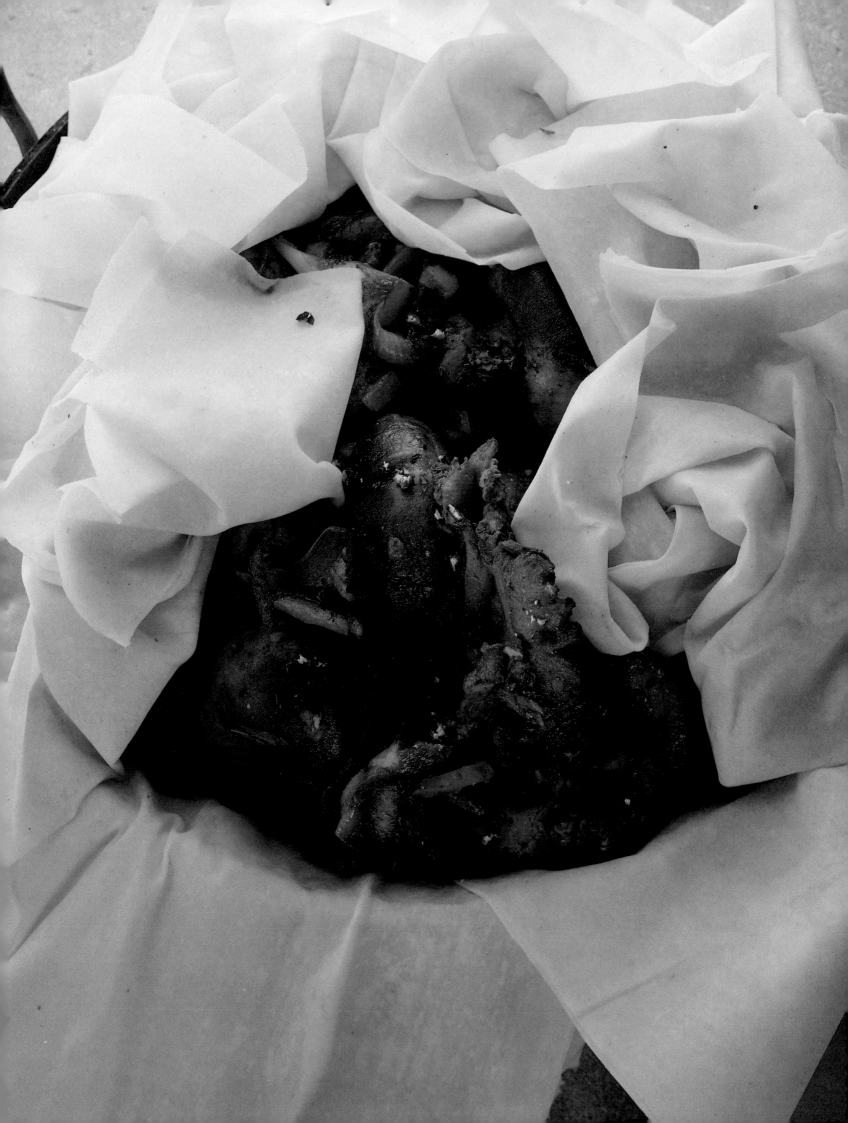

*Grilled
Marinated
Vegetables*

BROWN MUSHROOM SAUTE

The medium-sized slightly shaggy brown mushrooms are best for this dish. Use the darkest ones you can find.

**230g/8oz mushrooms
2 cloves garlic, chopped
3tbsp olive oil
half a lemon
1tbsp chopped parsley
salt and freshly ground pepper**

Remove the mushroom stalks and sauté them with the garlic in the olive oil. Make sure the garlic doesn't burn and become bitter. Slice the mushroom caps and add them to the pan. Cook over a low heat for 10 minutes, tossing occasionally. Squeeze in the lemon juice, throw in the parsley and season with salt and a couple of grinds of pepper.
Serves 2 as a side dish.

● Serve with grilled meat or with a cheese soufflé.
● Use fresh wild mushrooms if you can find them.

A PUREE OF WHITE VEGETABLES

**6 small turnips
1 medium celeriac, about
455g/1lb
1 medium potato
1 onion
1 small fennel bulb
2 cloves garlic, peeled
2 sprigs of thyme
60g/2oz butter, diced
60ml/2fl oz double cream
salt and freshly ground pepper**

Peel the vegetables and cut into rough chunks. Put them into a pan with the garlic and herbs. Add a little salt and bring to the boil. Cover then simmer for about 20 minutes, or until the vegetables are quite soft.
Drain all the vegetables, reserving the liquid for stock, and remove the garlic and herbs. Mash the vegetables with a potato masher or whizz them in a food processor until puréed. Return the purée to the saucepan, add the butter and cream and season with pepper.
Serves 4 as a side dish.

● Serve with roast lamb or chicken.
● You can vary the quantities of each vegetable depending on their availability and your mood.

GRILLED MARINATED VEGETABLES

The flavours, and particularly the aroma, of these marinated vegetables will make you think of Provence. They are the same ingredients that go into a traditional ratatouille except that here they are grilled on a skewer instead of being made into a stew. Serve with a spoonful of garlic mayonnaise.

**FOR THE MARINADE:
2 cloves garlic, finely chopped
1tbsp herbs, parsley, basil, and
thyme, finely chopped
salt and freshly ground pepper
230ml/8fl oz olive oil
FOR THE SKEWERS:
4 small aubergines
2 peppers
4 courgettes
6 tomatoes**

Put the garlic, chopped herbs and seasoning in a large basin and pour in the olive oil.
Slice the aubergines into pieces about the thickness of two £1 coins. Halve and slice the peppers into strips about 2.5cm/1in wide. Cut the courgettes into thick chunks, the tomatoes in half and put all the vegetables into the olive oil marinade. Mix thoroughly so that all the vegetable pieces are well covered, then set aside for at least an hour for the vegetables to absorb some of the aromatic flavours.
Skewer the vegetable pieces on 12 kebab sticks, or soaked bamboo skewers. Put the vegetable kebabs on the grill and brush continually with any marinade left in the bowl. Depending on the heat of the grill they will need about 8-10 minutes; turn once.
Enough for 6, served with an accompaniment.

MUSHROOMS

As well as the well-known cap mushroom, available in several sizes, other mushrooms have become generally available.
● *Cep.* Also known as Porcini or Boletus, the cep is the most prized of all the mushrooms. Short and fat, ceps are perfect for slicing and grilling or for frying in butter with parsley and a little garlic. Look out for them in late summer and autumn.

● *Oyster Mushroom.* Pale soft grey or a gentle creamy yellow, the oyster mushroom is available in good greengrocers and several supermarket chains. It is particularly good sautéed or stir-fried.
● *Shiitake.* The most firm-textured of the mushroom family, the shiitake is very popular in Chinese and Japanese cooking. The meaty texture and rich fla-

vour make it an ideal addition to casseroles. Shiitake are available all year round and keep better than most.

GRILLED RED PEPPER AND AUBERGINE TART

Vegetables that benefit most from the heat of the grill are peppers, tomatoes, aubergines and onions. Chop up chargrilled tomatoes, skins and all, and season with salt and pepper for an instant sauce. Enjoy them as a companion to grilled meat or fish, or use them here.

200g/7oz puff pastry
olive oil
2 medium aubergines
salt and freshly ground pepper
4 red peppers
2 medium onions
1tbsp chopped basil
2tbsp chopped flat-leaved parsley
1tbsp extra virgin olive oil
1tbsp red wine vinegar

Roll out the pastry thinly, place a dinner plate in the middle and cut round it. Place the pastry disc on a baking sheet, brush with a little olive oil and bake in a preheated oven at Gas Mark 6 (200°C, 400°F) for 7-10 minutes until crisp and golden. Cool on a rack.

Slice the aubergines into 5mm/¼in rounds, brush with olive oil, season with salt and pepper, then grill on both sides until golden and soft. Transfer to a bowl.

Grill the peppers until they blacken. Put them in a bowl and cover with a plate to let the skins steam loose. Slice the onions and brush with oil. Grill until golden and slightly caramelized, then add to the aubergine.

Peel the peppers, saving their juices, then slice them into thin strips and add, with the juice, to the aubergine and onion. Add the chopped herbs, the extra virgin olive oil and red wine vinegar. Toss gently. Slide the pastry on to a plate and top with the dressed, grilled vegetables. Eat immediately.
Serves 4.

Grilled Red Pepper and Aubergine Tart

GRILLED CORN ON THE COB

This is a recipe for cooking sweetcorn on a barbecue. Allow 1 corn cob per person. Peel back the green husk surrounding each ear of sweetcorn, a leaf at a time, without detaching it from the corn. Pull away the silky fibres surrounding the corn. Fold the husk back in place. Soak the corn in cold water for about 15 minutes to stop the husks burning. Drain, and lay the still wet corn on the grill over the fire.

Cook, turning often, for 15-20 minutes, by which time the husks will have turned black. Open the husks and rub the corn with butter. Serve hot.

GRILLED RADICCHIO

1 large round radicchio
3tbsp olive oil
salt

Cut the radicchio into four through the core, so that the leaves remain attached. Place the quarters in a shallow dish, drizzle over the olive oil and season with a little salt. Cook under a pre-heated grill until the edges start to crisp, turn the pieces over and grill the other side. Serve hot.
Serves 2 as a side dish to complement grilled fish, vegetables or chicken.

SWEETCORN BAKED IN THE ASHES

Of all the vegetables that can be baked on a fire, corn cobs must be among the most welcome, with their buttery sweetness. If you cannot find corn that has its entire husk left on (street markets are a better bet than supermarkets), pierce the end of each cob with a skewer and get a strong-armed volunteer to hold them over the fire for 15 minutes or so.

4 ears of sweetcorn in their husks
butter
salt and freshly ground pepper

Carefully pull back the husks from the corn and remove the silky threads, then fold back the husks. Bury the corn in the ashes of the fire. After 30 minutes the husks will be quite dark and crisp. Peel them away and discard them. Smother the corn cobs with butter and season generously with salt and pepper.
Serves 4.

GRILLING VEGETABLES

● Almost all vegetables taste better grilled over charcoal. The wood adds a subtle smokiness to the vegetables.
● Add thyme and rosemary to the embers for a herby fragrance.
● Marinating the vegetable pieces in olive oil and herbs adds to their flavour.

● Most suitable for grilling are sliced aubergines and peppers, halved courgettes and tomatoes. Surprisingly good contenders for the barbecue are onions and fennel; sweetcorn, ideally still in its husk, and mushrooms also grill well on a barbecue.

● Place the vegetables on the grill when the flames have died down and the embers are glowing. The correct temperature is when the coals are coated with grey ash.
● Brush the vegetables continually as they cook, with olive oil and herbs, to prevent the pieces from drying out.

TAMATAR BHUGIA

This is a recipe from *Curries and Bugles* by Jennifer Brennan (Viking, 1990).

60ml/2fl oz vegetable oil
1tsp cumin seeds
1 large onion, peeled and finely chopped
5 cloves garlic, smashed, peeled and chopped
1tsp garam masala
2.5cm/1in piece of fresh ginger, peeled, thinly sliced and shredded
2 small green chillies, seeded and cut into thin strips
8 large tomatoes, seeded, skinned and cut into 2.5cm/1 inch chunks
1tsp salt
2 heaped tsp brown sugar
1tbsp unsweetened desiccated coconut
2tbsp chopped fresh coriander leaves

Heat the oil in a wok or saucepan over a medium heat and fry the cumin seeds until they are lightly browned. Add the onion and garlic and fry, stirring, until the onion is soft. Stir in the garam masala and add the ginger and chilli strips. Continue to fry and stir the mixture for 2 minutes.

Now add the tomatoes, salt and sugar and bring the mixture to the boil. Sprinkle in the coconut and stir. Cover the saucepan and reduce the heat to low. Simmer for 10 minutes, lifting the cover and stirring from time to time.

The finished dish should have a little sauce but should not be like soup, and the tomato pieces should still be discernible. Transfer to a serving dish and sprinkle with the chopped coriander leaves. Serve with Grilled Prawns (see page 36).

CABBAGE STUFFED WITH BACON AND LENTILS WITH MUSTARD SAUCE

Dark green Savoy cabbage is in the shops from late autumn. The large outside leaves are perfect for stuffing.

4 large green cabbage leaves
110g/4oz smoked bacon (optional)
1tbsp vegetable oil
110g/4oz red cabbage, shredded
1tsp juniper berries, lightly crushed
2 apples
2 heaped tbsp hazelnuts, toasted
2tbsp wine or cider vinegar
1tbsp redcurrant jelly
60g/2oz brown lentils, cooked
salt and freshly ground pepper
FOR THE SAUCE:
140ml/¼ pint double cream
3tbsp Dijon mustard
salt and freshly ground pepper

Wash and blanch the cabbage leaves, and place under running water; then set aside.

Cut the bacon into strips, if using, and place in a shallow pan; cook until it starts to crisp, then remove with a draining spoon. Place in a large basin. Add 1tbsp oil to the pan, add the red cabbage and stir in the juniper berries. Cook until the cabbage is bright and shiny and has softened a little, but still retains its crunch. Remove with a draining spoon and add to the bacon.

Chop the apples, but do not peel them. Add to the pan with the hazelnuts and raisins. Cook over a gentle heat until the apples colour a little. Splash in the wine or cider vinegar, standing back from the pan so that your eyes do not sting, then stir in the redcurrant jelly. Allow to bubble, then stir into the bacon and cabbage. Stir in the cooked lentils. Season with the salt and pepper.

Spread out the four cabbage leaves, divide the stuffing between the four and fold each leaf to make a parcel. Secure with string and pack into the steamer. Steam, covered, for about 8 minutes, until thoroughly hot.

Meanwhile, make the mustard sauce. Pour the cream into a shallow pan. Stir in the mustard and season with the salt and pepper. Taste for seasoning, adding more mustard if you wish. Allow the sauce to bubble for 2-3 minutes. Lift the cabbage parcels from the steamer, place two on each plate and remove the string. Serve with mustard sauce. Serves 2 as a main course.

GRILLED POTATOES WITH GARLIC AND THYME

4 large potatoes
4tbsp olive oil
2 cloves garlic, minced
the leaves from 2 sprigs of thyme
salt
60g/2oz butter

Cook the potatoes in salted boiling water, drain them and peel off the skins. Slice the potatoes thickly and put them in a bowl.

Pour over the olive oil and add the garlic and thyme. Toss the potato slices very gently, taking care not to break them. Spread the potatoes out on a grill pan, pour over any oil from the bowl and sprinkle with salt. Drop a small knob of butter on each slice and cook under a hot grill until sizzling.

Eat the potatoes with grilled or baked fish, or with a green salad.
Serves 4.

*Potatoes
Rolled in
Bacon*

STEAMED POTATOES WITH PARSLEY AND GARLIC

When the wait for native, spring new potatoes seems unbearable, I often pick out some of the smaller, young main-crop potatoes and cook them with their skins on. The red-skinned Desirée is a particularly good variety for steaming.

**8 small potatoes, scrubbed not peeled
coarse sea salt
2 plump cloves garlic, unpeeled
a large knob of butter
4 heaped tbsp fromage frais or other soft curd cheese
6 sprigs of parsley, coarsely chopped
freshly ground pepper**

Place the potatoes, still wet, in a steamer basket and sprinkle generously with salt. Add the garlic cloves to the steaming water beneath. Steam for 10-15 minutes, testing the potatoes every few minutes with the point of a knife for tenderness.

After 10 minutes, remove the garlic peel with the point of a knife and chop the cloves finely. Melt the butter in a small saucepan over a low heat. Add the chopped garlic and allow to cook slowly, the butter gently frothing, until the garlic is soft and slightly golden.

Remove the potatoes from the steamer, divide between two warm plates and cut them in half. Stir the fromage frais and the parsley into the garlic butter and season with the pepper; spoon over the halved potatoes. Serves 2 as a side dish.

POTATOES ROLLED IN BACON

Starchy foods, such as pasta, rice and potatoes, make good party fare. They are cheap, satisfying and marvellous for soaking up the alcohol. I think potatoes, in one form or another, go down best of all. Try rolling them in bacon, then roasting in the oven, and serve them piping hot.

These potatoes can be prepared a few hours in advance and put in the oven during the party. The recipe makes enough for four; for party quantities just multiply as necessary.

**12 small potatoes
12 rashers streaky bacon
285ml/½ pint vegetable or chicken stock
freshly ground pepper
60g/2oz butter**

Preheat the oven to Gas Mark 6 (200°C, 400°F). Peel the potatoes, roll a rasher of bacon around each one and place in a well-buttered ovenproof dish. Pour over the stock, grind over a generous amount of fresh pepper and dot with small pieces of the butter.

Cook uncovered in the preheated oven for about 50 minutes, basting a couple of times, until most – but not all – of the stock has evaporated. Serve hot. Serves 4.

● Prepare some of the potatoes without the bacon, for people who don't eat meat.
● Dust a little paprika over the potatoes as they come out of the oven.
● This is one occasion (probably the only one) where the saltiness of a stock cube is actually preferable to home-made stock.

Baked Anchovy and Dolcelatte Potatoes

NEW POTATOES EN PAPILLOTE

Cooking the smallest of new potatoes in a parcel seals in their nutty aroma. Take the parcel from the oven and open it at the table, to get the full fragrance of garlic and butter.

500g/1¼lb very small new potatoes
sea salt
2 sprigs of fresh tarragon
85g/3oz butter
4 cloves garlic, peeled

Preheat the oven to Gas Mark 6 (200°C, 400°F). Wipe the potatoes. Cut two discs of greaseproof paper or cooking parchment, one with a 23cm/9in diameter, the other with a 23.5cm/9¼in diameter.

Place the smaller of the two discs on a baking sheet, put the potatoes on the paper and sprinkle with a tablespoon of water. Season with the salt and tarragon, then place the butter and the garlic in among the potatoes.

Place the second piece of paper on top and secure it by folding the edges over tightly to seal. Place in the preheated oven for 25-30 minutes, until the parcel is puffed up and the potatoes tender to the point of a knife. Serves 4.

BAKED ANCHOVY AND DOLCELATTE POTATOES

6 fat cloves garlic
4tbsp olive oil
4 large baking potatoes
sea salt
8 anchovy fillets
1tbsp chopped flat-leafed parsley
2 tomatoes, peeled, seeded and chopped
salt and freshly ground pepper
60g/2oz dolcelatte, Cashel Blue, or other soft blue cheese

Place the garlic cloves in a small dish, pour over the olive oil and bake in a preheated oven at Gas Mark 6 (200°C, 400°F).

Wash the potatoes, insert a metal skewer into each one, shake off most of the water and roll them in sea salt. Bake in the preheated oven until the skewers come out easily.

After about an hour, when the garlic is soft in the centre, remove the dish from the oven and push the garlic through a sieve into a small bowl. Discard the skins and reserve the purée.

Take the cooked potatoes out of the oven, but leave it switched on. Slice a lid off each potato and scoop out the filling into a bowl with a teaspoon. Mash with a potato masher or fork. Try to avoid puncturing the potato skin.

Chop four of the anchovy fillets and add them to the potato, along with the remaining anchovies. Stir in the garlic purée, parsley, tomatoes and salt and pepper.

Spoon the mixture into the potato shells. Divide the blue cheese into four and place a piece on top of each potato. Replace the potato lids and return to the oven for 7-10 minutes, until the potatoes are hot and the cheese is melted and bubbling. Serves 4.

POMMES DE TERRE A L'HUILE DE NOIX

Patricia Wells's book *Bistro Cooking* (Kyle Cathie Limited, 1990) is a welcome addition to anyone's kitchen shelves. The book feels just like an old friend and is full of recipes from the long-established and now ultra-chic Paris bistros. This recipe, for herby, nutty sautéed potatoes, is typical.

1kg/2¼lb small, firm smooth-skinned potatoes
75ml/2½fl oz best-quality walnut oil
freshly grated nutmeg
salt and freshly ground pepper
4 cloves garlic, finely minced
1 small bunch of parsley, minced
1 small bunch of chives, minced

Peel and thinly slice the potatoes, then wrap them in a thick towel to absorb any liquid.

In a large frying pan (preferably cast-iron or non-stick), heat the oil until hot but not smoking over medium-high heat. Add the potatoes and sauté them for about 20 minutes, shaking the pan from time to time, until they are thoroughly cooked and browned on both sides. Season to taste with the nutmeg, salt and pepper as the potatoes are being tossed.

To serve, sprinkle the garlic, parsley and chives over the potatoes and toss to blend well. Serves 4.

New Potatoes en Papillote

*Potato and
Herb Terrine*

POTATO AND HERB TERRINE

Layers of waxy potatoes sandwiched with cheese, cream and herbs make a creamy, rich gratin. When served cold it can be cut like a terrine and eaten with a leafy salad.

**3 eggs
cayenne
455g/1lb crème fraîche
salt and freshly ground pepper
1 handful of fresh herbs, chopped
(a mixture of any of the
following: sorrel, chervil or
tarragon, but try to include
parsley and chives)
1 large handful of spinach leaves,
blanched, drained and finely
chopped
85g/3oz Gruyère, finely grated
butter
1kg/2¼lb waxy potatoes,
scrubbed and sliced as thick as a
10p coin**

Preheat the oven to Gas Mark 4 (180°C, 350°F). Break the eggs into a small bowl and beat lightly with a fork. Sprinkle over a little cayenne and stir in the crème fraîche, salt and pepper, then add the chopped herbs and spinach and half of the Gruyère to the mixture.

Generously butter a large loaf tin, spread a little of the crème fraîche mixture on the bottom and cover it with a layer of sliced potatoes. Sprinkle over a little of the remaining Gruyère and then some more of the crème fraîche mixture. Continue layering the potatoes, cream and cheese until you have used it all up, ending with the Gruyère as the top layer.

Place in a roasting tin and pour in enough hot water to come half-way up the sides. Cover with kitchen foil, put in the preheated oven and bake for 1½ hours. Remove the foil for the last 15-20 minutes of cooking time to let the top brown.

Switch off the oven and leave the dish in there for 15 minutes. Take it out of the oven and turn the potatoes out on to a hot serving dish or spoon it straight out of the loaf tin.

This terrine is exceedingly good served cold. Leave it for at least 2 hours or preferably overnight, then loosen the terrine from its tin by running a knife around the edges. Turn it out and slice it into thick wedges.
Serves 6.

ROAST POTATOES WITH OLIVE OIL, GARLIC AND THYME

The best thing about roast potatoes is the crispy skin. Cutting the potatoes into a fan shape enables a larger surface area to crispen in the oven; they are especially tasty when cooked around the roast.

**8 medium potatoes
4tbsp olive oil (not your best)
4tsp red wine vinegar
salt and freshly ground pepper
4 large cloves garlic, peeled and
halved
some sprigs of thyme
bay leaves**

Preheat the oven to Gas Mark 6 (200°C, 400°F). Hold each potato firmly on the chopping board with one of the flat sides towards you. Make regular slices, the thickness of a pound coin, vertically through the potato, leaving 1 cm/½in at one end uncut to hold the slices together.

Turn the potato so that the flattest side is facing upwards. With the heel of your hand, press down firmly; the potato slices will fan out.

Place the potatoes in a roasting tin, pour over the olive oil and vinegar and season with the salt and pepper. Place half a peeled garlic clove, a sprinkling of thyme leaves, a bay leaf and a thyme sprig on top of each potato and cook in the preheated oven for 50-60 minutes, preferably around the roast.
Serves 4.

POTATO VARIETIES

- *Pink Fir Apple.* An old-fashioned variety easily recognized by its pink skin and firm yellow flesh. Good for salads.
- *Desiree.* Another pink-skinned variety, this time rounder and much larger than the fir apple. A new hybrid, this, good for boiling and roasting.
- *Maris Peer.* An early season potato which is dry and floury and good for mashing.

- *King Edward.* The most famous of the potato varieties. An excellent all-rounder, particularly suitable for mashing and for chips. Tends to break up in the water, therefore not the one for boiling.
- *Cara.* A very popular potato similar to King Edwards. Easily recognized by its pink eyes and pale creamy coloured skin.

- *Jersey Royal.* Tiny little potatoes with a fine flavour. Their flaky skins should be gently wiped rather peeled. Jersey Royals first appear in May, with their season continuing to early autumn. Easily recognized by their kidney shape and the fact that they are usually packed in sand.

Baked Potatoes with Mint and Parsley Pesto

POTATO GNOCCHI

Substantial enough to eat as a main course, these soft potato balls can be served with something as simple as warm, spicy pesto, either home-made or from a jar.

1kg/2¼lb floury potatoes
salt
2 small eggs, lightly beaten
300g/10½oz plain flour
butter
1 jar of pesto

Put the potatoes in a saucepan, cover with water and bring to the boil, then add salt and simmer until tender. Drain and peel them, then mash until smooth.

Add the eggs and most of the flour and mix until you have a soft dough. Break off pieces of the dough and roll them into strips, about as thick as a sausage. Cut each strip into 3.5cm/1½in pieces to make the gnocchi. Roll each piece down the prongs of a fork to give indentations for the sauce to stick to.

Bring a pan of water to the boil, add salt, and boil the gnocchi until they rise to the surface. Remove with a draining spoon and put into a shallow dish. Rub a knob of butter over the gnocchi and serve with the pesto sauce.

For the pesto sauce: tip the contents of the jar into a small saucepan, add a large knob of butter and gently heat it until it starts to bubble.
Serves 4 as a main course.

BAKED POTATOES WITH MINT AND PARSLEY PESTO

Simple dishes needing little preparation are the stars of 1990s cooking. For this recipe, choose King Edward or Maris Piper potatoes.

8 medium potatoes
salt
6 cloves garlic
30g/1oz fresh mint
30g/1oz fresh parsley
75g/2½oz Parmesan cheese
140ml/¼ pint olive oil

Scrub and salt the potatoes and bake them in a moderately hot oven.

While they are baking, prepare the pesto. Finely chop the garlic and the mint and parsley. Add the Parmesan and mix all the ingredients together well. (You can use a pestle and mortar or a food processor for this, if you have either.) Slowly dribble in the olive oil while stirring the mixture until well blended.

Split open the cooked potatoes and spoon the pesto over them.
Serves 4.

POTATOES IN WHITE WINE

I have a soft spot for the spud. Lindsey Bareham's *In Praise of the Potato* (Michael Joseph, 1989) is the bible of potato cookery. This is one of her recipes, which is delicious served with chicken.

2 rashers of smoked streaky bacon, diced
700g/1½lb small potatoes
30g/1oz butter
1 bay leaf
140ml/¼pint white wine
140ml/¼pint stock
salt and freshly ground pepper

Blanch the bacon in boiling water for a couple of minutes, then drain. Put in a pan with all the other ingredients and simmer until the potatoes are cooked.
Serves 4.

Potato Gnocchi

PASTA, GRAINS & PULSES

Comfort food is brought up to date as the textures and flavours
of Europe's traditional staples are rediscovered by modern cooks.

Pasta, grains and pulses are some of our most comforting and satisfying foods. While pasta has become our most satisfying fast food, pulses like beans and lentils and the whole grains of warm-climate cooking – couscous from North Africa, bulgar from the Middle East and polenta from Italy – are perfectly at home with slow-cooking stews and casseroles.

PASTA

Pasta is one of the oldest foods yet a quite recent arrival in the British kitchen. Although it can be bought fresh or dried it is the packets of dried pasta that have proved to be so useful. It takes very little time to turn almost any dried pasta into a satisfying meal, and the fresh variety can be ready in minutes.

DRIED PASTA

When buying dried pasta it is important to look out for the words *pasta di semolina di grano duro* on the packet. This means that the pasta is made from semolina from Durum wheat which produces a hard flour and gives body to the pasta. (Made with ordinary flour the pasta would be soft and have no bite to it). Such pasta will be a creamy yellow in colour. Generally speaking, the best is made in Italy.

Grocers always stock a greater variety of dried pasta than of fresh. There is a shape for every occasion, flat sheets of lasagne for layering with rich fillings, small deeply textured shapes designed to scoop up sauce, and tubular pastas for stuffing.

FRESH PASTA

Most supermarkets offer a selection of freshly prepared pasta, while traditional Italian grocers may stock up to eight or ten different varieties. Fresh pasta is found in boxes or vacuum packs or sold loose by the pound. The best fresh pasta also contains semolina flour made from Durum wheat.

Fresh does not always mean better. I have found fresh pasta from Italian grocers to be far superior to those varieties prepacked and sold in supermarkets, some of which can lack 'bite' when cooked. The most popular fresh pastas are sheets of lasagne, ribbons such as fine taglierini, medium fettucine and wide tagliatelle, and stuffed pastas such as ravioli.

COOKING PASTA

Whichever pasta you choose it will be best when sauced simply and sparingly. A small amount of robust sauce is better than large quantities of insipid liquid. Although most pasta sauces are easy to prepare at home, some of the bottled sauces, especially those made in Italy, are extremely good. In particular, look out for black and green olive pastes, which can be stirred into warm pasta, just as you would use pesto, the basil and garlic sauce. Jars of vegetables, such as aubergines and artichokes, can also be used. Drain them of their liquor and then toss with cooked pasta and some garlic and parsley.

GRAINS

Although we eat grains and cereals in bread and confectionery, it is only quite recently we have learned to enjoy whole grains such as couscous, bulgar wheat and wild rice. Polenta has been a staple food in Italy for centuries but has only just reached the more fashionable tables here. Grains are, above all else, a most comforting and frugal food.

Bulgar, also known as cracked wheat or spelt in any number of ways, is popular in Tabbouleh, the refreshing Middle-eastern dish spiked with lemon juice and mint. Fold sliced fruits such as fresh apricots or peaches into the earthy grain for a summer salad or starter. Couscous takes a little longer to prepare, but can be partially cooked in advance. Traditionally served with lamb, it is often served on its own padded with dried fruit and shelled pistachio nuts.

As well as being satisfying and comforting, grains are a good source of fibre. Wholewheat grains are those which have not had their husk removed during refining and are an even better source of fibre, but do take longer to cook.

PULSES

For those who have always enjoyed flageolets, haricots, lentils and chick peas, it is amusing to watch these humble foods be embraced by smart restaurant-goers of the nineties. It is also heartening as they are some of the most nourishing of all foods.

Lentils are the dullest of things when boiled, but reach new heights when tossed in a sharp vinaigrette and partnered with redcurrants or chopped fresh mint. Chick peas make an original alternative to potatoes when mashed with generous amounts of butter.

Traditional dishes such as bean-bakes spiced with mustard and molasses are the most warming of all winter foods. In summer those same beans can be served warm with olive oil and a handful of crisp green beans as a side dish. One myth about lentils needs exploding; they do not require soaking, and neither do they take very long to cook.

It is important to buy beans from a shop with a high turnover, as they do not keep indefinitely and the older they are the longer they take to cook. Most beans tin badly, loosing their bite and becoming soft on reheating; flageolet and haricot beans are quite good but must be thoroughly drained of their canning liquid. Chick peas are virtually indestructible, and can be whizzed to a spicy purée in minutes.

page 89
Tortelloni
with
Parmesan
and Pine
Nuts

TORTELLONI WITH PARMESAN AND PINE NUTS

This is a simple tortelloni with melted butter and toasted nuts. Use pastas stuffed with ricotta and spinach, artichoke paste or pumpkin.

6tbsp pine nuts
tortelloni for 2
110g/4oz butter, melted
Parmesan cheese

Toast the pine nuts under the grill until they are golden, shaking them occasionally to prevent them burning.

Cook the tortelloni in boiling, salted water. They are ready when they come to the surface. Drain and transfer to a warmed serving dish. Pour over the melted butter and scatter with the pine nuts and some Parmesan cheese. Serve at once.
Serves 2.

TAGLIOLINI ALFREDO

230ml/8fl oz double cream
60g/2oz butter
60g/2oz freshly grated Parmesan
freshly ground black pepper
tagliolini for 2

Bring the cream and butter to the boil in a saucepan, then simmer for a minute. Throw in half the Parmesan, stirring until smooth, and season with a little black pepper.

Cook the tagliolini in plenty of boiling, salted water and drain, then toss in the sauce and add the rest of the Parmesan. Serve at once.
Serves 2

BUTTERED NOODLES WITH LENTILS AND BASIL

230g/8oz brown lentils
1tsp olive oil
bay leaf
1 clove garlic, peeled
200g/7oz fat noodles
100g/3½oz butter
2 small leeks, thinly sliced
1tbsp chopped parsley
1tbsp shredded basil leaves
salt and freshly ground pepper

Rinse the lentils and put them in a saucepan with the oil, bay leaf and garlic. Add water to cover and simmer with a little salt for 25 minutes until tender but firm.

Cook the noodles in a pan of salted boiling water. They will take about 7 minutes to become soft. Remove from the heat and drain, not too thoroughly, then return the damp noodles to the saucepan and set aside.

Melt half the butter in a pan, and when it starts to sizzle add the leeks and cook until soft. Let them brown a little before adding the herbs. Drain the lentils and add them, with the drained pasta, to the leeks. Stir in the remaining butter; season with salt and pepper and serve while hot. Serve with a casserole or roast meat.
Serves 4 as an accompaniment, 2 as a main dish.

PAPPARDELLE WITH OLIVE PASTE

There are many good olive pastes on the market, but when I prepare my own I make a much coarser mixture, chopping the ingredients rather than processing them to a cream. When shopping for the capers needed for this recipe you may come across two types: those in brine and those in salt; I think the ones in salt have a better flavour.

60g/2oz black olives
4 anchovy fillets, rinsed and dried
1 dried chilli, crushed
1tbsp capers, rinsed
3tbsp olive oil
2 sun-dried tomatoes, soaked for 10 minutes in boiling water, then chopped
2tbsp chopped parsley
pappardelle for 2
freshly grated Parmesan

Stone and chop the olives finely, but not to a purée. Chop the anchovies and add them with the chilli and capers to the olives. Warm the olive oil in a shallow pan and stir in all the ingredients except the pasta and the grated Parmesan.

Cook the pasta in boiling, salted water, then drain and add to the olive paste. Tip into a warmed serving bowl and scatter over a handful of freshly grated Parmesan.
Makes enough for 2 servings of pasta.

Pappardelle with Olive Paste

WHOLEWHEAT PASTA GRATIN WITH RED ONIONS AND THYME

2 medium-sized red onions
30g/1oz butter
1 clove garlic
chopped leaves from two sprigs of thyme
280g/10oz dried wholewheat pasta
1 litre/1¾ pints rich cheese sauce, well seasoned
4tbsp chopped parsley
salt and freshly ground pepper
1tbsp grated Parmesan cheese

Peel and slice the onions thinly. Place them in a pan with the butter, chopped garlic and thyme. Cover the pan with greaseproof paper and a lid (so that the onions soften without burning), and cook slowly over a low heat until sweet and translucent.

Cook the pasta until tender (about 8 minutes) in boiling salted water, then drain. Mix the pasta with the cheese sauce, parsley and onions. Check the seasoning. Place in a deep baking dish, scatter over the Parmesan and bake at Gas Mark 5 (190°C, 375°F) for 25-30 minutes till bubbling and crisp on top.
Serves 6 as an accompaniment, 4 as a main course with salad.

● Almost any pasta can be used in a gratin. Nib-shaped *penne*, thin tubular *macaroni* and spiral *fusilli* are perhaps the most appropriate.
● Serve this gratin with roast lamb or chicken.
● Substitute yellow onions if you prefer them.
● Look out for the Italian Paolini brand of wholewheat pasta at your local health food shop – it is made with organically grown durum wheat and is the best I have come across.

Wholewheat Pasta Gratin with Red Onions and Thyme

FETTUCCINE WITH GREMOLATA, FRIED CRUMBS AND MELTED MOZZARELLA

3 cloves garlic, peeled and chopped
grated zest of 1 lemon
a handful of chopped parsley
60g/2oz butter
2 cupfuls of fresh white breadcrumbs
fettuccine for 2
2tbsp virgin olive oil
200g/7oz mozzarella, in 1cm/½ inch cubes

Make gremolata by mixing together the garlic, lemon zest and parsley. Set aside.

Melt the butter in a shallow pan over a gentle heat and when it starts to foam, add the breadcrumbs. Cook until they are golden, tossing continuously and taking care not to let them brown.

Cook the pasta in boiling, salted water, then drain. Tip into a warmed serving dish and toss with the gremolata, fried crumbs, olive oil and mozzarella. Serve at once.
Serves 2.

STEAMED BROCCOLI WITH MUSTARD NOODLES

400g/14oz noodles or fettuccine
455g/1lb broccoli
60g/2oz butter
1tbsp Dijon mustard
salt and freshly ground pepper
2tbsp chopped parsley

Drop the noodles into plenty of boiling salted water and cook rapidly until they are *al dente*. Trim the broccoli and divide into large florets, cutting the stalks into chunks. About 5 minutes before the pasta is cooked, steam the broccoli over boiling water until tender but still crisp.

Drain the noodles, melt the butter in the same saucepan and add the mustard. Return the noodles to the pan. Season with black pepper and add the chopped parsley. Heat through, stirring until very hot.

Place the noodles on 4 hot plates and add the steamed broccoli.
Serves 4 as a main dish.

COOKING PASTA

● Give pasta enough water to move about in: about 4 litres/7 pints of water for each 455g/1lb pasta, in a large saucepan that leaves plenty of space above the level of the water. Add a tablespoon of sea salt for each 4 litres/7 pints as the water comes to the boil. Put the pasta in when the water is boiling.
● Add all the pasta at once to ensure even cooking. Cover the pan with a lid to ensure the water returns quickly to the boil. When the water boils, re-move the lid and turn down the heat to a rolling boil, making sure the water does not boil over.
● The pasta is cooked when it is *al dente*. This means 'firm to the bite'. It is extraordinarily easy to overcook pasta and difficult to give timings.
● To be sure not to overcook pasta, test both dried and fresh types continually during cooking. Fresh pasta is cooked when it has risen to the surface of the water, is firm and slightly tacky to the touch.

● Start testing fresh pasta ribbons after 45 seconds of boiling, dried pasta after 8 minutes. It is done when it offers some resistance to the teeth. On no account should it be soft.

MUSHROOM LASAGNE

**2 large onions, peeled and
roughly chopped
2tbsp olive oil
bay leaf
sprigs of thyme
2 cloves garlic, peeled and sliced
455g/1lb mushrooms, sliced
butter
230g/8oz fresh lasagne
200g/7oz tomato sauce
salt and freshly ground pepper
200g/7oz mozzarella
40g/1½oz butter
40g/1½oz flour
850ml/1½ pints milk
4tbsp grated Parmesan**

Cook the onions in the olive oil over a
medium heat until they are translucent.
Add the herbs and the garlic. Stir in the
mushrooms and cook, covered with a
lid, until the mushrooms are soft and
their juices have started to run.

Butter a 30cm/12 in gratin dish.
Cover the base with a layer of lasagne.

Stir in the tomato sauce and a cupful
of water into the mushroom mixture.
Season with salt and pepper and simmer for 5 minutes, uncovered. Spoon
half of the mushroom mixture over the
pasta in the dish. Slice the mozzarella
and lay it over the mushrooms. Lay the
remaining pasta on top and then spoon
over the rest of the mushroom mixture.

Heat the oven to Gas Mark 6 (200°C,
400°F). Melt the butter in a pan, add the
flour and stir until they are combined.
Cook, stirring for 4-5 minutes.

Bring the milk to the boil and pour it
into the butter and flour, stirring until it is
smooth. Add salt and pepper, then
cook over a low heat for 5 minutes.
Pour on top of the mushrooms in the
dish and scatter over the Parmesan.

Bake in the preheated oven for about
40 minutes, until golden.
Serves 4.

*Mushroom
Lasagne*

TORTELLONI WITH BLUE CHEESE

This recipe is good with any blue
cheese, such as Gorgonzola, dolcelatte
or that delicious hybrid with layers of
dolcelatte and mascarpone. Any pasta
can be used, but I like spinach tortelloni,
because of its affinity with blue cheese. It
is very rich, so serve in small portions
with a chicory salad.

**spinach tortelloni for 2
230g/8oz soft, creamy blue
cheese, at room temperature
60g/2oz butter, cut into small
pieces
freshly ground black pepper**

Cook the pasta in boiling salted water,
then drain. Mash the cheese and butter
together in a large, hot serving bowl,
until it is melted and creamy. Toss the
pasta with the cheese and butter in the
bowl and give it one or two grinds of the
peppermill.
Serves 2.

APRICOT TABBOULEH

Bulgar wheat is available from health
food shops and delicatessens. Lots of
lemon juice is important here, so be
generous. The nutty flavour of the
wheat combines well with the fresh
green of the herbs and the surprising
addition of ripe apricots.

**85g/3oz bulgar wheat
60g/2oz (a good handful) parsley
30g/1oz mint
juice of 2 lemons
2tbsp olive oil
salt and freshly ground pepper
4-8 small spring onions
230g/8oz (about 6) apricots or
110g/4oz dried apricots soaked
for 1 hour**

Place the bulgar wheat in a pudding
basin and pour over enough cold water
to cover it completely. Allow this to
stand for 15 minutes while you prepare
the rest of the salad.

Chop the parsley and the mint quite
finely. Mix the lemon juice, olive oil and
salt and pepper in the dish in which you
are to serve the salad. Chop the onions
into small pieces.

Peel the apricots if you wish; if they
are very ripe the skins will come off
easily. Otherwise place the fruit in a
basin, cover with boiling water, leave for
a minute then peel with the point of a
sharp knife. Cut each apricot in half, remove the stone and chop the fruit into
large pieces.

Drain the water from the bulgar
wheat and, squeezing the grains in the
palm of your hand to remove the excess water, drop each handful of wheat
into the dish containing the dressing. Stir
in the chopped herbs, spring onions and
chopped apricots. Leave the salad for 10
minutes or longer for the flavours to
blend thoroughly, then serve with long,
crisp lettuce leaves, or, if possible, fresh
vine leaves.
Serves 4 as an accompaniment or 2 as a
main course dish.

● Makes a particularly good accompaniment to roast lamb dishes.

Date and Pistachio Couscous

KASHA

Kasha is another name for buckwheat. It is the seed of a herbaceous plant and has a wonderful nutty flavour. It is particularly popular in Eastern Europe and in France — when crushed it becomes an essential ingredient of the famous buckwheat *crêpes* you find on street corners in Paris. This recipe is based on one in the 28-page American book, *The Arcadia Cookbook* by Anne Rosenzweig (Abrams, 1986), which comes in the form of an accordian-fold seasonal mural by Paul Davies.

**2tbsp butter
I medium onion, finely chopped
455ml/16fl oz vegetable or
chicken stock
170g/6oz buckwheat (kasha)
salt and freshly ground pepper**

Melt the butter in a saucepan and when it starts to sizzle, add the onion and cook till soft. Add the stock and bring to a simmer. In a separate pan, cook the buckwheat over a lively heat for a few minutes, tossing the grains around so that they brown but do not burn. Pour the stock over the kasha, season and simmer for 15-20 minutes, until the liquid is absorbed.

Serves 6 as an accompaniment to roast meats or baked vegetables.

DATE AND PISTACHIO COUSCOUS

**230g/8oz medium couscous
a little vegetable oil
110g/4oz dried apricots, sliced
110g/4oz prunes, stoned and
sliced
85g/3oz pistachios, shelled
85g/3oz stoned dates, chopped**

Wash the couscous in a sieve, tip the grains into a shallow pan and sprinkle with water. Leave to swell for 10 minutes. Rub a drop of oil into your hands, and sift the couscous with your fingertips to separate the grains (most therapeutic this).

Transfer the couscous to the top of a steamer. Cook, without a lid, for 20 minutes. Remove the top part of the steamer and tip the couscous into the shallow pan again. Spread the grains out and sprinkle over a glass of cold water and a teaspoon of salt. Oil your hands again and break up any lumps. Allow the grains to dry for 10 minutes. At this point you can store the couscous in the fridge until you need to use it.

Return the grains to the steamer and cook for a further 20 minutes (or 30 if you have refrigerated it). Stir in the fruit and nuts. Remove from the steamer and serve.

Serves 4 as a side dish.

• The traditional accompaniment to Moroccan-style casseroles (*tagines*) of meat and vegtables, couscous is especially good with roast duck.

• It is particularly good if you stir in a knob of butter just before serving.

• For more information about the history and cooking of couscous, I recommend Paula Wolfert's *Good Food From Morocco* (John Murray, 1989).

SWEETCORN FRITTERS WITH CHILLI BUTTER

Although these little fritters make an original starter, you can also serve them as a main dish. Make them larger, if you wish, and serve them with a salad such as tomato and fresh coriander.

FOR THE FRITTERS:
2tbsp wholemeal flour
1tbsp plain flour
salt
1 egg
3tbsp milk
110g/4oz tinned sweetcorn, drained
FOR THE BUTTER:
1 small red chilli, fresh or dried, or ¼tsp chilli powder
60g/2oz butter
salt
juice of half a lemon

oil, for frying

Place the flour and salt in a small basin. Separate the egg; add the yolk to the flour and place the white in a small separate basin. Stir the milk into the flour and mix thoroughly. Add the sweetcorn and leave for 30 minutes in a cool place. Although not absolutely necessary, this resting of the batter before cooking allows the starch cells to swell, which will give a lighter fritter.

Meanwhile, make the butter. If using a whole chilli, cut it in half, remove the seeds and white inner membrane. If it's fresh, chop it very finely, almost to a purée; if dried, crush it to a powder using a pestle and mortar or a spice mill. Alternatively, you can crush it in a small basin with the end of a rolling pin. Cream the butter in a small basin until soft, stir in the crushed chilli or chilli powder and a little salt. Stir in the lemon juice. Refrigerate until needed.

Beat the egg white with a whisk until it

is stiff and fluffy, as if making a meringue. Using a metal spoon, fold it gently into the sweetcorn batter. Heat enough oil in a shallow pan to come 1 cm/½ inch up the side.

When the oil is hot, drop in table-spoons of the batter. They should sizzle immediately. Cook 5 or 6 fritters at a time, for 3-4 minutes. Lift each fritter with a palette knife; if it is golden on the bottom, turn it over to cook the other side.

When all the fritters are golden and crisp, drain them on kitchen paper. Remove them to a warm serving plate and drop teaspoons of the chilli butter on to each hot fritter.

Makes 12 small fritters; serves 2 as a starter.

ONION SKIRLIE

A traditional Scottish dish that works well as a side dish for grilled fish and roast meats. In her informative paper-back *Scottish Cookery* (Richard Drew, 1989), Catherine Brown suggests it also makes a good stuffing, particularly for game.

60g/2oz dripping or butter
1 large onion, finely chopped
110g/4oz coarse oatmeal
salt and freshly ground pepper

Melt the dripping or butter in a shallow pan. Add the onion and cook until soft. Sprinkle in the oatmeal and season. When all of the fat is absorbed, which should be a couple of minutes, the skirlie is ready. Serve hot.
Serves 2 as a side dish.

● Serve with grilled mackerel, trout or black pudding. As a side dish for roast chicken it is hard to beat.

GRAINS

Grains have been raised to a new smart status by enterpris-ing young chefs. Although stocked by supermarkets and grocers, the best place to find them is in health food stores and Italian delis. They go stale quite quickly, so it is best to transfer them to kilner jars once opened.
● *Kasha.* Another name for buckwheat, this is a favourite staple in Eastern Europe. It is not actually a grain, but is, in fact, the seed of a plant related to rhubarb. Use it as you would rice in a risotto, the texture will

be slightly different, but quite pleasing to eat. It probably has the most strident flavour of the grains.
● *Couscous.* Couscous is made from semolina, the fine grains of which are wet through then rolled in flour. Steaming is the most appropriate method of cooking, and more often than not, butter is folded in at the end of cooking.
● *Bulgar.* Bulgar can be spelt in several ways, but it is all the same product – cracked wheat. Much of it needs no cooking, just a good soak

before squeezing out the water and then wringing dry. Dress it with a sharp citrus vinaigrette and add finely chopped parsley or coriander for a quickly prepared refresh-ing salad.
● *Cornmeal.* The most popu-lar use of cornmeal at present is polenta, the yellow maize-meal mush made fashionable by new-wave Italian restaurants. It is just as good whether eaten wet or allowed to set then sliced and fried till crisp. I find the coarse-textured polenta gives a more interesting tex-ture when cooked.

SPICED BROWN RICE

4 cardamom pods or
½tsp ground cardamom
½tsp coriander seeds or
½tsp ground coriander
I dried or I small fresh chilli
I onion
3 cloves garlic
salt and freshly ground pepper
4tbsp groundnut oil
2.5cm/I inch piece fresh ginger
455g/Ilb long-grain brown rice
570ml/I pint vegetable stock

For whole spices, split the cardamom pods open and grind the seeds with the coriander seeds and the dried chilli, if using. A spice mill or pestle and mortar is best. Peel and finely chop the onion. If using a fresh chilli, finely chop it. Crush the garlic with a little salt.

Heat the groundnut oil and add the ground spices. Gently cook for little more than a minute, then add the onion and garlic. Cook for 2 minutes. Peel and grate the ginger and add to the pan.

Stir in the rice, season with salt and pour in the vegetable stock. Cover and simmer for 45 minutes or until the rice is cooked. Check the liquid often, as you may need to top it up. Season with ground pepper before serving.
Serves 4

VEGETABLE COUSCOUS

Don't be put off by this long list of ingredients – the stew is no trouble to put together and will take less than an hour from start to finish. The Harissa Sauce used in the recipe is available from good supermarkets and delicatessens, but sambal oelek, the Indonesian spice paste, can be used instead.

455g/Ilb couscous
30g/Ioz butter
I large onion, peeled and cut into
sixths through the root
2.5cm/I inch piece of fresh
ginger, peeled
Itsp turmeric
½tsp mild chilli powder
I cinnamon stick
½tsp freshly ground black
pepper
a pinch of saffron
3 medium carrots, scrubbed and
roughly chopped
2 medium potatoes, scrubbed
and cut into thick slices
½ a small pumpkin, peeled,
seeded and sliced
I medium can chick peas,
drained of their liquor
60g/2oz raisins
2tbsp chopped flat leaf parsley
2tbsp chopped coriander leaves
FOR THE RED PEPPER SAUCE:
Itsp Harissa Sauce
Itbsp lemon juice
Itbsp virgin olive oil
a little fresh coriander

First prepare the couscous. Place it in a fine sieve and wash thoroughly. Spread out on a baking sheet and leave for 10 minutes, then run the grain through your fingers to break up any lumps. Leave for another 20 minutes. Place the couscous in a colander over a pan of simmering water and steam, uncovered, for 20 minutes. Tip the couscous on to the baking sheet again and leave for 10 minutes while you prepare the stew. With a little oil rubbed into the palm of your hands, break up any lumps. Melt the butter in a heavy-based pot.

Cook the onion until it is soft and yellow, and has slightly caught at the edges. Shred the ginger finely, stir into the onion with the spices and fry for 2 minutes. Add the root vegetables and the pumpkin. Sweat the mixture over a medium heat for a few minutes, then add the chick-peas and raisins with 570ml/I pint water. Bring to the boil, then simmer for 25-30 minutes, until the vegtables are tender. Stir in the herbs and check the seasoning.

Give the couscous a second steaming in a colander over water or over the stew. If the colander does not fit exactly over the cooking pot, wrap a tea-towel around the join so that no steam escapes from the sides.

While this is cooking, make the red pepper sauce. Spoon 6tbsp of the broth from the vegetables into a dish and stir in the Harissa Sauce, lemon juice, olive oil and coriander.

To eat, serve a mound of couscous to each person, spoon on the vegetable stew and sprinkle over a little of the sauce.
Serves 6.

Vegetable
Couscous

WILD AND BROWN RICE PILAFF

85g/3oz wild rice
570ml/1 pint water
455ml/16fl oz vegetable stock or
water
2tbsp olive oil
1 small onion, finely diced
bay leaf
170g/6oz brown rice
salt

Place the wild rice in a sieve and rinse it under running water. Salt the water, bring it to the boil and add the wild rice. Let it simmer for half an hour, until all the water is absorbed.

Bring the stock to the boil. Heat the oil in a saucepan. Add the diced onion and the bay leaf to the oil and cook, stirring occasionally, until the onion is soft, for about 5 minutes. Add the brown rice, a little salt, and the stock.

Cover the pan and leave to simmer for 40 minutes, checking occasionally that the liquid hasn't evaporated, and adding more if necessary. Stir the wild rice into the brown rice and serve. Serves 4 as a side dish.

● Serve this pilaff with vegetable or meat casseroles.

Polenta

POLENTA

The Italians have appreciated polenta, which is made from cornmeal, for centuries. Now the word is spreading!

¾ litre/1½ pints water
salt
170g/6oz coarse cornmeal

Bring the water to the boil, add salt and pour the cornmeal into the boiling water. Stir quickly to stop lumps forming, reduce the heat and leave to simmer and thicken for 20 minutes. Stir as often as you can.

When the polenta comes away from the sides of the pan, turn it out on to a wooden board. Shape into a loaf with a spoon and leave for an hour or so to set, then slice it like thick toast.

Fry the slices in hot oil for a few minutes, or grill them on each side with a sprinkling of Parmesan until a crust forms. Serve plain or with a hot tomato and chilli sauce.
Serves 2

MILLET CASSEROLE WITH PISTACHIO NUTS

One-Course Feasts by Colin Spencer (Conran Octopus, 1991) is a collection of original vegetarian recipes, which includes this nutty casserole.

75g/3oz pistachio nuts, shelled
and peeled
40g/1½oz butter
2 cloves garlic, crushed
110g/4oz millet
285ml/½ pint stock
sea salt and freshly ground
pepper
75ml/3fl oz dry vermouth

Roughly grind 60g/2oz of the pistachio nuts, reserving the remainder. Melt 30g/1oz of the butter in a thick-bottomed flameproof oven dish and stir in the garlic and millet, then add the stock and the ground nuts. Bring to the boil, then simmer for 20 minutes. Season to taste. Stir in the reserved whole pistachio nuts, the dry vermouth and the remainder of the butter.
Serves 6.

GRILLED MARINATED TOFU

If you have tried tofu once and didn't like it then I urge you to have another go, this time marinating it with garlic, soy sauce and ginger.

2 cloves garlic, peeled and sliced
115ml/4fl oz olive oil
115ml/4fl oz red wine vinegar
115ml/4fl oz soy sauce
285ml/½ pint water
2.5cm/1 inch knob of fresh ginger, peeled and grated
455g/1lb tofu

Place the garlic, oil, vinegar, soy and ginger in a saucepan, add the water and bring to the boil. Place the tofu in a shallow dish, pour over the hot marinade, let it cool and leave in the fridge for an hour or two. Cut the tofu into chunks and place in a shallow pan. Grill, turning the chunks occasionally until they start to crisp.
Serves 4 as a side dish.

● Serve with stir-fry vegetables, chicken or noodles.
● Try threading the marinated tofu on to skewers with tomatoes and mushrooms and serving with rice.

CHICK PEA PUREE

Chick peas are one of the few foods that emerge from a can in good shape. If using dried ones, soak them overnight then boil them for a couple of hours.

Drain a can of chick peas, tip them into a saucepan and cover them with water or stock if you have some. Throw in a few herbs (some parsley stalks and a sprig of thyme would be nice, and a bay leaf). Salt the water and bring to the boil, then add half the chick peas' weight in peeled and diced potatoes. Simmer for 15 minutes or until the potatoes are tender. Drain and mash with a potato masher or, better still, push through a sieve. Stir in a generous knob of butter and a grind of black pepper. Serve warm.

● Serve with grilled meat and kebabs.

DAHL

1 onion, finely sliced
60g/2oz clarified butter or ghee
1 tsp turmeric
1 tsp ground cardamom
1 tsp cayenne
2 bay leaves
salt
230g/8oz lentils

Cook the sliced onion in the butter or ghee until soft and brown. Stir in the spices, add the bay leaves and season with a little salt. Cook for 3-4 minutes on a medium heat, then set aside.

Cook the lentils in enough salted water to cover. After 25 minutes, cover the saucepan and turn down the heat. Cook for about 20 minutes until soft, then stir in the onion mixture. Beat well until mixed – the consistency should be that of a rough purée. Serve hot with rice.
Serves 2.

PULSES

● *Lentilles de Puy.* By far the most chic of the pulses, Puy lentils are slate-blue/green in colour and really quite tiny. They keep their shape when cooked and are particularly flavoursome.

Cook them for 15 minutes then test to see if they are tender – they may need another 5 or so minutes. They also make a fine salad, particularly when dressed with a lemony vinaigrette.

● *Brown Lentils.* Slightly larger than Puy lentils, brown lentils have an earthiness to them which makes them particularly good for winter soups. They cook, without any pre-soaking, in 15-20 minutes.

● *Flageolet Beans.* Probably the most prized of all the beans, pale green flageolets are wonderfully versatile. They have a mild nutty flavour and go well with lamb and even fish. Soak them for at least 3 hours then cook them in unsalted water for 45 minutes. Salt them at the end of their cooking, dressing them with olive oil and perhaps a little garlic.

● *Black-eyed beans.* Round to slightly oval, black-eyed beans are creamy white in colour with a little black 'eye'. They tend to turn slightly darker when cooked, which will take 45-60 minutes. They should be soaked for a good 3 hours before cooking.

● *Mung Beans.* These are tiny, oval beans, a sort of dull green in colour. Although most people recommend soaking them for a few hours, I quite often cook them without, adding 10-15 minutes on to the cooking time. They are at their best when sprouted in a salad sprouter and eaten raw or in a salad.

● *Split Peas.* Green split peas need no soaking and cook to a purée in half an hour or so. Use them in soups.

MUSTARD AND MOLASSES BEAN HOTPOT

These are the ultimate baked beans, not as tomatoey but spicier than the norm.

455g/1lb assorted dried beans
397g/14oz can tomatoes
3tbsp molasses or black treacle
3tsp dry English mustard
salt and freshly ground pepper
2 onions, peeled but not chopped
110g/4oz piece of salt pork or salami

Rinse the beans in a sieve under running water. Place them in a large saucepan, cover them with water and bring them to the boil; cover with a lid. Reduce the heat and leave to simmer for about 5 minutes. Remove them from the heat and leave them, still covered, for 2 hours. Without draining them, bring the beans to the boil and turn the heat down to simmer gently for about 1 hour. Do not add any salt at this stage; it would only toughen the beans.

Preheat the oven to Gas Mark 2 (150°C, 300°F). Chop the tinned tomatoes roughly with a knife while still in the tin, to avoid the juice running everywhere. Then pour them into a saucepan with the molasses and the mustard. Bring to the boil, stirring until the molasses has dissolved. Season with salt and pepper. Remove from the heat.

Drain the beans, reserving the cooking liquor. This is best done by positioning a sieve or colander over a large basin placed in the sink. Return the beans to the saucepan with the 2 peeled whole onions. Bury the piece of pork or salami at the bottom of the pan and pour over the tomato stock. Add 570ml/1 pint of the reserved liquor.

Bake for 1½ hours with the lid on. After that time, remove the lid, stir well and bake for a further 25-30 minutes until the top has formed a crust.

Serve the dish hot, with the pork or salami divided between the plates, and with plenty of bread to mop up the juice.
Serves 4.

LENTILLES DE PUY AND PAPPARDELLE

Serve this dish of contrasting textures as a side dish, or as a main course with a tomato-based salad.

230g/8oz Lentilles de Puy
salt
230g/8oz pappardelle
115g/4oz butter
4 shallots, peeled and diced
2tbsp shredded basil leaves
ground black pepper

Wash the lentils in a sieve under running water. Place them in a saucepan with enough water to cover, add salt, and cook them until tender, about 15-20 minutes.

Cook the pasta in plenty of boiling salted water till *al dente*. Drain, and set aside.

Cook the shallots in half the butter until soft. Drain the lentils, add them with the noodles to the softened onions and season with the remaining butter, basil leaves and freshly ground pepper. Serve 4 as a side dish.

HOT BROWN LENTILS WITH MINT VINAIGRETTE

Scent a basic vinaigrette with shallot and mint. Mint is a pungent, refreshing herb; you'll need only a dozen or so leaves for a side salad for 4.

Make a vinaigrette by combining a finely chopped shallot with 2tbsp white wine vinegar in a bowl, add a little salt and pepper and whisk in 6tbsp extra virgin olive oil. Stir in the mint and drizzle over 230g/8oz warm brown lentils.

Serve as a side dish to a simple grilled, steamed or baked fish.

HOT FLAGEOLET AND RUNNER BEANS IN OLIVE OIL

Soak 200g/7oz flageolet beans for 2 hours in cold water. Drain, then simmer gently in fresh water for half an hour.

Cut the tops from 170g/6oz runner beans and slice them diagonally into thick diamond-shaped pieces. When the flageolets are tender, yet still have bite, add the runner beans. Cook them for no more than 2 or 3 minutes, drain and place in a large basin.

Squeeze the juice of a lemon over the beans and grind over a little salt and black pepper. Pour 4 tablespoons of extra virgin olive oil over the hot beans and toss them gently; the dish will smell invitingly fruity. Serve with a helping of crusty bread so as not to waste any of the dressing.
Serves 4 as a starter.

LENTIL, HAZELNUT AND REDCURRANT SALAD

Use brown lentils or, if you can track them down, the dark green Puy lentils, which are stocked by most good delicatessens and wholefood shops.

170g/6oz lentils, Puy or small brown
170g/6oz redcurrants or whitecurrants
60g/2oz whole hazelnuts
4 chives, chopped
1tbsp olive oil or ½tbsp each of olive oil and hazelnut oil
juice of 1 lime
salt and freshly ground pepper

Cook the lentils in boiling, salted water for 10-12 minutes. Drain and rinse in a sieve, under cold water. Put them into the serving bowl.

Top and tail the currants and add to the lentils. Place the hazelnuts on a baking sheet or on the grill pan and toast under a hot grill for 4-5 minutes until the skins start to blister. Remove the nuts from the heat and rub them with a tea towel until the skins start to flake off. Stir them into the lentil and fruit mixture.

Place the chopped chives in a small basin, add the oil and the lime juice, season with the salt and pepper and mix them thoroughly with a fork or small whisk. Pour this over the lentils and toss gently so as not to mash the currants. Spoon on to plates and serve with bitter red radicchio leaves.
Serves 4 as a starter or a side dish with grilled liver or baked mackerel.

BOSTON BAKED BEANS

This is an American friend's version of the famous one-pot dish.

455g/1lb white haricot or pink borlotti beans
30g/1oz butter
1 onion, chopped
2 cloves garlic, peeled and crushed
50ml/2fl oz molasses
1tbsp dry mustard
2tbsp Dijon grain mustard
1tbsp paprika
2tbsp Worcestershire Sauce
2 mild fresh chillies
a sprig or two of thyme
570ml/1 pint tomato juice
110g/4oz bacon in the piece
salt and freshly ground pepper (optional)

Soak the beans overnight. Melt the butter in a heavy-based pot, add the onion and garlic and cook on a low heat until transparent. Stir in the rest of the ingredients, add the drained beans, and place the piece of bacon in the middle. Bring to the boil, turn down the heat and simmer for 15 minutes.

Cook in a preheated oven at Gas Mark 4 (180°C, 350°F) for about 2 hours, until the beans are tender. Check the seasoning, adding salt and pepper if you think it needs it. Cut the bacon into pieces as you serve.
Serves 6.

SIMMERED LENTILS

Boston Baked Beans

230g/8oz green lentils
1 carrot, 1 small onion, 1 stick celery, finely diced
3 cloves garlic, peeled
4 sprigs of parsley
bay leaf
salt and freshly ground pepper
olive oil

Rinse the lentils. Put them in a saucepan, salt them and just cover them with water. Add the vegetables, garlic and herbs. Bring to the boil, turn the heat down and simmer for 20 minutes. The lentils should be firm but tender. Drain the little liquid that remains, reserving it for a soup or stock. Remove the bay leaf, parsley and garlic and season with pepper. Drizzle over a little olive oil and serve.
Serves 4 as a side dish.

● Serve with smoked fish, roast poultry or game.
● Look out for the fashionable small green *lentilles de Puy* from France, which have a wonderful nutty aroma. Failing that, use the small brown variety.

CHEESE & EGGS

The original convenience foods: readily available,
easy to store and quick to prepare for kitchen
classics and smart new ideas.

Cheese and eggs are probably the two most versatile additions to the storecupboard. An endless number of snacks, salads and meals can be made from either: indeed, it is difficult to think of life without them.

CHEESE

It is now easier than ever to buy traditionally made British cheeses. Grocers, local markets and cheese specialists are taking a great interest in our regional cheeses and offering a better stock than many of the supermarkets.

Traditionally produced 'artisan' cheeses are often made with unpasteurised milk, and have a deeper, more lively flavour than the bland 'block' cheeses of the big manufacturers. These traditional cheese-makers mostly operate from small farms with little encouragement from the 'powers that be'. Fortunately, there is a growing interest in 'real cheese' and it is now being stocked at a wide range of outlets, including some supermarket chains.

A little while spent in a cheese specialist's can be very rewarding. These shops are only too happy to let you taste as many cheeses as you want before you decide which to buy. I prefer to have just one, or perhaps two, cheeses around at once rather than have lots of little bits on a board. As I am particularly fond of goat's and sheep's milk cheeses I try to have one of these at home, too.

I find that a little cheese and some fruit is often all I need for lunch, but often use cheese in a salad such as a plate of tomatoes and soft, milky mozzarella. If I have really good pears then I serve them with peco-rino cheese and sometimes with huge shelled walnuts.

Sharp salty cheeses are particularly good in salads; try Greek feta with a truly ripe melon and a handful of ripe olives. Goat's cheese fans may enjoy its combination with beetroot or like to try it cubed and

wrapped in sharp sorrel leaves, then baked in the oven till melting.

Generally, I prefer to eat fine cheeses as they are with bread or biscuits, but if I cook with them at all it is in a very unfussy way. I have enjoyed grilling cheese such as Cypriot Halloumi marinated and grilled or a

tasty English variety such as Cheshire served with sizzling pears straight from the pan.

EGGS

The egg is an indispensable food. It can be boiled, baked, poached, fried, scrambled or beaten into an omelette, but it also plays a vital supporting role in custards, meringues, butter sauces and cakes. Eggs

also play a major part in a vegetarian diet, although they are unacceptable to vegans, who do not eat any dairy products.

There are three main methods of egg production. Eggs marked 'free range' imply that the hens have continuous daytime access to outdoor runs. Sometimes you will also find details of the hens' living conditions and diet on the box. These are the ones I always buy, and not just because I prefer my eggs to come from 'happy hens', I do believe they taste much better. 'Barn' or 'perchery' eggs are from hens that are permanently kept indoors; and you can be sure that unmarked eggs are from battery farms, where the hens are kept caged.

Eggs are graded according to size and labelled from size 0 to 7. Size 0 weighs 75g and over, size I weighs 70-75g, size 2 is 65-70, and 3 is 60-65. It is important to choose the right egg for the job. Most recipes are designed to use size 3 eggs, which are the most accessible and moderately priced. Larger sized eggs are usually used when the eggs are to be served whole, such as when they are boiled or poached. Although brown eggs look more wholesome than white ones, they taste no different. The colour depends on the breed of hen and has nothing to do with flavour.

When you get your eggs home they should be stored in a cool place with the pointed end downwards. It is not necessary to keep them in the fridge. Eggs will generally maintain their freshness for a fortnight if kept in the right conditions. To test an egg for freshness drop it into a large glass of water. If it sinks to the bottom it is fresh; if it floats throw it out, as it will be too stale to eat.

Duck and goose eggs have a rich flavour. Their generous size makes them good for baking, but they should be thoroughly cooked and not served soft-boiled as ducks and geese are not too fussy about where they lay their eggs.

PAN-FRIED PEAR AND CHESHIRE CHEESE SALAD

I large or 2 small pears
half a lemon
Itbsp walnut oil
2tbsp broken walnuts
a handful of salad leaves
60g/2oz Cheshire cheese

Wipe the pears, but do not peel them. Cut them in half and then into quarters. Remove the core and cut into thick slices, probably about 8 per pear. Squeeze lemon juice on to the flesh to prevent discolouring.

Heat the oil in a large shallow pan, place the pear slices into the hot oil and scatter over the broken walnuts. Cook the pears until golden and sizzling, turning them once.

Place a few salad leaves on two plates. With a palette knife, remove the pears and place them on top of the salad leaves.

Crumble the cheese into small pieces about the size of a walnut half. Divide the crumbled cheese between the plates, scattering it over the hot pears; it will soften a little but not melt. Squeeze any remaining lemon juice into the pan and spoon the resulting dressing with the walnuts over the pears.
Serves 2 as a starter or snack.

TOMATO AND MOZZARELLA CHEESE SALAD WITH BASIL AND OLIVES

4 very ripe tomatoes
2 balls mozzarella cheese
4tbsp extra virgin olive oil
10 basil leaves
salt
coarsely ground black pepper
12 slices salami, optional
16 black olives

Slice the tomatoes and the mozzarella into thick pieces. Pour the olive oil into a small basin, tear the basil leaves into pieces and stir into the oil. Season with salt and grind in some pepper. Lay the mozzarella, tomatoes and salami on 4 plates. Add the black olives and drizzle over the basil dressing.

Serve with country bread.
Serves 2-3.

GOATS' CHEESE BAKED IN SORREL

This recipe is loosely based on Jane Grigson's Cheese in Vine Leaves. Use spinach if you prefer, but it may need blanching in boiling water for a few minutes first so that the leaves are supple enough to wrap around the cheese.

20 sorrel leaves
4 × 60g/2oz goats' cheeses
olive oil for brushing
crusty white bread to serve

Preheat the oven to Gas Mark 6 (200°C, 400°F).

Using five or so leaves per cheese, wrap the goats' cheeses up and secure with a cocktail stick if necessary. Place them in an ovenproof dish, sprinkle with olive oil, then bake for 10 minutes. They are done when the cheese starts to soften and the colour of the sorrel leaves has changed from bright green to soft seaweed. Serve hot, spread on crusty white bread.
Serves 2 as nibbles.

HOT BEETROOT WITH GOATS' CHEESE

Now that many supermarkets are stocking small bottles of nut oils, such as walnut or hazelnut, you can afford to keep a few different types open simultaneously. Use them up quickly, as they are inclined to become rancid.

455g/Ilb small or medium raw beetroot
110g/4oz goats' cheese
2tbsp walnut oil
Itsp wine vinegar
salt and freshly ground pepper
2tbsp walnut halves

Without removing the tops or roots, gently scrub the beetroot with a vegetable brush. Heat some water in the base of a steamer to boiling, place the beetroot into the steamer basket and cover. Steam for 25-30 minutes, testing for tenderness with the point of a knife after about 25 minutes.

While the beetroot is cooking, crumble the cheese and then set aside. In a small bowl, mix the walnut oil and the wine vinegar, then season with salt and pepper. Chop the walnuts coarsely.

When the beetroot is tender, remove one at a time from the steamer. Hold the beetroot under cold running water and cut away the root and top with a small knife. Peel off the skin and return the beetroot to the steamer to keep warm. Repeat with each remaining beetroot.

Slice each beetroot into approximately 6 thin slices, hold each sliced bulb together, then cut down through the slices 6 times to create large matchsticks. Place these in a small, shallow serving dish and spoon over the crumbled goats' cheese.

Pour the dressing over and sprinkle the chopped walnuts on top. Serve immediately, or chill and serve cold.
Serves 2 as a starter.

MELON WITH FETA AND OLIVES

Salt brings out the flavour of melon dramatically. Feta cheese, with its savoury tang, does the same. Any really ripe melon is suitable.

2 ripe melons (charantais, ogen or cantaloup)
230g/8oz feta cheese
handful of black olives

Cut the melons in half, remove the seeds with a teaspoon, carefully saving any of the precious juices in a basin. Peel the flesh from the melon skin and cut into chunks about 2.5cm/1in square. Put the melon into the basin with the juices.

Crumble the feta into similar-sized chunks and scatter over the melon, then add olives. Chill well before serving. Serves 6.

GRILLED MARINATED HALLOUMI

Halloumi, or halloum, is a salty white cheese similar to the popular Greek feta in both taste and appearance. Originally made by bedouin tribes in the Middle East, it is now almost exclusively a Cypriot cheese. If your local supermarket does not stock it (usually next to the feta), look for it in Cypriot and Middle Eastern grocers. It has the advantage of travelling and keeping well, and its slight tang makes it good for outdoor meals.

230g/8oz block of halloumi
4tbsp olive oil
1tbsp chopped fresh thyme or coriander
pepper
lemon wedges for serving

Remove the cheese from its wrapping and pat dry with kitchen paper. Carefully cut it into slices. Lay the slices in a shallow dish, pour over the olive oil and sprinkle with the herbs. Leave for as long as you can (30 minutes minimum) for the cheese to absorb the flavour of the oil and herbs.

Pour the oil in which the cheese has been marinating into a frying pan and heat gently. Season the slices of cheese with pepper and cook in the hot oil for about 2 minutes on each side, until golden in patches. Hand out lemon wedges to those who like to squeeze a drop of lemon juice over the cheese. Serves 4.

MOZZARELLA WITH OLIVES AND CAPERS

If you are on the Continent look for ball-shaped mozzarella cheeses soaking in brine in local shops. In Britain some delicatessens and cheese shops now sell them, but you are more likely to find mozzarella in sealed plastic bags with salted whey inside. It is a fresh cheese so it should be eaten as soon as possible. The best quality is made from buffalo milk – look for cheeses marked Mozzarella de Bufala. The rest is likely to be made from cow's milk and is easily recognized by its firmer texture.

6 thick slices of mozzarella cheese
6 slices of large ripe tomato, preferably marmande
12 ripe olives, pitted
2tbsp capers in brine, rinsed
salt and freshly ground pepper
basil leaves, torn into shreds
chopped parsley
extra virgin olive oil

Lay the mozzarella slices on a plate or board. Place a slice of tomato on top of each piece, then add the olives, capers, salt, pepper and herbs. Drizzle generously with extra virgin olive oil. Serves 2.

● Another soft, fresh cheese for summer is Italian ricotta. Use it as a dip for raw vegetables such as peeled broad beans. Buy the smallest beans you can find to eat raw.

● *Feta.* A hard white crumbly cheese made from cow's, sheep's or goat's milk. Originally made in Greece, it is now also being produced on a small scale in Britain. It has an unusually salty flavour, making it most suited to tomato, melon or apple salads. It is widely available, usually sold in flat blocks wrapped in plastic.

● *Halloumi.* A Cypriot cheese, similar to, though milder in flavour than feta. It has a firm consistency and is particularly good for grilling or in the recipe above.

● *Mozzarella.* Genuine Italian mozzarella is the best for flavour, which is mild and milky, and for texture, which should be juicy and slightly tart. Danish imitations tend to be rubbery and dull. When melting mozzarella, it is important not to let the cheese overcook, which will render it rubbery and dry.

Mozzarella with Olives and Capers

Pears with Pecorino

FRITTATA

The frittata is the Italian answer to the French omelette. It differs from the French in that it is cooked slowly and at a low temperature. For best results you need to use a heavy-based frying pan at least 25-30cm/10-12in in diameter. If you prefer, instead of the cannellini beans, you can substitute other vegetables, such as sliced mushrooms, cooked artichoke hearts, blanched French beans or boiled asparagus.

**6 large eggs
salt and freshly ground pepper
4tbsp grated cheese (Parmesan
or gruyère)
2tbsp finely chopped parsley
230g/8oz cooked cannellini beans
60g/2oz butter
2 tomatoes, halved, seeded and
chopped**

Break the eggs into a bowl and beat gently with a fork. Add salt and a few turns of the pepper-mill. Fold in the cheese, parsley and beans.

Melt the butter in a frying pan set over a medium heat and when it starts to foam, tip in the eggs and beans, then add the tomatoes. Turn the heat down as low as it will go.

After 15 minutes the base of the frittata will be cooked and golden brown – check to see by lifting up the edge with a palette knife. The top of the frittata will still be runny. Hold it under a hot grill until it sets. Turn the frittata out on to a plate and cut it into wedges.
Serves 6 as a main dish.

PEARS WITH PECORINO

Pears are the traditional Tuscan accompaniment to pecorino cheese. Williams pears go particularly well, but it is important that they are ripe – if they smell sweet they will be ready. A soft pecorino is usually chosen to accompany fruit, although I often prefer a more mature, sharper cheese which has a deeper flavour.

Allow one pear per person, and 110g/4oz pecorino. Place the fruit and cheese on the table and let everyone help themselves. Alternatively, serve the pears peeled, cored and sliced on a plate, covered with thin slices of the percorino.

Pecorino is also good in salads. Vegetables such as baby broad beans, shelled but not cooked, and artichoke hearts, boiled until tender, are often tossed with slices of pecorino. Thin slices of prosciutto, Italy's cured ham, or even finely cut salami can be added along with olive oil and a little black pepper.

Frittata

CHEESE CROQUETTES

5tbsp olive oil or 110g/4oz butter
4 rounded tbsp flour
I wine glass sherry
285ml/½ pint chicken stock or milk
4tbsp strong cheese, grated
salt and freshly ground pepper
3-4tbsp seasoned flour
I egg, beaten with 2tbsp milk
4-5tbsp toasted breadcrumbs
oil for frying

Heat the oil or butter in a saucepan. Stir in the flour and let it froth up for a moment. Gradually beat in the sherry and the stock or milk with a wooden spoon. Stir in the grated cheese. Cook over a gentle heat until you have a very thick, soft sauce. Taste, and add salt and pepper.

Spread the mixture on a plate and cover with another inverted plate. Leave to cool and firm in the fridge for an hour or two, or overnight if possible.

When you are ready to cook, spread the seasoned flour on one plate, the egg and milk on a second, and the bread-crumbs on a third. With a knife, mark and then cut the filling into 20-25 short, stubby fingers. Roll each first in the flour, then in the egg mixture and then in the breadcrumbs.

Heat two fingers' depth of oil in a fry-ing pan. When it is lightly hazed, add the croquettes a few at a time and fry until they are crisp and golden. Serve with tomato sauce for dipping.
Makes 20-25.

Goats' Cheese and Tarragon Tarts

GOATS' CHEESE AND TARRAGON TARTS

230g/8oz pack of frozen pastry, thawed
I egg, beaten
4 × 2.5cm/I inch thick slices from a goats' cheese log
4tbsp chopped fresh parsley and tarragon mixed
freshly ground pepper

Preheat the oven to Gas Mark 7 (220°C, 425°F). Cut the pastry into 4 equal pieces and on a floured board, roll out each piece to a 13cm/5in square. Brush the edges of the pastry with a little of the beaten egg.

Put a slice of cheese in the centre of each piece of pastry. Sprinkle a table-spoon of the herbs on top of the cheese and season with the freshly ground pep-per. Draw the sides of the pastry up to form a pyramid. Press the pastry edges together half-way up the sides, leaving the centre open. Slide on to a baking sheet and bake for 15 minutes, or until puffed and golden.

Eat while the cheese is still melting. Makes 4 pastries, enough for 2.

HERBED GOATS' CHEESE

I small fresh goats' cheese for every 2 people
Itbsp mixed herbs per cheese

Chop the herbs and scatter on a small board or plate and roll the cheeses in them. Cut each cheese into slices about 2.5cm/Iin thick. serve with oatcakes, wholemeal scones or bread.

● Look out for fresh, soft goats' cheese at the cheese counter of supermarkets and delicatessens.
● Use a complementary mixture of herbs; try parsley, tarragon and chervil, or parsley, coriander and chives. Avoid using sage and rosemary.
● Slice log-shaped goats' cheeses from the supermarket into pieces 2.5cm/Iin thick, then press them, flat sides down, into the chopped herbs.

Cheese Croquettes

Boiled Eggs Dipped in a Nutty Spice Mixture

EGG ON TOAST

Beat an egg white until fluffy. Spoon it in rough peaks around the edge of a round of buttered toast. Drop an egg yolk into the centre and bake in a hot oven for 4-6 minutes, until the peaks of the egg white start to brown and the yolk just begins to set. Serve with a sprig of dill or tarragon.

● Serve poached eggs on a wholemeal muffin, instead of the usual toast, spread thickly with cream of sun-dried tomato.
● Scramble eggs in the usual way, then stir in any of the following just before the eggs begin to set; finely cut smoked salmon; thin shreds of Parma ham; onion rings which have been cooked in butter until golden brown; a spoonful of cottage cheese and chopped chives.
● Ambrose Heath was one of the most prolific food writers of the 1930s. This splendid way of cooking eggs with soured cream is his:

Cut 7.5cm/3in-diameter rounds of bread and cut 4cm/1½in circles out of the middle of each. Lay the remaining rings of bread in a buttered ovenproof dish and pour as much soured cream over them as they will absorb. Break an egg into the middle of each ring. Sprinkle with salt and pepper, and pour a teaspoon of milk over each egg. Bake at Gas Mark 6 (200°C, 400°F) for 15 minutes.

BOILED EGGS

Boiled – or, more accurately, simmered – eggs can be cooked to varying stages of softness, depending on how you like them. Carefully lower an egg, on a spoon, into a pan of simmering water. Let it cook for 3-4 minutes for a soft white and runny yolk, 6-7 minutes for a firm white and soft yolk, and 10 minutes for firm whites and yolks.

● Dip baby asparagus spears, blanched till tender, in a softly boiled egg as a light snack or lazy breakfast.
● Dip a shelled medium boiled egg, with a firm white and soft yolk, in a nutty spice mixture. Make it by dry-frying 60g/2oz pumpkin seeds, 3tbsp coriander seeds, 60g/2oz sesame seeds and 60g/2oz shelled hazelnuts in a pan until aromatic. Grind in a coffee-grinder or food processor, then stir in ½tsp salt and a few grinds of black pepper. Add a little chilli powder if you like a really spicy dip.
● To avoid a grey ring forming around the yolk of a hard-boiled egg, time the boiling carefully so that you do not overcook the egg, then remove it from the simmering water and leave it under running cold water for a few minutes.
● If you eat your eggs soft boiled – that is, with a runny yolk – make sure they are very fresh and come from hens that have been tested for salmonella.

HERB CUSTARDS

These little custards are a savoury version of a baked sweet custard and are rather like a quiche without the pastry. Flavour them with whichever herbs you have to hand and serve with toast and perhaps a few leaves of frisée or chicory, for supper or a light lunch.

4 eggs
115ml/4fl oz milk
3tbsp double cream
a little salt
4tbsp chopped herbs

Set the oven at Gas Mark 6 (200°C, 400°F). Beat the eggs, milk and cream and season with a little salt. Stir in the chopped herbs. Pour into three buttered cups or ramekins. Bake in a roasting tin filled with enough water to come half-way up the sides of the cups for 20-25 minutes. The custards are done when they are firm in the middle. Leave to cool for 5 minutes, then run a knife round the edge of each custard and turn them out.
Serves 3.

Herb Custards

SOUFFLE OMELETTE WITH CORIANDER PESTO

3 cloves garlic
2tbsp pine nuts
4 stems fresh coriander
2tbsp grated Parmesan
2tbsp olive oil
3 eggs, separated
60g/2oz butter
salt and freshly ground pepper

Crush the peeled garlic cloves in a food processor or mortar. Add the pine nuts and the fresh coriander leaves stripped from their stems, and pound or process until you have a thick paste. Stir in the Parmesan, then slowly add the olive oil, stirring all the time. (Pesto will store in the fridge in a screw-top jar for a week or two. Add a little olive oil to cover.)

Beat the egg yolks with half of the butter and a little salt and pepper for a few seconds. It is not important that the butter does not mix smoothly. Beat the egg whites until stiff.

Melt the remaining butter in an omelette pan. Mix the beaten yolks and whites together and tip into the pan when the butter starts to sizzle and foam. Cook until the omelette is golden on the underside, lifting with a palette knife to check.

Soufflé Omelette with Coriander Pesto

Spoon half of the coriander pesto on to the omelette. Shake the pan to release the omelette, then lift the half nearest the handle and fold over the rest with the help of a palette knife or spatula. Tip out on to a warm plate and eat straight away.
Serves 1 with enough pesto for 2.

BAKED CHEESE EGGS

This is a quick supper dish for one. If you don't have any chutney, try olive paste or artichoke paste from a jar.

2 heaped tbsp spicy chutney
110g/4oz coarsely grated Gruyère or Emmental cheese
1 large egg

Set the oven at Gas Mark 4 (180°C, 350°F). Spread the chutney in the bottom of a small round dish and cover with half the cheese. Break the egg and drop it on to the cheese, then top with the rest of the cheese. Bake for about 10 minutes, until the cheese is melted and golden. Serve with toast.
Serves 1

ZABAGLIONE

The Marsala you need for this creamy classic is the sweet variety rather than the dry. I have made it with sweet sherry, which was quite successful too. A few words of advice when preparing zabaglione: do not let the water boil, as the cream may become too hot and curdle; keep whisking all the time (it is important to have an electric whisk for this); and don't attempt to serve zabaglione when you have guests, unless they are the sort who will happily come and talk to you in the kitchen while you are preparing it.

8 egg yolks
60g/2oz sugar
115ml/4fl oz Marsala

Put the egg yolks and sugar in a medium-sized bowl and place it over a saucepan of gentle simmering water. Using an electric whisk, beat the eggs and sugar until they start to thicken, then gradually add the Marsala, whisking continuously. When thick and creamy, pour into glasses and serve.
Serves 4.

● If you do not have any Marsala you could use sweet sherry, Grand Marnier, a sweet white wine or even orange or lemon juice. Serve crisp biscuits or sponge fingers alongside.

EGGS

● *Quail's Eggs.* Now much easier to find, quail's eggs can be bought from butcher's shops and supermarkets. Most of them are farmed, which explains their availability and reasonable price. Quail's eggs are especially suitable for serving hard-boiled, dipped in celery salt, though they can be used soft-boiled, and carefully shelled, in a leafy salad.

● *Goose Eggs.* These are available from Easter onwards and are much prized for their rich taste and colour. Approximately twice the size of a hen's egg, they make a fine addition to cakes, giving a good colour to sponge mixtures. Because of the goose's ability to lay her eggs in unhygienic places, the eggs should be well cooked.

● *Unusual Eggs.* Butcher's shops and fishmongers often offer a supply of more unusual eggs. Many of these are worth a try. Pheasant or partridge eggs are available occasionally, when game dealers have a surplus – serve them hard-boiled in salads or coated with a herb mayonnaise.

SALADS

The salad has been redefined to become an integral part of everyday
eating whether as a main dish or refreshing accompaniment.

No section of the supermarket shelves has become more inticing than the salad section in recent years. My local store invariably carries six or seven types of lettuce, including long-leaved crunchy Cos, tight-leaved iceberg and a selection of fancy-leaved ones such as browny-red oak-leaf and pink-tinged but dull-flavoured lollo rosso. Unusual salad leaves such as smooth-leaved purslane, soft-textured lamb's lettuce and spicy rocket appear in the more enterprising supermarkets, if not at local greengrocers.

Salad mixtures, such as the French *mesclun*, save you having several different types of lettuce in the fridge at once. Leafy salads benefit from the simplest of dressings, perhaps a mustardy vinaigrette. They are also one of the best ways to use a nut oil such as hazelnut or walnut which is difficult to match with, say, tomatoes or peppers.

A classically made tomato salad is hard to beat when dressed with fruity olive oil, freshly ground black pepper and some shredded basil. A few simple embellishments can take it to new heights; matched with slices of buffalo mozzarella and black olives it can be substantial enough for lunch. Add a generous amount of dressing and chunks of country bread to give a classic Panzanella.

Brighten up everyday ingredients with unusual but complementary dressings: radishes with dill-scented cream, mushrooms with lemon and basil and fennel with a sharp pepper and citrus dressing.

Fruit can work well in a savoury salad if it is chosen wisely. Figs combine successfully with yoghurt and ripe pears are a particularly refreshing match for air-dried ham such as Cumberland or Parma. For a summer lunch whizz avocados up for a dressing for alph-alpha sprouts or fill ripe nectarine halves with a minty bulgar wheat stuffing. Simple ideas for *al fresco* eating include a halved and chilled papaya stuffed with wild rice and shredded Parma ham or an interestingly textured salad of flageolet beans with raw peas.

Winter salads tend to be more substantial and rely less on leafy bases. A composite salad with ample proportions of hot and cold ingredients is often the answer for a winter lunch; try black pudding grilled with apple rings and dressed with a mustard sauce, or Jerusalem artichokes boiled or roasted and scattered with toasted hazelnuts. Recipes for both these salads are in this chapter.

DRESSINGS FOR SALADS

Oils

The simplest is often infuriatingly difficult to achieve. Unctuous green olive oil dribbled over a perfectly ripe tomato, peppered with a spicy basil leaf and a little salt makes the perfect late summer dish, aromatic and sensual when all the elements are right, very dull when not. The most basic and exquisite of all dressings, neat olive oil, is native to the Mediterranean and has been used since before Christ. It was brought to our attention in Britain by Elizabeth David in the 1950s, before which our dressings were confined to egg- and vinegar-based creams.

Oil extracted from the olive falls into three main categories; finest of all is the single estate extra virgin olive oil, an unrefined oil made from the first pressing of olives from one grower. Next comes extra virgin olive oil which is also from the first pressing of the olives but may be a blend from different growers or even different countries. Both should contain less than 1 per cent oleic acid.

Any oil with more than 4 per cent oleic acid must be refined. A bottle labelled 'pure olive oil' is likely to contain a refined oil which has been given flavour with the addition of some extra virgin oil. It is best to try as many oils as you can to see which you prefer. You may find that a peppery Italian extra virgin suits your taste for pouring over hot vegetables whilst a more subtle fruity oil, say from Provence, is more suitable for everyday cooking. I find that two open at once is pretty much essential.

Vinegars

The word vinegar comes from the French *vin aigre* or sharp wine, and its acetic acid content is responsible for its pungency. Wine vinegar is just one of the growing range of vinegars suitable for dressings. Vinegars now come in many forms, from the delicate champagne suitable for sweet green leaves, to more assertive versions with chillies, garlic and peppercorns.

Fruit vinegars were part of the now passé nouvelle cuisine movement and smack of the more pretentious elements of restaurant cooking. This is a pity because the best of these make deeply scented and fruity dressings. The popularity of herb vinegar grows. Basil, tarragon, mint and rosemary vinegars can all be found in specialist shops and add variety to any dressing in which they are used. They are particularly suitable for dressings for cold meat and poultry salads.

The most talked-about vinegar at the moment is balsamic, or *aceto balsamico*. Initially off-putting because of its price, the investment soon pays off. This dark reddy brown Italian condiment is made from sweet wine aged in wooden barrels and has a rich smooth flavour. Just a teaspoon will give a warm, soft sharpness to red wine or Spanish sherry vinegar dressings. In the autumn and winter cider vinegar adds clear fruity notes to any dish. Mixed with the warming tones of honey, it will lift celery, apple and walnut salad from its apathy and give a new voice to bacon-scattered spinach.

A simple dressing composed of just a few ingredients is more likely to flatter a salad than a complicated one which will just confuse the issue. A simple vinaigrette made with four times as much oil as vinegar beaten gently with a fork in a basin containing a little mustard, pepper and salt is often quite enough for most salads. Fresh herbs can be used, too; try adding chopped dill to potato salads, fresh mint and chives to bulgar wheat and, of course, fresh basil to tomato salads.

page 119
Panzanella

PANZANELLA

This salad, substantial enough to be a main course, is made with tomatoes, onions and coarse country bread. The ingredients are mixed then left for a while to soak up the olive oil and wine vinegar dressing.

**4 slices of coarse-textured white bread
6 ripe tomatoes
½ cucumber, cut into cubes
I medium onion (red if possible)
small bunch of parsley, chopped
6tbsp extra virgin olive oil
2tbsp wine vinegar
salt and freshly ground pepper**

Tear the bread into small pieces and put in a serving dish. Sprinkle just enough cold water over it to make it wet but not soggy. If the bread becomes too wet, wring it out and then crumble it up again.

Cut the tomatoes, without peeling them, into bite-sized pieces, and add them with the cucumber to the bread. Slice and add the onion. Add the parsley, pour over the olive oil and vinegar and season with salt and freshly ground black pepper. Stir well, then leave for at least 30 minutes to allow the flavours to blend.
Serves 4.

SIMPLE LETTUCE SALAD

A lettuce salad is so simple that it risks being overlooked. Use crisp little gem lettuce or mild and floppy butterhead (not the utterly tasteless iceberg).

**a good handful of lettuce leaves per person
FOR THE DRESSING:
salt and freshly ground pepper
Itbsp white wine or champagne vinegar
5tbsp extra virgin olive oil**

Wash the lettuce leaves gently without leaving them to soak.

Mix the seasonings with the vinegar and stir in the olive oil. The dressing will not be improved by whisking or shaking; it just needs a gentle, thorough mix. Before serving, make sure that the leaves are dry, so as not to make the dressing watery, then toss the lettuce leaves in the dressing.

Serve with grilled rump steak and French fries.
Serves I.

TOMATO SALAD

Allowing 2 or 3 tomatoes per person, wipe them thoroughly or rinse under running water. I have never found it worth the trouble to peel them. No more than 10 minutes before eating, cut each tomato (a serrated knife is the easiest) into 3 or 4 not-too-thin slices. Season lightly with coarse salt and black pepper. Dribble a teaspoon of extra virgin olive oil over each tomato and scatter a shredded basil leaf or two over the fruit. Eat straightaway, wiping the plate with country bread.

HOT CABBAGE AND BLACK PUDDING SALAD

**110g/4oz red cabbage
110g/4oz dark green cabbage
110g/4oz cubed fat bacon
I clove garlic crushed with a little salt
Itbsp mustard seed
Itbsp oil such as groundnut
I apple
a few sage leaves, torn into small pieces
230g/8oz black pudding
FOR THE DRESSING:
2tsp grain mustard stirred into
Itbsp wine or cider vinegar
4tbsp light oil (e.g. sunflower)
sea salt and freshly ground pepper**

Finely shred the red and green cabbages, keeping them separate.

Place the cubes of bacon in a large heavy frying pan or wok. Cook them until the juices start to run, then add the garlic. Cook the bacon and garlic for a minute, taking care that the garlic does not burn. Add the red cabbage, stir and cook for 2 minutes before adding the green cabbage. Cook until the green cabbage turns a bright green, then tip into a large warm basin. Add the mustard seed to the pan and add to the cabbage mixture when the seeds start to pop.

Pour the oil into the pan and heat till it sizzles. Core the apple and slice into 6 rounds, and add to the pan. Sprinkle in the sage and slice the black pudding into 8 thick slices. Add them to the pan and turn with the apple when they start to crisp on one side.

Mix together the dressing ingredients. Divide the cabbage between 2 plates and top with the apples and black pudding. Spoon over the dressing and eat while the salad is still hot.
Serves 2 as a main course.

Hot Cabbage and Black Pudding Salad

PEPERONI ARROSTITI

Peppers – red, yellow and green – are an integral part of cooking in Tuscany. This grilled pepper salad is a bright dish full of sunny flavours. Best eaten for an outside lunch, it is especially good piled on to bruschetta (Italian-style garlic bread).

4 medium red or yellow peppers
4 cloves garlic, peeled and finely chopped
2tbsp finely chopped flat-leaf parsley
8tbsp extra virgin olive oil
salt and freshly ground pepper

Char the skin of the peppers under a hot grill, turning them as the skins blacken. Peel off the skins with a sharp knife, catching any juice that runs out in a bowl.

Remove the stalk, core and seeds, then cut each pepper into long thick slices. Lay the slices on a serving plate. Add the garlic, parsley and olive oil to the pepper juices in the bowl and mix well. Season to taste with salt and pepper. Spoon over the peppers and leave to marinate for at least an hour. Serve with crusty bread to mop up the juices. Serves 4.

FENNEL WITH LEMON PEPPER DRESSING

When buying fennel look out for the smoother bulbs, as those with heavily ridged flesh may be tough and stringy. Serve with cold seafood or as an accompaniment to a baked fish dish.

2 large bulbs of fennel with their fronds
170ml/6fl oz natural yoghurt
1tbsp white wine vinegar
1tbsp fresh lemon juice
coarsely ground pepper

Wipe the fennel. Cut off the wispy fronds and set aside. Slice the bulb thinly, discarding the core if it is tough.

Bring a pan of water to the boil. Place a steamer basket or colander over the boiling water, add the sliced fennel and cover with a tight lid. Steam for 2 minutes.

Turn the yoghurt into a small basin, gently whisk in the wine vinegar and the lemon juice. Grind a generous quantity of black pepper into the dressing.

Turn the fennel on to a flat dish or bowl, pour over the dressing and scatter the fennel fronds over the salad. Serves 4 as a starter or as an accompaniment.

MOOLI AND PINK GRAPEFRUIT SALAD

Mooli has a flavour similar to that of small red radishes but is much gentler. Ordinary grapefruits can also be used if they are sweet.

1 mooli, about 340g/12oz in weight
2 pink grapefruits
juice of half a lemon
salt and freshly ground pepper

Peel the mooli and grate it coarsely. Cut the skin and pith from the grapefruit and remove the segments as whole as possible.

Sprinkle the lemon juice over the grated mooli and season with the salt and freshly ground pepper. Place the grapefruit segments on plates, with a spoonful or two of grated mooli in the middle, and serve.
Serves 4 as a salad.

Pinziminio

PINZIMINIO

One of the most fascinating works on Tuscan cooking also happens to be the most beautiful. *A Table in Tuscany* by Leslie Forbes (Penguin, 1989) is like a sketchbook with recipes; each page is exquisitely handwritten and illustrated by the author. As Leslie Forbes says, 'The best way to test the flavour of a good olive oil is to make pinziminio, nothing more than oil into which generous amounts of sea salt and black pepper have been ground.'

Grind sea salt and pepper into a bowl of extra virgin olive oil, the greener the better – reckon on about 60ml/2 fl oz per person. Choose the freshest and youngest green vegetables – fennel, artichokes, green beans and asparagus – and dip them into the seasoned oil.

AIR-DRIED HAM WITH PEARS

Air-dried ham, in the style of Parma, makes a simple lunch or starter. Later in the year I would eat it with ripe purple figs or melon, but in the spring the perfect accompaniments are watercress and chilled pears with a squeeze of lime and a grind of pepper.

4 large pears
1 lime
4 large handfuls watercress
12-16 slices air-dried ham
freshly ground pepper

Wash and slice the pears, peeling them if you wish. Squeeze lime juice over each slice and chill in the fridge. Wash the watercress and place on four plates.

Arrange the slices of ham and the chilled pears over the watercress, seasoning with just a little pepper.
Serves 4.

MUSHROOMS WITH BASIL AND LEMON

230g/8oz medium-sized
mushrooms cut into quarters
2tbsp wine vinegar
juice and grated rind of 1 lemon
15-20 basil leaves
2 large sprigs of parsley
140ml/¼ pint olive oil
1tsp coriander seeds
1 finely chopped chilli
salt and freshly ground pepper

Tip the mushrooms into a basin and pour over the vinegar and lemon juice only. Set aside for an hour.

Chop the herbs finely, add to the oil with the lemon rind and spices and pour over the mushrooms. Serve cool, with smoked fish, poultry or game, or as a salad with crusty bread.
Serves 4.

SPROUTED SALAD WITH AVOCADO DRESSING

1 ripe avocado
230g/8oz thick yoghurt
black pepper
110g/4oz sprouted mung beans
60g/2oz sprouted wheat seeds
230g/8oz Caerphilly or white
Wensleydale cheese
bunch of watercress

Mash the avocado with a fork in a small basin until it is smooth. Stir in the yoghurt, then grind over a little black pepper and mix thoroughly. You will get a smoother dressing in a blender or food processor – if you can be bothered to wash it all out afterwards.

In a salad bowl, toss the mung beans and the wheat seeds together. Crumble the cheese into rough pieces and add to the beans. Spoon the avocado dressing over and fold in gently.

Wash the watercress, cutting off and discarding the coarsest stems. Scatter the watercress on 2 plates and spoon the cheese and sprouted salad on top. Serves 2 as a light lunch or supper with plenty of crusty wholemeal bread.

FLAGEOLET AND RAW PEA SALAD

110g/4oz mixed flageolet
cannellini or pinto beans, cooked
and cooled
455g/1lb peas in their pods
2-3 sprigs fresh mint leaves
2tbsp white vinegar
6tbsp olive oil
salt

Put the beans in a salad bowl. Shell the peas and add them to the beans. Tear the mint leaves to little pieces and drop into a small dish. Pour in the vinegar and oil and add a little salt. Mix gently and pour over the beans and peas.
Serves 4-6 as a side dish.

- Take the cooked beans to a picnic in a sealed container.
- Use fresh peas straight from the pods for this recipe – oversweet little frozen numbers will not do. Get everyone to help with shelling the peas – but don't expect all the peas to make it as far as the salad.
- Sugar snap peas – when you eat the whole pod – are good in this salad.

The classic French dressing:
½ tspn salt
½ tspn freshly ground black pepper
2 tbsp white wine vinegar
8 tbsp extra virgin olive oil

Dissolve the salt with the pepper in the vinegar in a small china bowl. Stir in the olive oil, using a fork or a small whisk.

- *Herb Vinaigrette:* add 2 tbsp chopped fresh herbs to the above recipe. Choose from parsley, chervil, tarragon, basil and mint, or a mixture.
- *Garlic Vinaigrette:* pound a peeled clove of garlic to a purée with a little salt. The easiest way to do this is with the flat blade of a knife. Mix it with the salt and pepper before adding the liquids.

- *Mustard Vinaigrette:* add 1 heaped tspn of mustard to the above recipe. Choose from a variety of mustards such as green peppercorn, seeded Dijon, or tarragon. Stir the mustard into the vinegar, salt and pepper.
- *Lemon Vinaigrette:* substitute freshly squeezed lemon juice for the wine vinegar.

PAPAYA WITH PARMA HAM AND WILD RICE

Wild rice is a grass, rather than a true rice, from North America and the Far East. It has a nutty flavour and a soft crunchy texture which complements the tender flesh of papaya particularly well. Wild rice is expensive, so buy it a couple of ounces at a time for an occasional indulgence. For this recipe you can substitute long-grain brown rice instead.

30g/1oz wild rice
2tbsp pine nuts
I lime
2 thin slices of Parma ham
salt and freshly ground pepper
I ripe papaya

Cook the wild rice in simmering salted water for 45 minutes. It should still have some bite to it. Drain any excess water – there will not be much – and pour the rice into a basin. Cook the pine nuts under a hot grill until golden brown to bring out the full flavour.

Squeeze the lime and add the juice to the wild rice. Shred the Parma ham into matchstick pieces. Stir into the rice and season with black pepper; it is unlikely that you will need any salt.

Cut the papaya in half. Scoop out the black seeds with a teaspoon and discard. Spoon the wild rice and nut filling into the scooped out papaya.
Serves 2 as a starter.

Papaya with Parma Ham and Wild Rice

RADISHES WITH DILL CREAM

2tsp white wine vinegar
2tbsp chopped fresh dill
285ml/½ pint soured cram
2 bunches radishes, washed and chilled

Stir the vinegar and fresh dill into the soured cream and serve chilled with crisp radishes.

● Keep radishes crisp by leaving them in cold water for an hour before use.
● As a variation, use tarragon or chervil instead of the dill.
● Sharpen the dip with lemon juice instead of vinegar if you prefer.

WARM NEW POTATO SALAD WITH CHIVE DRESSING

The potatoes can be peeled after cooking or left unpeeled – the flavour of the salad is not altered, but it looks much neater with peeled potatoes. Snip the chives with scissors into approx. 1cm/½in lengths. This salad is especially good as a partner for cold roast lamb.

680g/1½lb new potatoes
2tbsp white wine vinegar
4tbsp olive oil
salt and freshly ground pepper
2tbsp snipped chives

Wipe or scrub the new potatoes, boil until tender, then skin them if you wish while they are still hot.

To make the dressing, stir the wine vinegar into the oil, season with the salt and pepper and add the chives. Drop the potatoes, while they are still warm, into the chive dressing and leave for at least 15 minutes, for the flavours to blend, before serving.
Serves 4 as an accompaniment.

Radishes with Dill Cream

SPINACH AND PUMPKIN SEED SALAD

Many shops now sell spinach already washed. If you buy loose spinach from the greengrocer make sure that you wash it thoroughly, as sand and grit tend to hide in the deep veins of the leaves.

2tbsp pumpkin seeds
2tsp wine vinegar
2tsp grain mustard
salt
4tbsp groundnut oil
4 large handfuls of young spinach leaves, washed
4 lightly hard-boiled eggs, quartered

Toast the pumpkin seeds under a hot grill for about 5 minutes, shaking the pan now and again so that they brown evenly.

In a salad bowl, mix the vinegar and mustard with a little salt and stir in the oil. Tear the spinach into shreds and toss in the dressing with the eggs. Scatter the pumpkin seeds on top.
Serves 4.

Nectarines with Bulgar and Mint

NECTARINES WITH BULGAR AND MINT

**60g/2oz bulgar wheat
a handful of chopped parsley
a handful of chopped mint
the juice of 1 lemon
2tbsp olive oil
half a small cucumber
2 thin slices of Parma ham
shredded (optional)
6 chopped radishes
salt and freshly ground pepper
4 ripe nectarines**

Cover the bulgar with cold water and soak for 15 minutes. Place the parsley and mint in a basin with the lemon and olive oil. Chop the cucumber into small dice and then add it, with the ham, radishes and seasoning, to the herbs mixture in the basin.

Squeeze the water from the bulgar with your fist and toss into the mixture. Combine thoroughly. Halve and stone the fruit, place on a large plate and spoon the bulgar on top of each half. Serves 4.

FIGS WITH YOGHURT DRESSING

**12 fresh figs
6tbsp chopped walnuts
280g/10oz natural yoghurt, chilled
3 slices Parma ham, finely shredded**

Wipe the figs, cut a 2.5cm/1in cross into the top of each one with a sharp knife and squeeze slightly so they open out to show the centre of the fruit.

Make the dressing by folding the chopped walnuts into the chilled yoghurt. Spoon the dressing over the figs, scatter the Parma ham on top and serve chilled.
Serves 4 as a light lunch or as a savoury starter.

SPRING LEAVES WITH HOT BACON DRESSING

For each person take two large handfuls of spring leaves: tiny spinach, little gem lettuce, watercress, lamb's lettuce and even baby dandelions. Wash them and shake dry, then place in a large china bowl. Scatter 2tbsp per person of fresh uncooked peas or a few mange-touts over the leaves. Set aside while you make the bacon dressing.

Allowing two rashers of streaky bacon per person, cut the bacon into thin strips, fry until crisp, then toss over the leaves. Without washing the pan, add 1tbsp each of olive or walnut oil and cider vinegar and heat until bubbling, scraping up any residue from the bacon. Pour the hot dressing over the leaves and season with salt and freshly ground pepper. Serve immediately.

HOT ARTICHOKE AND HAZELNUT SALAD

**455g/1lb Jerusalem artichokes
4tbsp hazelnut or walnut oil
40g/1½oz shelled hazelnuts, skinned and chopped in half
1 lemon
salt and freshly ground pepper
chopped parsley**

Set the oven at Gas Mark 6 (200°C, 400°F). Wash the artichokes and peel if the artichokes are large, or scrub hard with a vegetable brush if very young.

Place them in an ovenproof dish, pour over the oil and the hazelnuts. Bake for 25-30 minutes until the artichokes are tender and the hazelnuts are roasted.

Remove from the oven and pour the oil into a small basin. Add the juice of the lemon and season with salt and pepper. Mix the dressing with a fork or a small whisk. Slice the artichokes into 1cm/½in-thick pieces. Pour over the dressing while the vegetables are still steaming. Scatter over the chopped parsley.
Serves 2 as an accompaniment.

Figs with Yoghurt Dressing

HOT PUDDINGS

Nostalgic and warming, crisp tarts and spiced sticky puddings
are an occasional indulgence that everyone deserves.

The British and Americans excel at home baking. Our hot fruit pies, sweet baked fruits and the stickiest of steamed puddings are loved the world over. The French seem to produce the finest of light-crusted open tarts, often filled with apples, pears or apricots. To be really good, all home baking should include butter, not margarine, free range eggs and only truly ripe fruits.

BAKED FRUITS

Baked fruits are welcome all year round. Apples, dripping with butter and honey and dried fruits, are the easiest of puddings to prepare, and can be left to look after themselves in the oven with only the need for occasional basting. Other fruits can be baked, too. Bananas take on a rich sweetness when they spend a little time in a hot oven. They can also be grilled with fresh lime juice and scented with honey.

TRADITIONAL PUDDINGS

We have a great tradition of warming winter puddings, hot sweet food to fight the cold. There has been something of a renewal of interest in this hearty food of late, with even the smartest restaurants boasting a handful of nursery puddings on their menus. Bread and butter pudding has been the darling of restaurant chefs in the past few years, though rarely have their gilded lilies been as good as the established recipes.

A favourite of mine is a baked lemon sponge where the lemon and eggs sink to the bottom to form a sharp citrus custard and the sponge floats to the top. I am sure it would work just as well with oranges, particularly blood oranges – now ridiculously labelled as ruby oranges – which would give a most spectacular colour and flavour.

Figgy pudding is traditionally made with raisins rather than figs but try making a steamed pudding with a layer of figs at the bottom, having first cooked them in port to give a rich syrup. Spice the syrup with ginger, cinnamon and nutmeg, allowing the only sweetness to come from the dried fruit itself. Make custard if you have the patience or serve the pudding with dollops of yoghurt.

Treacle pudding is probably the pudding most inclined to induce nostalgia. I have a soft spot for a pudding which is so unashamedly sweet and sticky. It is for food like this that I need to remind myself that there is no unhealthy food, only unhealthy diets. This is a hot pudding, like many fruit pies, that deserves thick, yellow cream rather than a hot sauce.

SPICED PUDDINGS

Spices are synonymous with hot puddings. Baked apples would not be the same without their sprinkling of cinnamon, or bread and butter pudding without its grating of nutmeg. Cinnamon resembles a tight roll of dusty brown paper, tattered at the ends. It is the thinly rolled bark of a tree harvested in southern India and Sri Lanka, then left to dry in the sun where it develops its characteristic curl.

Use cinnamon to flavour custard. In Morocco it really dazzles when sprinkled with icing sugar to represent the sun's rays on crisp pastries. Take this as inspiration and store the sticks in a jar of caster sugar, to add to cream as an accompaniment to mince pies. You can also use the spicy quills to stir strong high-roast, after dinner coffee. Cinnamon's warm undertones go well with red wine and fruit such as poached pears and apples.

Nutmeg loses its perfume very quickly so buy whole nutmegs and grate them as they are needed; use the blade of a small knife to scrape away a little of the creamy brown crumbly spice from the hard oval nut. Grind it as fine as you can in a coffee grinder or pestle and mortar. Sweet milk puddings, either the creamy yellow Indian rice dishes or gently scented custards, all benefit from a little grated nutmeg.

Ginger is a versatile spice that is as happy in a meat dish as in any pudding. You can find knobbly beige fresh ginger in supermarkets and most greengrocers, but it is also sold dried, either whole or ground, or preserved in sugar syrup. The latter comes from China and is made with the youngest, tenderest parts; try using the sweet warming syrup over slices of mango, pineapple and papaya.

Cardamom's miniscule black seeds add a magical fragrance to syrups for hot winter fruit puddings such as baked banana with orange juice, or a creamy rice pudding. Grind them finely as you need them, as cardamom's subtle spiciness is most volatile.

TARTS

Pastry making is not difficult and is immensely satisfying. Fruit tarts – perhaps an individual apple tart or a deep-filled plum pie – are at their best when served warm, almost straight from the oven. Some of the most attractive fruit tarts are those made without the formality of a tart ring; just the pastry folded round the edges of the fruit and allowed to form its own shape. A wobbly-edged home-made fruit tart has far greater appeal for me than any of the 'India-rubber perfections' seen on many hotel patissier's trolly.

A favourite of mine, but one that must be eaten in its entirety the moment it is assembled, is that made from layers of filo pastry piled with warm fruits.

ACCOMPANIMENTS FOR HOT PUDDINGS

Thick unpasteurised cream is my choice for adorning steaming hot puddings, though it is not always easy to find. Heavy yellow cream always has a sharper, richer flavour than thin white cream, which is often quite bland. Avoid the UHT creams, which have undergone a heat-treatment process that renders them thin, tasteless and unappetisingly grey in comparison.

Try flavouring softly whipped cream with spices; cloves, roasted in a low oven till deeply fragrant, can be crushed finely and stirred with caster sugar into the cream as an accompaniment to mince pies or a steamed pudding.

MILLE-FEUILLE OF ORCHARD FRUITS

This flaky fruit pastry is especially good eaten with thick, golden cream. It is important not to let the moist fruit filling and the pastry layers meet until the last moment.

**230m/8fl oz cider or apple juice
½ stick cinnamon
4 cloves
2 long strips orange zest
900g/2lb pears or apples
455g/1lb plums, washed, halved
and stoned
30g/1oz butter
3 sheets filo pastry
powdered cinnamon
1tbsp icing sugar, optional**

Preheat the oven to Gas Mark 7 (220°C, 425°F). Bring the cider or apple juice to the boil in a small heavy-based saucepan. Add the cinnamon, cloves and orange zest and simmer for 7-8 minutes – the liquid will have reduced by half.

Peel, core and roughly slice the pears or apples and add to the juice. Simmer, covered, for 15-20 minutes, until the fruit is tender but not mushy – there should still be a little crunch. Stir in the plums, replace the lid and cool; this is all the cooking the plums need.

Melt the butter and allow to cool a little. Lay a pastry sheet with the longest edge towards you, fold over in half like a book. Repeat for the other 2 sheets. Scoring round a 15cm/6in plate or dish, cut 2 circles on each sheet – you should just be able to fit them into the area. (You will be left with 12 circles.) Separate the pastry scraps left by the circles so that they dry out and can be used for decoration.

Brush some of the melted butter on 3 of the circles and sprinkle a little cinnamon on each of them, then top each circle with another piece of pastry and butter that too; again dust with cinnamon and top with a third and fourth piece of pastry. Brush the top piece of pastry on each of the 3 piles with butter. Crumble all the pieces of dried-out, leftover pastry and scatter them on top of one of the 3 pastry piles; dribble with any remaining butter.

Lay the piles on a baking sheet, one at a time, and bake for 4-5 minutes, watching carefully. Then remove them with a fish slice to a cooling rack. The last pile of pastry with the topping on may take a couple of minutes longer.

Serve at room temperature and, no more than a few minutes before you wish to eat, layer the crisp pastry with the cooked fruit, with the decorated circle on top. Dust with a little icing sugar if you wish. Cut with a large sharp knife. Serves 4 as a pastry or pudding.

GRILLED STUFFED PEACHES

Follow the recipe for Grilled Peaches with Honey and Cinnamon (right), but omit the butter. Before you add the spiced honey mixture, place a spoonful of the following stuffing into the centre of each peach.

**60g/2oz ricotta cheese
2tbsp toasted ground almonds or
6 Amaretti biscuits, crushed**

Spoon over the honey and place under the grill until the almond cheese stuffing starts to brown. Serve hot, pouring the spiced honey from the baking dish over the peaches. Serves 4.

GRILLED PEACHES WITH HONEY AND CINNAMON

These peaches can be cooked whole or in halves.

**4tbsp honey
juice of 1 lemon
a little ground cinnamon
4tsp butter (preferably unsalted)
4 ripe peaches**

In a small basin mix the honey with the lemon juice and add the cinnamon, I suggest about ½ level tsp, or a good pinch.

Unless you are serving the peaches whole, cut them in half and remove the stones. Place the peach halves in a basin and pour over just enough boiling water to cover them. Leave for a few seconds then remove the skins with the point of a knife.

Lay them flat side up in a shallow ovenproof baking dish. Place ½tsp butter on top of each peach. Brush or spoon the spiced honey and lemon mixture over the peaches and place under the grill. Cook them until the honey starts to bubble and the peaches turn a rich golden brown.

Serve the peaches hot with vanilla ice cream or with natural yoghurt. Serves 4.

'FIGGY' PUDDING

The best dried figs are sold loose, but prepacked ones are perfectly suitable for cooking. Remove hard stems with a sharp knife. Figgy is actually an old West Country term which refers to anything full of raisins or currants such as traditional Christmas pudding.

455g/1lb dried figs
140ml/¼ pint port or strong tea
½tsp powdered ginger
½tsp powdered cinnamon
a few grinds of nutmeg
FOR THE SPONGE:
110g/4oz butter
110g/4oz soft brown sugar
2 eggs
60g/2oz fresh brown breadcrumbs
grated rind of an orange
110g/4oz self-raising flour
½tsp each ginger and cinnamon

Baked Bramleys with Vine Fruits and Honey

Chop all but 6 of the figs into quarters and place in a saucepan with the port or tea and the spices. Bring to the boil and simmer gently for 10 minutes. Remove from the heat, lift the figs out with a draining spoon and reserve. Reduce the port syrup to 4tbsp, by boiling rapidly over the heat.

Butter a 900ml/1½-pint pudding basin, place the 6 whole figs in the bottom, followed by the port syrup. Set aside. Beat the butter and sugar till fluffy and pale coffee-coloured. Add the eggs, one at a time, and beat in. At this point the mixture will curdle, but don't panic; just add the breadcrumbs and the grated orange rind. Sift together the flour and spices, and add the cooked figs. Fold this into the egg and butter mixture.

Spoon the mixture into the basin containing the whole figs. Smooth the top with a spoon. Cut out a circle of greaseproof paper or muslin to overhang the top of the basin by 7.5cm/3in.

Lay the circle flat on the table, and make a 1cm/½in deep pleat in the middle. Place over the pudding basin, holding the pleat together, and tie with string. Place a pleated muslin cloth over the basin and tie the cloth with string beneath the ridge of the basin. Make a handle to lift the pudding, by drawing the loose ends of the cloth over the basin, knotting them together.

Place the basin on a trivet in a deep pan, with enough boiling water to come two-thirds of the way up the sides of the basin. Steam for 1 hour. Remove from the heat, discard the muslin and paper, and serve hot with very cold cream. Serves 4.

BAKED BRAMLEYS WITH VINE FRUITS AND HONEY

2tbsp dark raisins
4tbsp light raisins
6 large dried apricots, chopped
60g/2oz walnuts, chopped
2tbsp brandy
4 large cooking apples, such as Bramleys

Mix together the raisins, honey, apricots, walnuts and brandy to make a stuffing. Remove the cores of the apples with a corer or a knife. Slice the skin of the apples around the middle and set them in a roasting tin. Fill up the holes in the apples with the stuffing mixture and bake at Gas Mark 6 (200°C, 400°F) for about 45 minutes to an hour, until they are fluffy and starting to ooze out of their skins.
Serves 4.

'Figgy' Pudding

CHUTNEY MARY'S BAKED BANANA

Itbsp finely grated fresh root
ginger
115ml/4fl oz golden syrup
Itbsp rum
85g/3oz brown sugar
juice of 1½ lemons
juice of ½ orange
4 bananas
I orange, peeled and cut into
segments

Squeeze the grated ginger in a garlic press to obtain the juice. Put the golden syrup, rum, brown sugar, lemon, orange, and ginger juice in a saucepan over a low heat for 5 minutes until the sugar has dissolved and the consistency is syrupy. Cut the bananas in half lengthwise and place in the syrup. Cook on a low heat for about 5 minutes, turning the bananas carefully as they cook. Transfer to an ovenproof serving dish and add the orange segments. Leave to cool for 2-3 hours.

Place under a hot grill just before serving.

Serves 2.

BAKED BANANA WITH CARDAMOM AND ORANGE

Minuscule black cardamom seeds add a magical fragrance to pilaffs or syrups for winter fruit salads. Keep the seeds in their pods until you need them, rather than buying them ready-ground.

4 bananas
4tbsp brown sugar
60g/2oz butter
4 cardamom pods
I small orange, squeezed

Preheat the oven to Gas Mark 6 (200°C, 400°F). Cut the bananas into slices about 1cm/½in thick. Put them in a baking dish, sprinkle with sugar and dot the butter in little pieces on top.

While the bananas bake for 7-8 minutes, remove the little black cardamom seeds from their husks and crush them roughly. When the bananas are done, take them out of the oven and scatter them with the cardamom seeds and drizzle with orange juice.

Serves 4.

HOT POACHED PEARS WITH CINNAMON AND HONEY

6 Comice or Conference pears
half a lemon
I bottle red wine
I cup water
2 cinnamon sticks
8 cloves
pared rind of a small orange
2 mace blades, optional
4tbsp honey

Peel the pears with a vegetable peeler, rubbing the cut side of the lemon over them to stop them turning brown. Put them in a stainless steel or enamel-based saucepan so that they sit snugly together.

Pour over the red wine and the water and throw in the cinnamon sticks, cloves, orange peel, mace and honey. Bring to the boil, then turn down the heat and leave to simmer for 35-45 minutes. The pears are ready when the point of a sharpish knife slides into the fruit without pressure.

Remove the pears with a draining spoon and put in a serving dish in a warm place. Turn up the heat to full, return the pan with its contents to the heat and let the liquid bubble away for 5 minutes, or until the wine and honey mixture has reduced to a slightly thickened juice.

Pour through a sieve into the serving bowl and serve warm. The poached pears are also good when chilled and eaten cold.

Serves 6.

FRUIT BOWL PUDDINGS

You often need look no further than the fruit bowl for inspiration for winter puddings.

● *Bananas.* Banana puddings are a great favourite – just think of baked bananas or the most lovely of nursery puddings, banana custard. Try them brushed with honey and grilled or baked in their jackets in a hot oven. Cream, or thick-style Greek yoghurt, are perfect partners for hot, sweet bananas.

● *Apples.* There are few more welcoming smells than that of apples baking in the oven. Try them sprinkled with brown sugar and cinnamon or cored and stuffed with vegetarian mincemeat. Apples can also be sliced thinly and pan-fried in melted butter and sugar. Serve with finely grated orange zest and cold, thick cream.

● *Pears.* One of the most simple pear puddings imaginable is also one of the most delicious: slice the pears into thick segments, fry in melted butter for a few minutes till golden and tender. Stir in a little caster sugar and a spoonful of brandy. Stir in a little butter and leave to reduce until thick and syrupy. Serve with vanilla ice cream on the side.

Hot Poached Pears with Cinnamon and Honey

ROSEHIP AND HIBISCUS PRUNES

Fruit and herbal teas make excellent marinades for dried fruit. Most rosehip tea is mixed with hibiscus, which is responsible for the brilliant red colour.

2tsp rosehip and hibiscus tea or 2 sachets
455g/1lb prunes

Pour 570ml/1 pint of boiling water on to the loose tea or sachets of tea and leave to brew until quite deep red in colour, about 5 minutes.

Add the prunes. Cover with a plate and leave until the prunes are plump and juicy and the tea has cooled.

To serve, either re-heat the prunes by bringing them slowly to boiling point, or serve at room temperature. Serve with thick Greek-style yoghurt.
Serves 4.

RAISIN AND COGNAC BATTER PUDDING

340g/12oz mixed vine fruits
115ml/4fl oz cognac
knob of butter
60g/2oz flour
pinch of salt
60g/2oz sugar
4 eggs
570ml/1 pint milk
2 egg yolks

Place the fruit in a small saucepan and add enough water to just cover them. Bring to the boil, remove from the heat and set aside for 10 minutes. Drain the fruits in a sieve, place in a basin and pour over the cognac. Leave overnight.

Set the oven at Gas Mark 5 (190°C, 375°F). Butter a 1.15 litre/ 2 pint baking dish. Sift the flour into a bowl, add the salt and the sugar. Beat in the eggs, milk and egg yolks.

Bread and Butter Pudding

Put the vine fruits in the baking dish, strain the egg and milk mixture over them and bake for 45 minutes until golden and well risen. Dust with icing sugar and serve warm.
Serves 4.

BREAD AND BUTTER PUDDING

It may be old-fashioned, but Bread and Butter Pudding is still the queen of nursery puddings.

butter
110g/4oz raisins
4 slices light wholemeal bread
3 eggs
1 egg yolk
60g/2oz caster sugar
230ml/8fl oz milk
230g/8fl oz double cream
vanilla pod or 1 tspn vanilla extract

Butter a 1 litre/1½ pints pudding dish and scatter the raisins over the bottom. Cut each slice of bread into 4 triangles (16 triangles in all) and lay them in the dish.

Beat together the whole eggs and egg yolk. Bring the milk and cream slowly to the boil in a pan to which you have added either the vanilla pod or the vanilla extract. Remove the pod (if using) and pour the hot milk and cream over the eggs. Ladle the mixture over the bread and place the dish in a roasting tin half-filled with water. Bake for 45-50 minutes at Gas Mark 3 (170°C, 325°F).
Serves 4.

STICKY TREACLE PUDDING

This is one of those sticky sponge puddings which seems to have been forgotten over the years – but it is still my favourite. Surprisingly quick to make, it can cook while you prepare the rest of the meal. If you need to keep it waiting, leave it in the steamer with the lid on but the heat switched off, and it will come to no harm for around 20-30 minutes. Serve it hot with cream.

4tbsp golden syrup
2tbsp breadcrumbs
140g/5oz butter, plus a little extra for greasing.
140g/5oz light brown sugar
2 eggs
2tbsp milk
140g/5oz self-raising flour

Butter a 1.15 litre/2 pint pudding basin. Mix the golden syrup and breadcrumbs, and pour into the bottom of the basin. Cream the butter and the sugar until light and fluffy. Break the eggs into a small basin and mix with a fork, then add gradually to the butter and sugar mixture. Fold in the milk and the flour.

Spoon the mixture into the pudding basin, on top of the golden syrup. Cover with a piece of pleated and buttered greaseproof paper. Tie with string and cover with foil or muslin, securing with string. Place the basin on a trivet in a large saucepan of simmering water. Cover with a lid and steam for 1½ hours.

Carefully remove from the saucepan, allow to cool for 5 minutes then remove the foil and paper. Invert the basin on to a serving dish.
Serves 6.

BAKED LEMON PUDDING

A sharp, lemony sponge pudding that makes its own sauce is the perfect finish to a light meal of fish.

85g/3oz butter, softened
170g/6oz demerara sugar
finely grated zest and juice of 4 lemons
4 large eggs, separated
60g/2oz flour
8tbsp milk

Grease the inside of an 18cm/7in soufflé dish with a tiny knob of butter. Preheat the oven to Gas Mark 4 (180°C, 350°F).

Using an electric or hand-held beater, cream the butter with the sugar until they form a creamy white, fluffy mass that will stand in soft peaks. Add the lemon zest and juice, then the egg yolks, one at a time, beating well after each one. The mixture may curdle at this point, but ignore its dubious looks and beat in the flour, adding the milk one tablespoon at a time.

With a wire or electric hand whisk, beat the egg whites until they are firm and stand in huge snowy peaks. Fold them gently into the mixture, softly but thoroughly, until all the whites are incorporated. Pour the mixture into the buttered soufflé dish, place the dish in a roasting tin and pour hot water into the tin until it comes half way up the sides of the soufflé dish.

Bake until the top of the pudding is risen and golden, about 45 minutes, and then serve hot.
Serves 4.

SCHIACCIATA CON L'UVA

This grape and chestnut bread was originally made in the Chianti-producing area of Tuscany. The addition of dark, juicy grapes – which were plentiful at harvest time – to a basic bread dough is typical of Tuscan cooking, appearing rich and extravagant, while really being extremely frugal. This dish was inspired by a recipe from Claudia Roden's classic work on Italian regional cooking, *The Food of Italy* (Arrow, 1990).

30g/1oz fresh yeast, or 2 sachets of dried yeast
170ml/6fl oz tepid water
340g/12oz plain white flour
110g/4oz caster sugar
pinch of salt
455g/1lb black grapes, seeded but not peeled
85g/3oz walnuts or canned chestnuts, drained and roughly chopped
60g/2oz caster sugar
2tbsp olive oil

Dissolve the yeast in the tepid water. Put the flour, sugar and salt in a large bowl. Pour the yeast mixture into the flour and mix well, first with a wooden spoon and then, when the mixture starts to come together, with your hands.

Take the dough from the bowl and put it on a clean, slightly floured work surface. Knead the dough with your hands, just as you would for bread, for at least 5 minutes. Place the dough back in the bowl, cover with a cloth and leave in a warm place until it doubles in size. This will take anything from 20 minutes to over an hour, depending on the warmth and humidity of the room.

When the dough is twice the size it was, cut it in half and roll or pat each piece out to a 1cm/½in thickness. Put one disc of dough on a floured baking sheet and cover it with half of the grapes, nuts and sugar. Place the second disc of dough on top and press the edges down to seal in the filling.

Brush with the oil and add the rest of the grapes, nuts and sugar. Bake in a preheated oven, at Gas Mark 4 (180°C, 350°F), for 45-50 minutes, until the top is golden brown and streaked with grape juice. Serve the bread warm or cold, in wedges.
Serves 6.

MULLED APPLE SAUCE

1 stick cinnamon, broken in half
3 whole cloves
3 whole allspice berries
2.5cm/1 inch strip orange zest
500ml/16fl oz cider or apple juice
6-8 tart apples, peeled, cored and coarsely diced
pinch of salt
60g/2oz light brown sugar
60-100g/2-4oz caster sugar
15g/½oz butter, softened

Place the cinnamon, cloves, all-spice and orange zest in a spice bag or on a square of cheesecloth and tie securely with string.

In a heavy saucepan, bring the cider to the boil over high heat. Add the spice bag, reduce heat to medium, and simmer until the cider is reduced to two-thirds of a cup (about 30 minutes). Discard the spice bag.

Add the apples, salt and brown sugar to the reduced cider. Cover and simmer over a medium heat, stirring frequently for about 20 minutes until the apples become mushy. Taste and add enough caster sugar to bring the mixture to the desired sweetness, then add the butter and stir until well blended.
Serves 4.

Schiacciata con L'Uva

STEAMED APPLES WITH APPLE BUTTER SAUCE

Any variety of dessert apple can be steamed quickly and successfully. This recipe takes about 10 minutes from start to finish. If you leave the skins on, the flesh will take on a subtle pink or green depending on your choice of apple. If you can, try to find an unfiltered English apple juice, which gives a better flavour.

230ml/8fl oz apple juice
2 dessert apples
40g/1½oz unsalted butter

Place the apple juice in a saucepan and bring to the boil. Cut the apples in half, peeling them if you wish. Remove the cores and place flat side down in a steamer basket. Steam them over the boiling apple juice for 4 minutes, or a minute or two longer for larger ones. Remove the apples from the steamer basket with a broad flat knife or fish slice. Place in a warm dish. Remove the steamer basket from the saucepan and allow the apple juice to boil and reduce for 4 minutes.

Cut the butter into small cubes and whisk into the apple juice, a couple of pieces at a time. As you whisk, the sauce will start to thicken. Pour the apple butter sauce over the steamed apples and serve, with thick yoghurt or cream if you wish.
Serves 2.

TARTE TATIN

The classic French upside-down tart of buttery pastry and caramelized apples.

FOR THE PASTRY:
170g/6oz cold butter, cut into chunks
230g/8oz plain flour
2 egg yolks
3tbsp caster sugar
FOR THE FILLING:
60g/2oz butter
4tbsp caster sugar.
3 apples, weighing about 455g/1lb in total, peeled, quartered and cored

Preheat the oven to Gas Mark 7 (220°C, 425°F). To make the pastry, rub the butter into the flour in a large bowl. Add the egg yolks, sugar and 2-3 tablespoons of cold water and stir until the mixture forms a ball. Wrap in greaseproof paper and leave to rest for 15 minutes.

For the filling, melt the butter and sugar in a 20-23cm/8-9in frying pan over a medium heat. When syrupy, add the apples and cook, stirring occasionally so they do not stick, for about 15 minutes, until they are tender to the point of a knife. Turn up the heat and cook the apples until they are a golden colour and the syrup is thick and brown. Remove from the heat.

Roll out the pastry to a shape 2.5cm/1in larger all round than the top of the frying pan. Fold this edge to make a rim around the edge, then place, rim side down, on top of the apples. Bake in the oven for about 40 minutes, until the pastry is golden.

Remove the tart from the oven. Place a heat-proof plate over the top and invert the dish to release the tart on to the plate. Serve at room temperature with thick cream or crème fraîche.
Serves 4.

APPLE VARIETIES

Several supermarket groups are encouraging their growers to produce old-fashioned apple varieties, and not before time. Up to twenty different apples are now to be found in their traditional seasons in some supermarkets and farm shops, hopefully putting an end to the flavourless and woolly imports that we have been offered for too long.

● *Cox's Orange Pippin.* A true Cox has a distinctive aromatic flavour, and is as good to cook with as it is to eat raw. Cox's keep their shape when cooked and retain much of their flavour. Best from late October on to well past Christmas.

● *Blenheim Orange.* A nutty flavoured apple with yellow flesh. Good for dessert eating and cooking, this is a late-fruiting variety.

● *Bramley.* Huge, bright green fruits, most often used for cooking. If you like fluffy, juicy baked apples then this is the one for you.

● *Egremont Russet.* A heavily scented, crisp-textured apple with a rough, reddish skin and white flesh, good for eating or cooking.

● *Ashmead's Kernel.* Green and yellow russeted skin with an aromatic white flesh, a sweet dessert apple that is also good for cooking.

● *Discovery.* A light green and pink-tinged apple, smaller than average, that heralds the start of the apple season. One of the most fragrant of fruits, best for dessert, and one variety where you can eat the entire apple.

● *Orleans Reinette.* A large apple with a sweet yellow flesh. Its flecked orange and yellow flesh is easily recognized – often sold in this country with a sticker of authenticity.

Tarte Tatin

APPLE FRITTERS

Fritters need to be cooked in small batches and eaten straight away. This is a good pudding to make if you can sit in the kitchen and eat the crisp fritters as they come sizzling out of the pan.

110g/4oz plain flour
pinch of salt
30g/1oz caster sugar
2 eggs, separated
115ml/4fl oz beer
1tbsp melted butter
4 apples, peeled and cut into
3mm/¼in slices
caster sugar for dusting

Sift the flour and salt into a large bowl, then add the sugar and the egg yolks and stir well. Pour in the beer and mix to a smooth batter. Leave to stand for 30 minutes to thicken, then add the melted butter. Beat the egg whites and fold into the batter.

Heat some groundnut or vegetable oil in a deep-fat fryer to 195°C, 385°F. Dip the pieces of apple first into the batter then into the hot oil. (Cook only a few at a time as overcrowding the pan will lower the temperature of the oil and lead to soggy batter.) Fry until crisp and golden, then drain on kitchen paper and dust with sugar.
Serves 4.

HOT MANGO WITH COCONUT AND ORANGE

1 ripe mango
8tbsp finely grated fresh coconut
(about half a coconut)
or 6tbsp grated dried (or
desiccated) coconut
1 knob of unsalted butter
1 orange

Peel the mango and pare slices about as thick as a pound coin, from all sides of the fruit. Scatter the coconut on a plate. Press the slices firmly into the coconut to coat each side.

Heat the knob of butter in a shallow pan; a frying pan will do nicely. When the butter starts to froth, add as many pieces of mango as will fit into the pan. When the coconut starts to brown, turn with a palette knife to cook the other side and transfer to a warm plate. Repeat with the remaining slices.

Serve with segments of orange, squeezing the juice over the fruit.
Serves 2.

BANANAS WITH HONEY AND LIME

Try to find limes which are turning yellow, as they are far juicier by then.

8 ripe bananas
2 limes
2tbsp honey

Peel the bananas and place them in the base of a foil-lined grill pan. Squeeze the juice of 1 of the limes over the bananas and brush with honey.

Place the bananas under a hot grill, rolling them over from time to time as they cook. They are ready to eat when they have turned golden but still hold their shape. Cut the other lime in quarters.

With a palette knife or slice transfer the fruit to a serving dish, pouring over any pan juices. Eat while still hot with a squeeze from the limes, and yoghurt or *fromage blanc*.
Serves 4.

MANGO, PAPAYA AND PINEAPPLE IN HOT GINGER SYRUP

7.5cm/3in piece of fresh ginger
110g/4oz sugar
285ml/½ pint water
1 large mango
1 papaya
1 small pineapple

Peel the ginger and slice into pieces as thick as a pound coin. Place the sugar in a saucepan with the water. Bring the water to the boil, add the ginger pieces and continue boiling until the liquid starts to thicken and takes on a very slight golden tinge. This will probably take about 5 minutes.

Meanwhile, peel the mango, holding it over a basin to collect the juice. Hold it gently but firmly in the palm of your hand. Cut the mango in half lengthways with a sawing movement, following the line of the flat stone with the blade of the knife. Remove the uppermost half, then remove the stone in the other half by loosening it with the point of a knife. Cut the 2 halves into thick slices. Add to the basin.

Slice the papaya in half, scoop out the seeds and discard, and peel the 2 halves. Cut the fruit into slices similar in thickness to the mango and add to the basin. Peel and slice the pineapple, cutting each slice into 6 segments. Add to the basin.

Remove the ginger syrup from the heat; pour carefully through a sieve over the tropical fruit in the basin. Allow to cool for a couple of minutes before serving.
Serves 4.

Apple
Fritters

HOT CARDAMOM RICE PUDDING

570ml/1 pint milk
230ml/8fl oz single cream
30g/1oz long-grain white rice
¼tsp ground cardamom
4tbsp sugar
2tbsp raisins

Pour the milk into a heavy-based saucepan and add the cream; stir to mix and bring slowly to the boil. Drop in the rice and the cardamom and leave to simmer very gently for an hour. Test the rice to see if it is cooked: it should just have a little bite.

Stir in the sugar and raisins and simmer for 5 minutes more. Eat warm. It is good to eat cold too, when it becomes thick and even richer.
Serves 4.

RICE PUDDING WITH LEMON AND ALMONDS

Although it can be eaten hot, this lemon-scented milk pudding is at its best when served very cold. It is important to toast the nuts under the grill, as this will impart a recognizable almond flavour to the cooked rice.

1 lemon
110g/4oz short-grain rice
570ml/1 pint milk
60g/2oz raisins
60g/2oz toasted flaked almonds
1tsp vanilla extract
85g/3oz sugar

Peel long, wide shavings of lemon rind from the lemon. Place the rind in a heavy-based saucepan with the rice, milk and 1.15 litres/2 pints water. Bring to the boil, reduce the heat and simmer for 15 minutes.

Add the raisins, toasted almonds, vanilla extract and sugar; stir and then leave the mixture to cool. Remove the strips of lemon and put the rice in the refrigerator until it is very cold.

Note: if you are intending to eat the pudding while it is hot, add the raisins and nuts after 10 minutes of simmering. Serves 6.

PEACH AND NECTARINE ALMOND CRUMBLE

A pudding such as a crumble, hot or cold, is usually made with apples until the rhubarb arrives, and is often forgotten completely in summer. Yet peaches are good cooked in this way, especially with an almond crumble. You can prepare, and even cook it, in advance and it is delicious served cold, topped with thick fresh cream or strained yoghurt.

1.35kg/3lb peaches and/or nectarines
2tbsp water
170g/6oz plain flour
85g/3oz ground almonds
110g/4oz chilled butter, diced
85g/3oz sugar

Preheat the oven to Gas Mark 6 (200°C, 400°F). Halve the fruit, remove the stones, and cut the peaches into 4. Place in the bottom of a large shallow pie dish or baking tin. Sprinkle with 2tbsp water. Place the flour and almonds in a large basin and rub in the butter with your fingertips. Stop when the mixture resembles coarse breadcrumbs. Stir in the sugar and then scatter the almond crumble on top of the fruit. Bake for 25 minutes.
Serves 6.

FREE-FORM FRUIT TART

FOR THE BASIC SWEET TART CRUST:
280g/10oz plain flour
3tbsp sugar
170g/6oz cold butter, in chunks
2 egg yolks, lightly beaten
FOR THE FILLING:
about 1kg/2lb apples, peeled and cored
230g/8oz frozen blackberries or blackcurrants, thawed
110g/4oz sugar
juice of 1 lemon
1tsp ground cinnamon
1 egg, beaten

First, make the sweet tart crust. Put the flour and sugar in a large mixing bowl and rub in the butter with your fingertips until the mixture resembles fine breadcrumbs. Stir in the egg yolks and enough cold water – about 2 tablespoons – to bind it. Roll the pastry into a ball, then flatten it and leave it to rest in the fridge for 15 minutes.

Preheat the oven to Gas Mark 6 (200°C, 400°F). Roll out the pastry to a width of 35cm/14in, then slide on to a baking sheet.

Slice the apples and toss them in a mixing bowl with the dark fruits, sugar, lemon juice and cinnamon. Pile in the middle of the pastry, leaving a 7.5cm/3in strip of pastry all round. Lift the edges of the pastry up and fold them over on to the fruit. Brush with a little beaten egg and bake in the oven for about 45 minutes, or until golden. Leave to cool slightly before lifting on to a serving plate. Eat with cream.
Serves 6.

Free-form
Fruit Tart

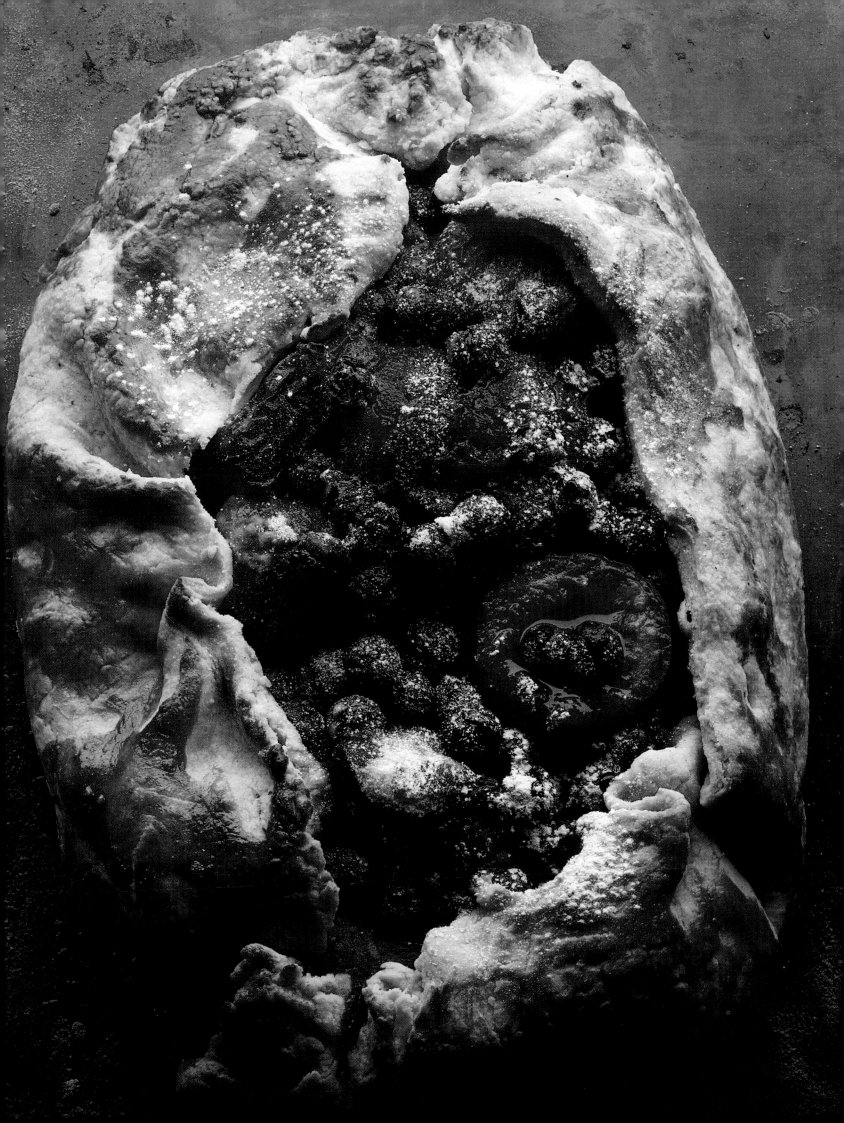

TARTES AUX POMMES

Rich shortcrust pastry is the usual base for a French apple tart but I prefer it made with a thin base of crisp puff pastry, brushed with a little fruit jelly and eaten very hot with cold, thick cream.

200g/7oz puff pastry
4 apples, cored and halved
a little caster sugar for sprinkling
apricot jam or fruit jelly for
brushing

Preheat the oven to Gas Mark 7 (220°C, 425°F). Roll out the puff pastry to a thickness of 7mm/⅓in and cut out 8 circles using a saucer.

Slice each apple-half thinly, holding the apple intact with your free hand. Lift the sliced apple with a palette knife on to the pastry discs and sprinkle with sugar. Slide the pastries on to a baking sheet and bake in the oven for 10 minutes, or until the pastry starts to colour.

Test the apples with the point of a knife; if it goes in easily they are cooked. Remove the tarts from the oven and brush the apple and surrounding pastry with a little jam or jelly. Return the tarts to the oven for about 5 minutes, until the jam starts to caramelize.
Serves 4.

Warm
Apricot Tart

WARM APRICOT TART

Use very ripe scarlet-blushed apricots for these tarts with thin, crisp pastry.

200g/7oz puff pastry
8 ripe apricots
caster sugar

Roll out the puff pastry to a thickness of 3mm/⅛in. Cut two 15cm/6in rounds of pastry and place on a baking sheet or wooden board. Chill in the fridge for 20 minutes.

Preheat the oven to Gas Mark 7 (220°C, 425°F) and place an empty bak-ing sheet in the oven. Bring a large pan of water to the boil. Immerse the apricots in the water, leave for 30 seconds and then remove with a slotted spoon.

Cut the apricots in half, peeling the skin with your fingers as you go. Re-move the stones. Place the apricot halves, flat side down, on the rounds of chilled pastry and dust with a little caster sugar. Transfer each one with a fish slice to the hot baking sheet. (This will stop the pastry going soggy on the bottom.) Bake for 10 minutes until puffed, crisp and golden. Serve warm with cream. Serves 2.

Tartes aux
Pommes

COLD PUDDINGS

On hot summer days the best desserts
are those that offer simple combinations of soft
scarlet fruits and unctuous cream.

At the heart of summer desserts are ripe fruits and fresh creams; plump locally-grown strawberries, deep-scented raspberries and sweet golden creams. Match the fruits to the creams for the simplest of seasonal puddings.

CREAMS

Mixed with softly whipped cream, fromage frais makes the exquisite summer dessert, Coeur à la crème. It is traditionally made in romantic heart-shaped china moulds; but any carton, can or sieve will do the trick, as long as it contains a few holes for the cheese to drain through. Improvise by piercing holes in a yoghurt or cream carton, or line a sieve with clean damp muslin. Once the pudding is un-moulded scatter it with fraises de bois – tiny wild strawberries.

Fromage frais can also be drained and used as a firm low-fat base for fruit desserts. Make a purée with plump hairy gooseberries or deep red raspberries, then fold in an equal amount of fromage frais and lace the mixture with a little whipped cream. Spoon into glasses or ramekins and serve cold from the fridge.

Petit Suisses are the most charming of creams. Eat them with a teaspoon or unwrap them on to small plates and surround them with purple blueberries or slices of fresh apricot as the perfect convenience dessert. My favourite combination is with very ripe blackberries and a drizzle of fresh cream; the surprising contrast between the sharp white cheese, the sweet yellow cream and the scent of ripe fruit is positively ambrosial.

Mascarpone is the most fashionable soft cheese for dessert use. Smooth, thick and addictive, it is a full cream product and the richest of all the soft cheeses and cultured creams. I like to eat it with crisp almond tuiles, high-bake water biscuits or sweet lacy wafers, but I have also made a seriously rich but irresistible

pudding by plumping raisins in a little cognac, stirring them into the cheese with toasted pine nuts, chilling it thoroughly, then serving with crisp brandy snaps. Dotted with bitter chocolate pieces, and a generous swig of rum or cognac, mascarpone also makes an original ice cream. Serve these rich puddings with strong black coffee.

Ricotta is another fresh cream cheese worth looking out for. It is instantly recognizable by its pudding basin shape, bright white colour and the embossed pattern made by the basket in which it is traditionally stored. Freshness is paramount, as ricotta is prone to sour easily. Do not buy any ricotta that shows signs of yellowing.

Ricotta can also be made into quick and delicious puddings. Sweeten it with a little sugar, fold in cream and rum, or, alternatively, pour a home-made fruit purée, such as apricot, over it.

FRUITS

Deep red raspberries make a wonderful summer treat if crushed gently with a fork then folded into sharp, thick yoghurt or, remembering their affinity with cream, layered between softly whipped cream and crisp puff pastry.

Blackcurrants have a rich powerful taste that makes an intensely flavoured purée. Simply cook with a little water and a sprinkling of sugar for four to five minutes until they start to burst, then sieve to remove the seeds. Pour the purée over poached pears or ice cream or stir into yoghurt as the Swedish do for breakfast. I also like to put blackcurrants into summer pudding.

Far too rare for summer pudding are yellow raspberries, which are a soft golden colour. Once difficult to find they are becoming more popular; like many soft fruits, they are perfect accompanied by a sweet dessert wine such as a Muscat or rich honey-yellow Sauternes. Luscious ripe, but not over-ripe, peaches and apricots can be sliced, dropped into a glass of white wine, then left for half an hour to give up some of their flavour to the wine without becoming too soft.

Both peaches and apricots have an affinity with almonds as they are closely related. An ice cream or blancmange flavoured with almonds makes an ideal accompaniment to a bowl of sliced apricots. The watchword for preparing fruits is simplicity. Try halved apricots filled with soured cream and chopped pistachio nuts, or raspberries and blueberries scented with rosewater.

Redcurrants and blackcurrants can be splashed with framboise, the raspberry flavoured eau-de-vie, or crème de cassis, which is based on blackcurrants. I also like to mix one tablespoon of cassis to four of blackcurrants, simmer them for four or five minutes till they start to burst, then spoon the syrup and fruit over vanilla ice cream.

page 149
Apricot
Amaretti
Trifle

APRICOT AMARETTI TRIFLE

I use the term 'trifle' rather loosely, as I think a true trifle should contain custard. Amaretti di Saronno macaroons make a convenient trifle base, but use sponge-cake if you prefer. Substitute a liqueur or eau-de-vie for the sherry if you like. Raspberries can be used instead of strawberries and half petit suisse to mascarpone if you have some. This recipe can be a base for your own ideas. A scattering of sugared rose petals would look pretty.

**455g/1lb apricots
255g/9oz amaretti biscuits
6tbsp sherry
455g/1lb strawberries
230g/8oz mascarpone
2 free range eggs, separated
60g/2oz caster sugar
230g/8oz crème fraîche or thick double cream**

Halve the apricots, remove stones and place the halves in a shallow pan of simmering water and cook for 4-5 minutes, until the tip of a knife will slide through them effortlessly. Drain and allow the fruit to cool.

Place the amaretti in a large china or glass bowl. Sprinkle over the sherry. Purée half the apricots in the blender and rub through a sieve. Pour the apricot purée over the amaretti biscuits.

Scatter the remaining apricots and the strawberries over the purée. Beat the mascarpone and the egg yolks in a bowl till creamy, beat in the sugar, then beat the egg whites until stiff and fold in gently.

Place the trifle in the fridge for at least 4 hours for the flavours to blend together. Spread the crème fraîche or cream over the top of the trifle.
Serves 6-8.

BURNT CREAM

Grilled puddings can be as straightforward as berries with whipped cream, sprinkled with sugar and browned under a hot grill, or as voluptuous as this traditional custard.

**455ml/16fl oz double cream
1 vanilla pod, split
5 large egg yolks
100g/3½ oz caster sugar**

Pour the cream into a thick-bottomed saucepan, throw in the vanilla pod, and bring slowly to the boil. Beat the egg yolks together with 2 tablespoons of the sugar until slightly thickened.

As soon as the cream starts to boil, pour it over the egg yolks and sugar. Remove the vanilla pod. Return the custard to the heat and cook over a low heat, stirring constantly, until it starts to thicken. On no account let it boil.

Pour the custard into an 850ml/1½ pints shallow dish and cool. Refrigerate overnight until it has set.

An hour or so before serving, preheat the grill until it is very hot – essential for the sugar to caramelize quickly. Sprinkle the remaining sugar over the custard. Put under the grill, as close to the flame as you can, and cook until the sugar caramelizes. Leave for one hour, in the cool, before eating.
Serves 4.

● Put a layer of fruit – ripe plums, sweet muscat grapes or blackberries – in the bottom of the dish before adding the custard.

● Stephen Bull serves rice pudding with a caramelized top in his brilliant eponymous restaurant in London. Make your own by topping chilled thick rice pudding with a thin layer of caster sugar and grilling as above.

DATE AND BANANA CREAM

This is my version of a traditional Middle Eastern pudding that I enjoyed in Marrakech.

**4 large bananas
230g/8oz dried dates
280ml/10fl oz single cream
2tbsp flaked almonds, toasted**

Slice the bananas about as thick as a £1 coin. Chop the dates roughly. Mix the fruits together and place in a serving dish. Pour over the cream and chill for at least 2 hours. Remove from the fridge, scatter over the almonds – even better if they are still hot from the grill – and serve.
Serves 4.

Burnt Cream

DRIED FIGS WITH HONEY AND THYME

**455g/1lb dried figs
1 litre/1¾ pints red wine
4tbsp honey
2 branches of thyme**

Place the figs in a saucepan with the wine, honey and thyme. Cook gently over a low heat for about 45 minutes until the figs are soft and the sauce has thickened slightly. Chill and serve with thick cream.
Serves 4-6

ALMOND BLANCMANGE

The affinity between almonds and peaches, apricots or strawberries is demonstrated here. A creamy old-fashioned blancmange, made from milk, which has been scented with almonds, is the ultimate accompaniment for soft summer fruits. You can serve this pudding with sliced ripe peaches and a glass of Sauternes, chilled in glasses with raspberries sprinkled on top, or set in a pretty mould, turned out and surrounded by poached apricots or very ripe English strawberries.

**230g/8oz whole almonds, peeled
4 bitter almonds or a few drops
bitter almond essence
340ml/12fl oz milk and water
mixed
1tbsp powdered or 4 leaves
gelatine
110g/4oz caster sugar
340ml/12fl oz double or whipping
cream**

Grind all the almonds in a food processor or chop them very finely with a heavy knife. Place them in a saucepan with almond essence if used and pour on the milk and water. Heat gently up to boiling point, but do not allow to boil.

Set aside for 10 minutes to allow the almonds to perfume the milk fully.

If you are using powdered gelatine, sprinkle it on to 115ml/4fl oz tepid water and leave for a few minutes to soften. Soak leaf gelatine in 115ml/4fl oz water for 5-10 minutes until it is soft.

Line a sieve with a double layer of muslin or a clean kitchen towel, and place the sieve over a bowl. Pour in the almond mixture. Lift the four corners of the cloth or towel and twist them tightly round until the almond milk starts to drip from the cloth into the bowl. Twist the cloth several times until all the almond milk has been extracted. Discard the almonds in the cloth.

Gently heat the almond milk in a small saucepan, adding the sugar and stirring until dissolved. Remove from the heat and add the softened gelatine. Stir until completely dissolved. Place the mixture in a bowl and leave in the refrigerator until it is tepid and on the point of setting. This can take anything from 5-15 minutes, so keep checking the mixture regularly.

While the almond cream is in the fridge, whip the cream until it forms soft peaks; it should not be stiff, but should just hold its shape when you lift out the whisk. Remove the almond cream from the fridge, when its consistency is liquid enough for it to slide off a spoon gently, and fold in the whipped cream. Pour into a 850ml/1½ pints dish and leave to set in the refrigerator for at least 2 hours.
Serves 4.

ALMOND CREAM WITH BLUEBERRIES

This rich pudding is similar to a cheese-cake, with its origin in *pashka* – the Russian Easter cake. Why keep such a good thing just for one day of the year?

**1kg/2¼lb cream cheese or
mascarpone
110g/4oz ground almonds
3 egg yolks
110g/4oz caster sugar
drop of vanilla extract
110g/4oz double cream
230g/8oz blueberries**

Line a sieve or colander, 20cm/8in in diameter and about 10cm/4in deep, with muslin or a cloth.

Mix the cheese and almonds thoroughly. Beat together the egg yolks and sugar until slightly fluffy, add the vanilla extract and fold into the cheese mixture. Gently whip the cream and fold in.

Turn the mixture into the lined sieve. Spread a layer of muslin or cloth on top of the mixture, then cover with a plate and a weight. Place in the refrigerator in a shallow dish or deep plate and leave overnight.

The next day, turn out on to a plate and serve with the blueberries.
Serves 8.

● Use real vanilla extract to flavour the cream. Avoid anything labelled 'essence' as it has little true vanilla flavour, and some brands can be positively nasty.
● Rosewater makes a refreshing change from vanilla; add 2tsp to the above recipe.
● The pudding can be made up to two days in advance if you wish.
● Take the almond cream to a picnic in its container and turn it out when you get there.
● Use blackberries or loganberries if blueberries are not available.

Almond Cream with Blueberries

RICOTTA WITH CHOCOLATE AND COGNAC

Ricotta is surprisingly cheap, and its mild cheesy taste can be a base for savoury and sweet dishes. You can use any thick dairy product in place of the fromage frais, or leave it out altogether for a firmer spread which could be used as a cake filling. Use unsweetened cocoa powder as drinking chocolate is not the same: Van Houten's is particularly good.

4tbsp raisins
1tbsp cognac
110g/4oz ricotta
4tbsp fromage frais, quark or petit suisse
2tbsp caster sugar
2tbsp cocoa powder
brandy snaps or biscuits to serve

Sprinkle the raisins with the cognac and set aside for 15 minutes for the fruit to absorb the spirit. Sieve the ricotta into a pudding basin and stir in the fromage frais, quark, or petit suisse. Fold in the sugar, cocoa powder and lastly the soaked raisins. Chill for 15 minutes or longer. Serve in tiny pots to spread on to crisp biscuits.
Serves 2 as a dessert.

GINGERED RICOTTA

110g/4oz ricotta
4tbsp fromage frais
1tbsp caster sugar
2tbsp ground almonds
2 lumps of ginger in syrup
2tbsp syrup from the ginger jar

Sieve the ricotta and stir in the fromage frais. Add the caster sugar and the ground almonds. Cut the ginger into small dice and fold in with the syrup.

Chill for at least 20 minutes for the flavours to blend, and serve in tiny pots or in a small bowl with crisp biscuits or brandy snaps to dip.
Serves 2.

COEUR A LA CREME WITH BERRIES

You will need some sort of mould for this dish. It can be made of china, steel or wood, or even waxed card, as long as there are draining holes in the base. I have used a flour sieve, a small colander or four small flower pots (new and well scrubbed) with equal success. A practical improvisation is to make holes in the base of four 230ml/8fl oz crème frâiche or fromage frais containers with a skewer. Use the pretty white china heart-shaped moulds if you have them. This quantity will fill a mould of about 850ml/1½ pints. Use a piece of damp muslin, or a new J-cloth, to line it.

455g/1lb fromage frais
170ml/6fl oz crème fraîche
1 egg white (free range)
2tbsp caster sugar
230g/8oz strawberries or raspberries for purée
230g/8oz blueberries, raspberries or strawberries

Line the moulds with the damp muslin, pushing the fabric well into the sides.

Place the fromage frais in a pudding basin and fold in the crème fraîche. Beat the egg white until stiff and fold it into the creams with the caster sugar.

Spoon the cream into the lined moulds and set on a shallow dish or deep plate, remembering that there will be some leakage from the moulds. Place in the fridge for at least 5 hours and preferably overnight.

Make a fine purée of the strawberries or raspberries by pushing them through a sieve. It is unnecessary to sweeten the purée for this dish. Chill before serving with the cream.

Turn out the cream on to chilled plates and surround with blueberries or other fresh berries.
Serves 4.

MASCARPONE WITH APRICOTS AND ALMONDS

Mascarpone is a rich Italian cream cheese, but you can substitute ricotta or fromage frais if you prefer. I like to use whole unskinned almonds for this recipe, but flaked almonds, toasted, are fine as an alternative.

230g/8oz ripe apricots
170g/6oz mascarpone cheese
12 whole almonds

Cut the apricots in half and remove the stones. Liquidize the fruit in a blender, adding 1tbsp water if it seems rather dry. Push the purée through a sieve using a wooden spoon.

Divide the mascarpone cheese in scoops between 4 plates. Spoon the purée around the cheese, allowing about 2tbsp per plate. Split each almond into approximately 4 thin slivers and scatter over the cheese and purée.
Serves 4.

Coeur à la Crème with Berries

CREMA ALLA MASCARPONE

This rich cream is well known in Italy, although I have rarely seen it on restaurant menus there. Surprisingly quick to make, it is also good if you throw in a handful of Amaretti di Saronno macaroons to add crunch.

2 free range eggs, separated
60g/2oz caster sugar
280g/10oz mascarpone
1tbsp brandy or kirsch

Cream the egg yolks with the caster sugar, add the mascarpone and beat until light and creamy. Add the brandy or kirsch. Whisk the egg whites until stiff and fold into the cream with a metal spoon. When the egg whites are thoroughly incorporated, spoon the cream into four large wine glasses, or six smaller ones.

Leave in the fridge for a couple of hours to chill thoroughly. Serve with crisp biscuits, such as almond brandy snaps. Alternatively, chill the cream in the bowl in which it is made then spoon it into the brandy snaps.
Serves 4-6.

MANGO YOGHURT FOOL

1 large or 2 small ripe mangoes
280g/10oz thick natural yoghurt

Peel the mangoes, holding them over a bowl to catch the juices. Remove all of the flesh from the stone and place in a blender or food processor. Add juices and liquidize to a thick purée. Place the yoghurt in a basin and gently stir in the mango purée.

Spoon the fool into 2 standard wine goblets. Place in the fridge for an hour or more.
Serves 2.

Strawberries with Black Pepper

RASPBERRY SYLLABUB

Recipes for syllabubs (cream flavoured with wine and brandy) appear in earliest cookery books. The addition of fruit is a more modern idea.

A small glass of white wine
1tbsp brandy
1 lemon
285ml/½ pint double cream
230g/8oz raspberries
2tbsp caster sugar

Pour the wine and brandy into a large pudding basin and add the thinly pared peel from the lemon. Set aside for a couple of hours. Remove the lemon peel and add the sugar to the alcohol. Pour in the cream and whisk till thick. Lightly crush the raspberries and stir into the cream. Serve with crisp almondy biscuits.
Serves 4.

STRAWBERRIES WITH BLACK PEPPER

Strawberries from Hampshire and Kent mark the start of the British berry season. You will need a 230g/8oz punnet for two people. Sprinkle the strawberries with a very little finely ground black pepper, then eat them in the sun, with your fingers. The spice subtly brings out the full flavour of the ripe fruit.

● Choose the deepest red fruits as they have a more intense flavour.

Raspberry Syllabub

Orange Juice Jelly

ORANGE JUICE JELLY

A jelly made from fresh fruit juice is a very adult affair, with little other than the shape to remind you of those childhood birthday parties. Most orange juice you buy in cartons is made from pasteurised juice, which has been reduced to a concentrate, frozen then traded on financial markets. It is a far cry from freshly squeezed fruit, which has an unbeatable taste and aroma. For this recipe either squeeze the juice yourself from small oranges, or buy the freshly squeezed variety commonly available in supermarkets.

**6 sheets of leaf gelatine or
15g/½oz powdered gelatine
I litre/1¾ pints fresh orange juice**

If you are using leaf gelatine, soak the sheets in a bowl of cold water for 5 minutes until they soften.

Warm half of the orange juice over a low heat and stir in the softened leaf gelatine. If you are using powdered gelatine, sprinkle it over the warm juice and stir until dissolved. Pour in the remaining cold juice, then tip into a jelly mould and leave to set in the fridge for 4 hours.

To turn out, run the mould briefly under the hot tap, without getting the jelly wet, then upturn the mould on to a deep plate or dish. Shake it confidently, and the jelly will slide right out.

Serve with brandied fruits, such as kumquats, and cream if you wish.
Serves 6-8.

STRAWBERRY FOOL

I like real pieces of fruit among the cream in my fools, but if you prefer a smoother texture then work the berries to a purée in a blender or push them through a sieve. If all the ingredients are used cold from the fridge, this can be eaten straightaway, otherwise chill it for an hour before serving. Sweeten the fool with a tablespoon of icing sugar if you must.

**230g/8oz strawberries
230g/8oz fromage frais
110g/4oz crème fraîche or thick
double cream**

Crush the berries in a pudding basin with a fork. Fold in the fromage frais and the crème fraîche, slowly but thoroughly.

Spoon into glasses or small pots and chill before serving. Crisp biscuits such as almond brandy snaps are good with this fool.
Serves 4.

SUMMER FRUITS WITH GERANIUM CREAM

**I lemon- or rose-scented
geranium leaf
110g/4oz caster sugar
whipping cream (see method)
soft summer fruits**

Make the geranium sugar a week or so before you intend to use it. Put a lemon- or rose-scented geranium leaf, which should be absolutely dry, into the caster sugar, and store in an airtight container. Over the next few days, the leaf will give up its scent to the sugar. Alternatively, use a vanilla pod.

Use 2-3tbsp of the scented sugar to sweeten 285ml/½ pint cream. Whip the cream and sugar slowly with a hand whisk until stiff.

Spoon it into little pots with soft summer fruits such as strawberries, raspberries and apricots, or lay the fruits in the centre of the table and let everyone help themselves, dipping the fruits into scented cream.

*Summer
Fruits with
Geranium
Cream*

SUMMER PUDDING

The quantities of berries used here are only a rough guide: you can use more or less of each, depending on what's available in the shops. I find that the more raspberries I use the less sugar is needed: it is actually possible to make the pudding using no sugar at all, if you wish.

8 slices white or fine wholemeal bread, crusts removed
230g/8oz blackcurrants
280g/10oz redcurrants
340g/12oz raspberries
170g/6oz caster sugar
cream or yoghurt to serve

Line a 1.7 litre/3 pint pudding basin with the bread, reserving some to cover the fruit. Remove the stalks from the fruit, place in a saucepan with 2tbsp water and the sugar. Cook gently until the currants start to burst their skins, and the juice becomes a rich purply-red, which will take about 5-7 minutes.

While the fruit is still warm, spoon it into the lined basin, and cover it with the rest of the bread. Put a plate on top and press down with a heavy weight. (The weights from a pair of scales, or a couple of full milk bottles, will do the trick.)

Stand the pudding basin on a plate and leave overnight in the refrigerator. Reserve any of the juice that has been pressed out of the pudding and pour it into a small jug. Turn out the pudding on to a serving plate, pour over the reserved juice so that the bread is completely covered, and serve with cream or yoghurt.
Serves 6.

MELON WITH SUMMER FRUITS AND CHAMPAGNE

The round green Charentais melons from France, with their fragrant apricot-coloured flesh, have the finest flavour but the more popular and cheaper Ogen variety is a good substitute for this recipe

110g/4oz blackcurrants or raspberries
2tbsp sugar (if using blackcurrants)
2 Charentais or Ogen melons
230g/8oz assorted berries and soft fruits: choose from raspberries, blueberries, strawberries, redcurrants, apricots, peaches, melon balls
½ bottle champagne or sparkling wine, chilled

If you are using blackcurrants, remove the stalks from the fruit and place them in a small saucepan with the sugar, and 1tbsp cold water. Cook gently until the sugar has dissolved and the fruit has burst, making a deep purple purée. Push the purée through a sieve with a wooden spoon to remove the skins and the seeds. When cool, put the purée in the refrigerator to chill. If you are using raspberries, place them in a sieve, wash them very gently under running water and then push them through the sieve with a wooden spoon. Reserve in the refrigerator.

Cut the melons in half with a sharp knife, either straight across or, if you have time, with a zig-zag line by making a series of small V-shaped incisions around the middle of the melons using a small sharp knife. Carefully pull the halves apart and scoop out the seeds. Remove a small slice from the base of each melon half so that it can stand up without wobbling.

Spoon the blackcurrant or raspberry

purée into the melon halves. Gently wash the berries and place them on top with slices of soft fruit or melon balls. Place each filled melon on a plate.

Pour the champagne into the melon halves at the table so that the fruits are surrounded by a foam of bubbles.
Serves 4.

FRUITS BRULEES

This is a dish of summer berries topped with whipped fresh cream and crisp caramel. Whichever fruits you choose try to include raspberries, peaches and bananas.

230g/8oz sugar
680g/1½lb mixed soft fruits, to include bananas, peaches and raspberries
340ml/12fl oz double cream

Put the sugar in a heavy-based deep saucepan and pour in enough water to cover. Set over a high flame to boil while you prepare the fruit.

Peel the bananas, halve, stone and slice the peaches and remove the stems and hulls from the raspberries. Place all the fruit in a serving bowl. Whip the cream until it forms soft peaks. Spoon the cream over the fruit.

The sugar in the saucepan will start to turn a pale golden caramel after about 10 minutes – watch it carefully as it may burn, but do not stir it. It is ready when it turns a shiny rich dark golden brown; take it off the heat before it starts smoking or it will be bitter. Immediately – taking care not to let it splash and burn you – pour the caramel over the cream and fruit. The cream will start to bubble a little and the caramel will set crisp. Serve within 30 minutes.
Serves 6.

Fruit Brulées

WINTER FRUITS IN MUSCAT DE BEAUMES DE VENISE

Winter Fruits

The principle of macerating fruits in sweet wine will also work with figs, kumquats, lychees and any dried fruits. Pierce the skins of dried fruits with a needle so that they soak up the wine quickly.

1 bottle of Muscat de Beaumes de Venise
230g/8oz prunes
1 pear, quartered and cored
2 small bunches of grapes

Pour the wine into a large screw-top or Kilner jar. Pierce the flesh of the prunes with a needle and drop them into the wine, then add the pear and the grapes. Seal the jar and place in the fridge overnight.

Just before serving, lift out the fruits with a draining spoon, pile them in a dish and pour a spoonful of the wine on top, or simply place the jar in the centre of the table and let everyone spear the fruits with wooden skewers.
Serves 4.

● Prunes are my favourite for macerating in sweet wine, but other dried fruits can be used too. Try hunza apricots, dried plums from Pakistan, or dried pears. Soak the hunza apricots in water first and then simmer till tender, before you soak them in the wine.

Winter Fruits in Muscat de Beaumes de Venise

WINTER FRUITS

Fruit is always a healthy, easy end to a meal. In winter, it can lighten the general gloom, especially if you choose unusual fruits such as dusty pink, fragrant persimmons and orange Sharon fruit.

Skin the Sharon fruit, slice it thickly and scatter with a chopped knob of preserved ginger.

Persimmons can be scooped out with a teaspoon and eaten with thick clotted cream.

PAPAYA WITH LIME

2 ripe papayas
1 lime

Cut the papayas in half from stalk to base and scoop out the round black seeds with a teaspoon. Place each half on a plate.

Cut the lime in half from the stalk end to the tip and then in half again, to give 4 easily squeezable segments. Place 1 on each plate. Before eating the fruit with a teaspoon, rub the lime over the cut edge of the papaya, or squeeze over the lime juice.
Serves 4 for breakfast.

COFFEE ICE CREAM PARFAIT

This grown-up version of an ice cream sundae is ideal when you have very little time in which to produce something to revel in. Serve it with wafer biscuits – crisp wafer scrolls filled with chocolate (from Italian grocers) go very well with this pudding.

1 litre/1¾ pints coffee ice cream
230ml/8fl oz coffee liqueur, such as Kahlua
115ml/4fl oz double cream
wafer biscuits

Soften the ice cream a little by leaving it at room temperature for 10 minutes. Divide the ice cream, alternating scoops of it with coffee liqueur, between four tall glasses. Set them in the freezer for 30 minutes. Whip the cream, sweetening it with a tablespoon of icing sugar if you wish, until it forms soft peaks. Spoon the whipped cream on to the ice cream, stick a wafer in, soda-fountain style, and serve.
Serves 4.

ICE CREAMS WITH LIQUEURS

Certain liqueurs have an affinity with ice cream and sorbets.

- Vanilla ice cream with Bailey's Irish Cream and grated dark chocolate
- Almond ice cream with poached dried apricots and Archers Peach Country Liqueur
- Mango sorbet with Cointreau and a squeeze of passion fruit
- Chocolate ice cream with a spoonful of crème de cacao
- Chocolate ice cream with raisins that have been soaked in whisky for an hour or two.

PASSION FRUIT AND MANGO WATER ICE

280g/10oz sugar
20 ripe passion fruits
1 ripe mango

Set the freezer to its coldest. Bring the sugar and 570ml/1 pint water to the boil in a heavy-based saucepan. Allow to boil for 5 minutes until it goes syrupy but shows no change of colour. Cool quickly by placing the saucepan into a sink of cold water, then place the pan in the fridge.

Cut each passion fruit in half and squeeze the flesh and seeds from 18 of them into a small sieve balanced over a 1.15 litre/2 pint pudding basin. Push the flesh through the sieve with the back of a spoon, working until you are left with nothing but dry seeds. Discard the seeds.

Squeeze the 2 remaining passion fruits into the purée, to add crunchiness, or sieve them with the rest if you prefer. Peel the mango, slice its flesh away from the stone and purée in a blender or food processor. Add the purée to the passion fruit, mix and stir in the syrup.

Put the mixture into the freezer and freeze until almost solid, around 1½-2 hours. Remove from the freezer, break up the mixture with a fork, and beat with a whisk, or with an electric mixer. Freeze again, for 3-4 hours. Remove the water ice from the freezer 15 minutes before serving.
Serves 6-8.

MASCARPONE AND CHOCOLATE-CHIP ICE CREAM

I like the contrast in texture between the creamy ice and the crunchy chocolate chips in this ice cream. Generally, I flavour it simply with a true vanilla extract, but a couple of tablespoons of rum or brandy can go down well too. Use a smooth curd cheese instead of mascarpone if you prefer.

280g/10oz mascarpone
2 free range eggs, separated
60g/2oz caster sugar
vanilla extract
60g/2oz bitter chocolate, chopped

Set your deep freeze or freezer compartment at its coldest. Beat the mascarpone and the egg yolks in a mixing bowl with a wooden spoon or electric hand beater. Add the sugar when the two are well mixed and beat until fluffy, for about 2 minutes, with an electric whisk. Add a few drops of vanilla extract, testing as you go, until the mixture tastes like extremely good vanilla ice cream. Stir in the chocolate chips, and any rum or brandy. Whisk the egg whites in a clean basin until they are stiff enough to stand up in peaks. Using a metal spoon, gently fold the beaten whites into the vanilla cream, making sure they are thoroughly incorporated.

Freeze the mixture, in a covered container, for 4 hours in the deep freeze. Alternatively, pour the mixture into an ice cream maker and follow the manufacturers instructions.

Remove from the freezer for 5-10 minutes before serving in order to allow it to soften a little.
Serves 4.

A simple scoop of ice cream can be turned into something more original by partnering it with the right ingredients.
- Almonds. These have an affinity with berry ices such as strawberry or raspberry. They are particularly suitable when flaked and toasted as they offer a change of texture, too. Try golden toasted almond flakes with strawberry ice and a handful of fresh berries.

- Walnuts. To get the most flavour from these meaty nuts they should be freshly shelled and toasted till fragrant. Sprinkle them over coffee ices.
- Pistachios. These little green nuts flatter strawberry or almond ices like nothing else.
- Chocolate Chips. A packet of finest quality chocolate chips is useful for adding crunch to chocolate or walnut ice creams.

- Honey. Runny, flower-scented honey can be drizzled over hazelnut or walnut ice creams.
- Flower Waters. A sprinkling of flower water adds a fragrant note to ices. Try rosewater on strawberry or raspberry ices or sorbets. Orange-flower water on apricot, peach or vanilla ice creams.

Passion Fruit and Mango Water Ice

CAKES & PASTRIES

A contemporary teatime combines store-bought basics
with old-fashioned baking. Even the richest, most elegant
cake can be assembled in minutes.

There can be few more satisfying ways of spending a rainy afternoon than baking cakes and pastries for tea – perhaps some simple shortbread or a plain sponge cake served with warm jam on the side. For a special occasion, try assembling a pyramid of choux pastry buns to produce a Croquembouche, the traditional French wedding cake, covering it in an unfussy way with powdered sugar.

A glass of milk and a plate of cookies is a substantial snack, especially welcome late at night or whilst working. It is a fairly easy task to make simple spice cookies at home, not much more complicated than making pastry. Florentines, those luxurious biscuits full of almonds and dried fruit, are a little more complicated, but well worth the effort.

Old-fashioned cakes such as gingerbread are on most people's lists of favourite foods. Use both powdered and fresh ginger to give warmth to a sticky ginger cake, which will be made all the better by being kept in a tin for a couple of weeks to make it even stickier.

There can be few things that suggest 'welcome' like being offered a slice of home-made cake. Some are quite simple and straightforward to make, only becoming complicated when you decide to decorate them.

A dusting of icing or caster sugar is much less fussy than messing about with piping bags and icings. Simplicity is the key here, and even celebration cakes look better with a 'forked' icing than some more elaborate design involving different coloured icings in numerous piping bags.

A striking way to decorate a cake can be as simple as using slices of glacé fruit, such as plums and apricots. Even simply chopped they can be piled in the centre to good effect, and a little dusting of icing sugar will make them look like jewels.

Chocolate, the darker the better, looks wonderful

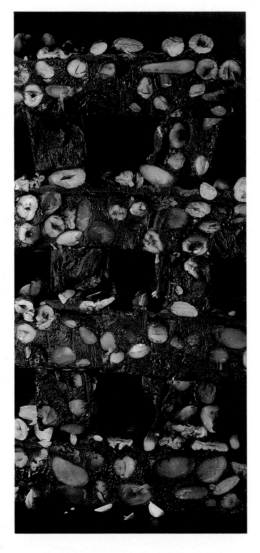

when melted and drizzled over a plain sponge cake. Just dip a spoon into the liquid chocolate and then drizzle it over the top of the sponge.

Some of the best tea-time recipes don't even need cooking: the richest of chocolate cakes can be made by simply melting chocolate and folding toasted nuts and eggs into the liquid chocolate. Cakes such as

these 'cook' in the fridge rather than the oven, and are just as suitable for tea or dessert.

Tea is so comforting, whether it is scones with jam and cream on blue and white plates served with a strong brew from a brown pot, or dainty sandwiches and crisp pastries with fragrant tea from elegant china. You can spend hours baking if you want to or you can throw a tea together quickly using a few shop-bought basics. Frozen puff pastry, for instance – although it won't taste as buttery as the home-made variety – makes a good crisp base for fresh fruit and real fruit jams.

Muffins, those doughy baps you toast so that they are crisp on the outside and warm and soft within, are perfect tea-time food – not just smothered in butter, but spread with soft cheeses and delicately flavoured fruit jellies. For a different dessert, try them filled with hot, stewed apple and a dollop of crème fraiche.

MAKING TEA

Teatime is a good time to entertain. Most of the food can be prepared in advance, leaving just the crumpets or muffins to toast and the tea to make. Nothing good will come from dipping a tea bag into a mug of boiled water. The most you can say of it is that it is warm and wet. Good tea needs to be made in a pot, preferably china which will not taint the flavour. Use loose tea, one teaspoonful per person and one for the pot, or the largest tea bags you can find – the leaves need plenty of room to yield their full flavour.

Tea must be made with freshly drawn water; using water that has been sitting for a while produces a flat-tasting brew. Warm the pot by swishing a little hot water round in it, then take the pot to the kettle so that the water is still boiling when it is poured on to the leaves. Put the lid on quickly so that none of the fragrant steam escapes.

SPICE BREAD

230ml/8fl oz milk, lukewarm
15g/½oz dried yeast
85g/3oz caster sugar
I egg
2 egg yolks
500g/1lb 2oz plain flour
2tspn ground ginger
2tspn ground cinnamon
¼tspn ground cloves
2tbsp poppy seeds
I tbsp caraway seeds, optional
pinch of salt
110g/4oz butter, softened but not melted
110g/4oz mixed chopped candied orange and lemon peel and dried fruits

Butter and line a 15cm/6in soufflé dish.

Pour the milk into a large china basin, sprinkle the yeast on top with a tablespoon of the sugar and mix until dissolved. Leave in a warm place until it has started to froth (this takes about 10 minutes, depending on the warmth of the room).

Beat the egg and the yolks lightly with a fork and pour into the frothy yeast mixture. Sift in the flour, spices, salt and the remaining sugar. Bring the dough together (easier with your hands than with a spoon); at this stage it will be sticky.

Using a well-floured pastry board or work surface, turn out the dough and place the softened butter in small knobs all over it. With one hand, knead the butter in; the dough will be sticky and shiny to start with, but after about 10 minutes you will find it becomes smooth and elastic.

Turn the dough into a lightly floured basin, cover with a tea-towel and place in a warm, draught-free spot. In about an hour it will have doubled in size. At this point, turn the dough out on to the board, pat it hard with your knuckles, and knead again, this time folding in the peel and dried fruits.

Prove the dough for a second time: shape into a ball and slide into the lined soufflé dish which should be returned to the warm place for 20 minutes. It should rise above the top of the dish.

Preheat the oven to Gas Mark 6 (200°C, 400°F). Bake the bread for 10 minutes then reduce the heat to Gas Mark 4 (180°C, 350°F). The bread is done when it is brown on the outside and sounds hollow when the bottom of the dish is tapped. This will take about 35-40 minutes more.

Leave to cool in the dish. Serve in wedges or slices, with honey if you wish.

DOUBLE GINGER GINGERBREAD

110g/4oz wholemeal flour
110g/4oz plain flour
2tsp baking powder
3 heaped tsp ground ginger
Itsp ground cinnamon
Itsp ground nutmeg
2tbsp ground almonds
110g/4oz butter
2 rounded tbsp black treacle
2 rounded tbsp golden syrup
2tbsp dark brown sugar
2 eggs, well beaten
Itsp bicarbonate of soda
85ml/3fl oz warm milk
170g/6oz chopped stem ginger
2tbsp rolled oats

Preheat the oven to Gas Mark 4 (180°C, 350°F). Butter and line a 20cm/8in loaf tin. Mix together the flours, baking powder and ground spices. Stir in the ground almonds. Melt the butter, treacle, syrup and sugar in a small saucepan. Stir in the spiced flour.

Mix well, remove from the heat and stir in the beaten egg. Dissolve the bicarbonate of soda in the warm milk and stir into the mixture with the chopped stem ginger.

Pour into the loaf tin and scatter the oats over the surface. Bake for 45-50 minutes. Allow to cool in the tin, then turn out and wrap in foil or greaseproof paper and keep in a biscuit tin for a few days before eating.

SIMPLE SHORTBREAD

It's hard to beat the tried-and-tested, six-four-two method of making this crumbly biscuit: that is, 170g/6oz plain flour, 110g/4oz butter and 60g/2oz caster sugar. Slowly combine the ingredients in a food mixer, or mix the butter and sugar by hand then gradually work in the flour. Spread the mixture on to a 18 × 28cm/7 × 11in baking sheet and bake at Gas Mark 2 (150°C, 300°F) for about 1 hour. While still warm, cut into fingers and sprinkle with caster sugar. Makes 8-10.

MUFFINS

Split, rather than cut, muffins in half after toasting, for a crisper, rougher texture. Spread them with butter or any of the following:

- Apples, cored and chopped, and cooked in a pan with a drop of water till fluffy, and a spoonful of crème fraîche.
- Thick orange blossom honey and thickly sliced bananas.
- Butter and cinnamon.
- Apple or blackcurrant jelly and fromage frais.
- Cottage cheese and stoned and sliced fresh apricots.
- Cashel Blue, Beenleigh Blue or Stilton cheese and sliced crisp pears tossed in apple juice.
- Peanut butter and raisins.

Double
Ginger
Gingerbread

LIME AND YOGHURT CAKE

This is a simple, plain sponge flavoured with lime and sweet wine. The middle of the cake should be slightly moist and the cake is at its best served warm straight from the oven. Serve it with a spoonful of top-quality jam, such as Bonne Maman apricot or greengage.

2 limes
4 tbsp thick yoghurt
4 tbsp double cream
I egg
255g/9oz plain flour
2 tsp baking powder
8 tbsp sunflower oil
4 tbsp sweet wine or sherry
230g/8oz caster sugar

Preheat the oven to Gas Mark 7 (220°C, 425°F). Line the base of a 25cm/10in sponge tin with greaseproof paper.

Grate the limes, using the fine side of the grater, into the bowl of a processor. Throw in the remaining ingredients and mix for 30 seconds, scraping down the side of the bowl with a rubber spatula until all the ingredients are thoroughly mixed. Alternatively, beat thoroughly with a wooden spoon until the ingredients are amalgamated.

Tip the mixture into the cake tin and bake in the oven for 35 minutes. The cake is cooked when a skewer inserted in the centre comes out moist but clean. Ease the cake away from the sides of the tin with a palette knife, allow it to cool in the tin for a couple of minutes, then turn out on to a cooling rack.

Peel the paper off the bottom of the cake, then place a serving plate over the cake and invert the plate, cake and rack. Remove the cake rack. Serve the cake slightly warm with thick yoghurt, warmed jam or poached seasonal fruits such as apricots or cherries. It will stay moist in a cake tin for several days.

Serves 8.

FLORENTINES

Take your time over these indulgent biscuits – they're worth it. Glacé cherries without any fluorescent colouring are available in many health food shops.

60g/2oz glacé cherries
140g/5oz flaked almonds
170g/6oz butter
110g/4oz sugar
3 tbsp double cream
85g/3oz mixed peel
30g/1oz plain flour
230g/8oz plain dessert chocolate

Preheat the oven to Gas Mark 4 (180°C, 350°F) and lightly butter and flour two large baking trays.

Wash and dry the cherries to remove the excess syrup and lightly crush the almonds. Melt the butter in a small, heavy-bottomed saucepan, add the sugar and bring to the boil. Add the cream, the mixed peel and the flour and stir for half a minute, then remove from the heat.

Drop heaped tablespoons of the mixture on to the two prepared baking trays, leaving a 10cm/4in gap between each heap. Pat the mixture down a little with the back of the spoon, then bake the first tray in the preheated oven for 7 minutes, by which time the biscuits will have spread. Ease the edges in with a round biscuit cutter or the lid of a jam jar so that the florentines are round and about 10cm/4in in diameter. Return them to the oven for 3-4 minutes until they are brown at the edges.

Remove from the oven and put the next tray in. As the biscuits cool, gently lift the edges of each one with a palette knife. This is not a job to be hurried. Ease the palette knife further under each biscuit until you can lift it off completely, steadying it with your other hand, and transfer to waxed paper to set. Repeat until all the mixture is used up.

When the biscuits are cool and set firm, melt the chocolate in a small basin over hot water. Dip each biscuit into the melted chocolate and leave upside down to set.

Makes about 20.

● *Cream of Tartar.* Also known as tartaric acid, cream of tartar is an essential ingredient of baking powder. It is made from powdered dried grapes and combines with baking soda to give a rise to cake mixtures. It is also used in sweet making.

● *Baking Soda.* This is sodium bicarbonate, and is responsible for producing a gas when mixed with an acid (such as sour milk) which will cause a cake to rise. It is one of the constituents of baking powder.

● *Wholemeal flour.* This can be from any grain, wheat, rye or barley. It is that which has had nothing removed, leaving the flour full of all its original nutrients. It is used in bread with great success, but almost always renders pastry and cakes heavy and dull.

● *Stoneground Flour.* Any flour labelled stoneground has been milled in the traditional way, using stones rather than mechanical rollers. Stoneground flours have more flavour than the modern ones.

● *White Flour.* This is lighter than wholemeal, and a lot less nutritious, as it has had its bran and wheatgerm removed during milling. It can be labelled 'plain' or 'self raising', the latter where a raising agent has been added. Flour from small millers is likely to be milled in the traditional way and be free from the preservatives and additives rife in many household flours.

Florentines

CROQUEMBOUCHE

This is a pyramid of crisp choux buns, piled up and covered with chocolate sauce or drizzled with icing. Make the buns a day in advance – leaving yourself plenty of time for the preparation - then fill and assemble them on the day of the party.

125g/4 fl oz water
50g/2oz butter, cut into even pieces
75g/3oz plain flour
½tspn salt
2 eggs, size 2 or 3

Put the water into a saucepan with the butter, then place over a low heat and bring to a simmer. Sift the flour and salt together.

When the water has come to the boil and the butter has melted, add the flour to the liquid all at once. Stir over a medium heat until the mixture comes together into a solid mass and leaves the sides of the saucepan.

Off the heat, add the eggs, one at a time, beating hard with a wooden spoon. Continue beating until the mixture is smooth and shiny. The pastry batter is now ready to use.

Preheat the oven to Gas Mark 6 (200°C, 400°F). Lightly butter two baking sheets. Spoon the choux pastry into little heaps about 3.5cm/1½ in in diameter on to the prepared baking sheets. Bake in the preheated oven for about 25-30 minutes, until crisp and golden brown. Allow the buns to cool on a wire rack.

• When the choux buns are cool, split them open and fill with whipped cream, then dust with icing sugar. You should also try:
• filling the choux buns with vanilla ice cream and pouring hot chocolate sauce over (see recipe, below)
• dipping each choux bun into a variety of pastel-coloured icings to give an alternative to chocolate; the effect is a dazzling, if slightly kitsch, party centrepiece
• the most effective presentation of this cake – making several small pyramids instead of one large one.

CHOCOLATE SAUCE

I have used this chocolate sauce recipe for years. It is delicious on steamed puddings, poached pears and for indulgent ice cream, banana and toasted nut concoctions.

170g/6oz good quality plain chocolate
60g/2oz unsalted butter
60g/2oz sugar
2 tbsp golden syrup
200ml/7fl oz milk

Break the chocolate into squares and melt it, with the butter, in a bowl over a pan of hot water. Stir in the sugar and syrup until dissolved, then pour in the milk and continue to cook for 10 minutes, until the sauce thickens.

MILLE-FEUILLES

Sandwiching crisp puff pastry with fruit and cream is a classic of the French kitchen. A packet of frozen puff pastry can be used to make mille-feuilles: cut in half and roll out each part very thinly, then prick with a fork and chill for 20 minutes. Bake at Gas Mark 7 (220°C, 425°F) for 8-9 minutes until dark golden brown.

When cool, spread one half with a good-quality jam or fruit jelly and top with fresh fruit. Spoon over some lightly whipped fresh cream and sandwich with the second sheet of pastry. Dust with sieved icing sugar.

Make a pattern on the top by heating a skewer for 5 minutes over a flame till red hot, then drawing it along the sugar to caramelize it. Repeat until you have several golden lines burnt into the sugar.

Fill the pastries with any of the following mixtures:
• Blackcurrant jam and poached fresh apricots.
• Whole strawberries and clotted cream.
• Sliced peaches sprinkled with lemon juice and raspberry purée.
• Traditional crème pâtissière: when cold, spread it between the pastry layers. Cover the top with sliced strawberries and brush with a little melted jam.
• Thickly sliced bananas stirred into strained Greek yoghurt. Spread thick honey on one of the sheets of pastry and top with the banana and yoghurt mixture. Place the other pastry sheet on top, spread with a little honey and scatter with a few toasted oat flakes.

Mille-Feuilles

CHOCOLATE NUT CAKE

Although good as a pudding in its own right, I think this is best with coffee; either as a slice mid-morning, or cut into small chunks and served as a *petit four* at dinner.

340g/12oz plain chocolate
200g/7oz unsalted butter
110g/4oz each hazelnuts,
almonds and brazil nuts
2 eggs
110g/4oz large raisins

Line a 20cm/8in square cake tin with greaseproof paper. Melt 230g/8oz of the chocolate and all the butter together in a heavy-based saucepan over a low heat. Spread the nuts on a baking sheet or grill pan and toast under a hot grill until the skins start to blister. Rub the nuts with a cloth, discard any of the skins which have flaked off and return the nuts to the grill to toast until they are golden brown.

Remove the chocolate from the heat when completely melted and stir in 230g/8oz of the toasted nuts, keeping the remaining 110g/4oz on one side. Beat the eggs lightly with a fork, and add to the chocolate and nuts along with the raisins. Spoon the mixture into the lined cake tin and leave to set in the fridge for 4 hours, or preferably overnight.

When completely set, remove from the tin and peel off the paper. Melt the remaining chocolate in a basin over simmering water. Pour the chocolate over the cake, sprinkle over the remaining nuts, and return to the fridge for 10 minutes until set. With a large heavy knife, cut the cake in half, then cut each half into six slices. Or keep in the fridge and cut a slice as you wish.
Makes 12 slices or 36 *petits fours*.

Chocolate
Praline
Truffle Cake

CHOCOLATE PRALINE TRUFFLE CAKE

Serve just a sliver of this cake, preferably with a little softly whipped cream. Add a tablespoon of cognac or rum to the recipe if you wish. It is particularly good served with a few fresh raspberries, or in the winter a spoonful of raspberry purée made from frozen fruit. If you like, top the cake with chocolate curls.

FOR THE PRALINE:
60g/2oz sugar
60g/2oz whole almonds
FOR THE TRUFFLE CAKE MIXTURE:
340g/12oz plain chocolate
170ml/6fl oz double cream
85g/3oz unsalted butter
cognac or rum, optional

To make the praline, place the almonds on a metal tray or grill pan and toast under a hot grill for 5-6 minutes. The skin will start to blister and brown. Rub the nuts with a cloth and discard any of the skins that have flaked off.

Put the sugar in a small, heavy-based saucepan and cook over a moderate heat, stirring as it starts to melt. Continue stirring until it has dissolved and started to turn a pale golden colour. It will be completely clear. With the pan still over the heat, the sugar will caramelize slowly at first, but should be watched carefully once it starts to take on a golden colour.

Stir in the toasted nuts and allow them to cook in the caramel for 1 minute. Remove from the heat and pour the mixture on to a lightly oiled baking sheet or metal tray – be careful as it will be very hot. Leave to cool for 15-20 minutes. Should any of the praline stick stubbornly to the pan, it can be removed easily with a little boiling water.

To make the truffle cake mixture; break the chocolate into pieces and place in a small bowl with 2tbsp of water, over a pan of simmering water to melt. Line the base of a 20 × 10cm/8 × 4in loaf tin with greaseproof paper.

Scrape the praline from the tray and break into small pieces. Place the praline in a plastic bag and crush with a heavy rolling pin. It can be crushed a little at a time in a food processor but I find it easier to produce pieces of a uniform size using the bag method.

Whip the cream until it can be gently drawn into soft peaks with the whisk, taking care not to over-beat. Cream the butter in a basin with a wooden spoon until it is light and fluffy, which takes about 2-3 minutes, then spoon in the melted chocolate, with the cognac or rum if you are using it. Stir well, but slowly, to mix thoroughly. Fold in the cream, and then the crushed praline. Spoon the mixture into the lined loaf tin and leave to set in the fridge for 2-3 hours, or overnight.

When the mixture has set, slide a warm knife down the sides of the loaf tin, and unmould the cake on to a serving dish. Keep covered in the fridge until you wish to serve it. It will quickly become very soft if left at room temperature.
Serves 8.

TREATS

Fun food, for friends and parties is an excuse
for extravagance. These sweets and snacks are easy
to prepare and always popular

Sometimes I long for something sweet. It is usually when I am drinking strong black coffee after a meal that I yearn to eat sugary, chewy and perfumed sweets. Turkish delight will do, scented with lemon or rose, bought from Middle Eastern grocery shops where it is piled high in wicker baskets; or perhaps sticky stem ginger coated in dark, bitter chocolate.

Many sweetmeats are easy to make at home. On a cold and rainy afternoon you can fill the kitchen with the scents of sweet making: almonds roasting, honey warming in a pot, spicy, buttery fudge simmering. For some recipes you will need a sugar thermometer and undivided attention, while others need nothing more than a few minutes' preparation.

Many of the basic ingredients may already be in your storecupboard. Syrups – either golden ones in their familiar green and gold tins or scented ones from the Lebanon – provide fudges and jellies with their velvety texture. Condensed milk, that peculiarly British sticky cream, finds a home in creamy brown-sugar fudge.

Glacé fruits are a favourite after-dinner treat; I find the best place to buy perfect specimens is in the food halls of department stores in London and Paris. Places such as Fortnum and Mason in London and Hédiard and Fauchon in Paris are usually beyond my budget, but they have a fast turnover in such confections and offer the best choice. However, the crispest and juiciest glacé fruits I have ever come across were piled high in the souk in Marrakesh.

Simply-made sweetmeats include prunes stuffed with honey, almonds and ginger and a cake made by pressing dried figs with fennel seeds and almonds under a weight for a couple of days. Chocolate truffles are also simple to make: the best are the simplest, made from just chocolate and cream. You can add butter but I think it makes the truffles very rich and heavy.

If truffles are to be good you must start with finest quality ingredients. Nothing can transform cheap bars of sickly chocolate and UHT cream into a plate of seductive truffles, so use the best you can afford. Good chocolate doesn't cost a fortune and is widely available; it has a clean sharp flavour, with an almost fruity after-taste and snaps crisply as you break it.

The quality depends on the percentage of cocoa butter, sometimes referred to as cocoa mass or cocoa solids, in the finished product. Chocolate that is to be melted for truffles needs to be at least 50 per cent cocoa butter – which rules out most of the household name bars with their high fat and sugar contents. Luckily, most grocers stock fine quality chocolate such as Valrhona.

Use the thickest and yellowest cream you can find for truffles. Pour it into a saucepan, and bring it gently to the boil, drop in the broken chocolate and stir until it melts. Remove from the heat and stir until the whole mixture is smooth. Refrigerate the mixture until it has set and scoop or roll it into truffles. It's that simple.

DRINKS

Sometimes traditional drinks just don't quite fit the bill. Neither coffee nor tea is right for the occasion, and fruit juice or alcohol isn't what you want, either. Try spicing your coffee with ground cardamom for a fragrant spiciness.

For a summer's day you can add sparkling wine to a fruit liqueur such as strawberry and top the jug up with ice cubes. If the weather is really hot and the sunshine really bright, you can make sun tea. Drop a tea bag into a large glass jar of cold freshly drawn water. Sit it in the sun for several hours and when the water is bright golden from the tea, pour the liquid over crushed ice and serve with orange and lemon slices and a sprig of borage, as you would a Pimms. Christmas parties really do need a bowl of punch if they are to go the right way. Punches made without care can be less than the sum of their parts, not to mention unpleasantly alcoholic; a simple one made with a few ingredients is a far better idea. In hot weather try a glass of punch made from bananas and rum, though this is only good when served very, very cold.

For serving with drinks, grissini are always popular. A smart way with them is to make several dips and scatter small bowls full of spice and nut mixtures to dip them into. Warming the grissini slightly in a hot oven makes them even more tempting. Popcorn is absurdly simple to make, and I think, far better to eat at the end of a party, when all but your very best friends have gone home.

page 176
Chocolate
Truffles
(recipe, page
182)

page 177
Grissini and
Dips

GRISSINI AND DIPS

Grissini are the breadsticks, crisp and light and as thin as a pencil, that you often find on the table in Italian restaurants. You can buy them in boxes at many grocers and delicatessens. Look out for the tastier wholemeal variety to be found in healthfood shops. Grissini store well and they are perfect dipping material.

Set a basket of grissini on the table with small dishes of simple, creamy dips such as fromage blanc, garlic mayonnaise, olive paste or blue cheese mashed with thick yoghurt. Add a few more smaller dishes of toasted sesame seeds, poppy seeds, toasted breadcrumbs, black sesame seeds and spice mixtures such as *dukkah*. Let everyone dip their breadsticks first into the creamy dips and then into the crunchy toppings.

● To make a spicy Middle Eastern *dukkah*, dry-fry 60g/2oz hazelnuts, 110g/4oz sesame seeds, 3tbsp coriander seeds and 2tbsp cumin seeds separately in a frying pan until golden and aromatic. Put them in a coffee grinder or food processor and blend until they are coarsely ground. (Be careful as over-blending will make the mixture oily.) Stir in ½tsp salt and ¼tsp ground black pepper and place in small dishes.

POPCORN

At a party, when all the food has gone, and it is very late, you can often feel peckish. The best answer is popcorn: not the horrid caramelly stuff you get at the movies, but the savoury variety that you can easily make at home using popping corn (available at most supermarkets) served with lots of butter and salt.

Heat a little oil in a deep saucepan. Throw in the popcorn, cover tightly and shake gently over a medium heat for about 5 minutes, until it has stopped popping. Lift the lid, tip the popcorn into a bowl, and pour over a little melted butter and a liberal dose of salt, then watch it disappear.

CHAROZETH

Sophie Grigson's daily recipe column in the *Evening Standard* is well known to Londoners. Fortunately, in *Sophie's Table* (Michael Joseph, 1990), she brings together some of those recipes for us all to enjoy. This recipe is a simplified version of traditional Jewish sweetmeats, which are full of apricots, dates and nuts.

30g/1oz walnuts
30g/1oz blanched almonds
60g/2oz pitted dried dates (not the sticky Christmas variety) or fresh dates
60g/2oz dried apricots
¼tsp ground ginger
¼tsp ground cinnamon
1 tbsp honey

Whizz all the ingredients together in a processor, chop the nuts and fruit very finely then mix in the spices and the honey. Roll teaspoons of the mixture into firm little spheres.
Makes 20.

PRUNES WITH HONEY, ALMONDS AND GINGER

Ideal with coffee, but better still with a glass of Calvados or *eau-de-vie*, these stuffed prunes are worth the little bit of fiddling involved. Soft juicy prunes do not need soaking, but larger, drier fruit should be soaked for an hour, before poaching gently in water or herbal tea for 40 minutes, then chilling and patting dry with kitchen paper.

110g/4oz ground almonds
2-3tbsp chestnut or heather honey
12 prunes
4 lumps crystallized ginger
6tsp redcurrant or apple jelly

Mix the ground almonds with enough of the honey to make a stiff paste. The amount of honey you need depends on the dryness of the almonds but will probably be about 2 tablespoons.

Slice the prunes across one of the flattest sides and pull out the stone with your fingertips.

Break off pieces of the almond and honey mixture and stuff them into the hollows in the prunes. Set the prunes on a dish, or in paper cases if you wish. Slice the ginger into thin pieces and press them gently on top of the prunes. Spoon a little of the fruit jelly over the ginger slices and serve.
Makes 12; enough for 4 as petits fours.

Prunes with Honey, Almonds and Ginger

PROVENCAL DRIED FIG CAKE

1kg/2¼lb dried figs
36 almonds
1 tsp fennel seeds
3 bay leaves

Split each fig in half horizontally. Line the base and sides of a 20cm/8 inch cake tin with greaseproof paper or, if you have some, fresh fig leaves. Place a layer of the halved figs in the bottom of the cake tin, then scatter a quarter of the almonds over, a pinch of the fennel seeds and one of the bay leaves. Continue the layers until all the ingredients are used up. Cover with greaseproof paper or fig leaves.

Place a plate on top and then a weight such as a heavy bowl. Leave in a cool place – not the fridge – for a few days. Remove the lining and cut the cake into slices.
Serves 8-10.

CRISP FLAPJACK

These flapjacks are crunchier and more buttery than the gooey version (right).

230g/8oz butter
230g/8oz demerara sugar
280g/10oz medium rolled oats

Preheat the oven to Gas Mark 6 (200°C, 400°F). Melt the butter in a heavy-based saucepan. Add the demerara sugar and stir until dissolved. Stir in the oats. Remove from heat and tip into a 30 × 20 cm/12 × 8in baking tin.

Bake for 15-20 minutes. The flapjack will appear bubbling and buttery. Leave it to cool, then cut into 15 (see sticky flapjack, above). Store in a tin to prevent the pieces from becoming damp.
Makes 15.

Sticky Flapjack

STICKY FLAPJACK

An easy way to measure the golden syrup is to weigh the sugar, leave it on the scale pan, then spoon out the golden syrup on top of it. Slide the sugar and syrup off into the saucepan. If you don't have a 30 × 20cm/12 × 8in baking tin, then improvise with whatever you do have; the flapjack will come to no harm.

280g/10oz butter
110g/4oz demerara sugar
230g/8oz golden syrup
230g/8oz jumbo rolled oats
230g/8oz medium rolled oats

Preheat the oven to Gas Mark 6 (200°C, 400°F). Place the butter, sugar and syrup in a heavy-based saucepan, heat until the butter is melted, then add the oats. Stir to mix well. Tip the mixture into a 30 × 20cm/12 × 8in baking tin and bake for 15 minutes until it is a pale golden colour.

Allow to cool a little before cutting. Mark 5 equal spaces along the longest side of the tin, and 3 along the other. Cut into 15 equal pieces.
Makes 15.

Provençal Dried Fig Cake

CHOCOLATE TRUFFLES

This is the simplest form of chocolate truffle and, I think, the best.

130ml/4½fl oz double cream
100g/3½oz plain chocolate,
broken into small pieces
60g/2oz cocoa powder for rolling

Pour the cream into a small saucepan and heat gently to boiling point. Remove from the heat and add the chocolate. Stir until the chocolate has melted and combined thoroughly with the cream. Transfer to a china or glass bowl, carefully scraping all the mixture from the saucepan. Leave the mixture in a cool place for 10 minutes to return to room temperature.

Whisk the truffle mixture by hand for 5 minutes, or for 3 minutes with an electric whisk. The mixture will become fluffy and paler in colour. Place the bowl in the fridge for 10 minutes, until the mixture is firm enough to handle.

Sieve approximately two-thirds of the cocoa powder on to a tray. Take spoonfuls of chocolate truffle out of the bowl with a teaspoon and, using a second, clean teaspoon, push the truffle on to the cocoa-covered tray. Sieve over the remaining cocoa. Dip your fingertips in the cocoa powder and gently roll the mixture into truffle shapes – round but with slightly flattened sides. Do not roll for more than a few seconds as the chocolate will melt and become completely round, losing the flattened detail.

Chill in the fridge until ready to serve. All truffles can be stored in the fridge in an airtight container and should be eaten within three or four days.
Makes 15 large truffles.

ALMOND BRANDY SNAPS

These crisp biscuits are easy to make: the tricky part is knowing when to remove them from the tray. I prefer to curl them loosely round a rolling pin than roll them traditionally round the handle of a wooden spoon. This way they are easier to fill, with Crema alla Mascarpone (see page 157), crème fraîche or fromage frais and fruit.

2tbsp caster sugar
2 heaped tbsp golden syrup
60g/2oz butter
3 heaped tbsp plain flour
1 level tsp ground ginger
1tsp brandy
2 heaped tbsp shredded almonds

Preheat the oven to Gas Mark 2 (150°C, 300°F). Lightly butter a baking sheet. Too much butter will alter the consistency of the mixture while it is cooking.

In a small saucepan melt the sugar, golden syrup and butter. As soon as it starts to bubble, remove from the heat and stir in the flour, ground ginger and brandy, and then sprinkle in the shredded almonds.

Using a teaspoon, place 6 blobs of the mixture on the buttered baking sheet, each about the size of a large walnut half. There is no need to flatten them, they spread naturally in the oven to over 4 times their size, so bear this in mind when spooning out the mixture.

Bake the biscuits, in 2 batches, for about 10-12 minutes. When cooked they will be flat and a rich golden brown colour. Leave the biscuits on the baking sheet for 5 minutes or so until they become cool enough to roll.

This is where the fun starts. Holding the baking sheet with an oven glove and using a palette or other blunt-edged knife in the other hand, loosen each biscuit from the tray, one at a time - they should still be hot. If the biscuit sticks to the palette knife or tears, then leave it to set a little longer. Lift the snap with the palette knife and your fingers. Wrap each biscuit round a rolling pin with your hands, gently pressing the biscuit to fit the rolling pin.

Work quickly, as once the biscuits have cooled they won't budge from the baking sheet. If you prefer, wrap the biscuits tightly around a wooden spoon handle to make them into crisp rolls, instead of curled biscuits.
Makes 12 large brandy snaps.

Almond
Brandy Snaps

● *White Truffles.* Truffles can also be made from white chocolate. Melt the same quantity of chocolate as in the recipe (above, left) very carefully over hot, but not boiling, water. (The bowl must not touch the water.) Avoid stirring white chocolate as it can be more temperamental than dark chocolate and is more likely to become grainy on heating.

● *Dipped Truffles.* Complete the basic truffle recipe, but do not roll in cocoa powder. Chill the truffles. Melt 170g/6oz plain dark chocolate in a small basin over a pan of simmering water. When completely liquid, remove from the heat. Gently press a fork into each truffle, dip into the chocolate then roll immediately in cocoa powder until covered. Set each truffle on a tray lined with greaseproof paper. Refrigerate till set.

The truffles will have a crisp coating with a dusty bloom.

● *Praline Truffles.* Make half the quantity of the praline given in the recipe for Chocolate Praline Truffle Cake (page 175) and grind to a fine powder. Fold into the basic truffle mix when it has cooled, but before it has been whipped. Then whip the mixture as usual. Scoop or roll into balls when set; and dip, if you wish, into melted chocolate, as above.

MARSHMALLOWS

Marshmallows are some of the easiest confectionery to make, although watching the mixture thicken as you pour the hot syrup on to the beaten egg whites is more akin to chemistry than cooking. Make sure you use vanilla extract and not essence.

455g/1lb granulated sugar
1 tbsp liquid glucose
9 sheets of gelatine
2 egg whites, size 1
1 tsp vanilla extract
icing sugar
cornflour

Put the granulated sugar, glucose and 200ml/7fl oz water in a heavy-based saucepan. Bring to the boil and continue cooking until it reaches 127°C/260°F on a sugar thermometer.

Meanwhile, soak the gelatine in 140ml/¼ pint cold water. Beat the egg whites until stiff. When the syrup is up to temperature, carefully slide in the softened gelatine sheets and their soaking

Marshmallows

water. The syrup will bubble up so take care not to burn yourself. Pour the syrup into a metal jug.

Continue to beat the egg whites – preferably with an electric whisk – while pouring in the hot syrup from the jug. The mixture will become shiny and start to thicken. Add the vanilla extract and continue whisking for about five to ten minutes, until the mixture is stiff and thick enough to hold its shape on the whisk.

Lightly oil a shallow baking tray, about 30 × 20cm/12 × 8in. Dust it with sieved icing sugar and cornflour, then spoon the mixture over and smooth it with a wet palette knife if necessary.

Leave for at least an hour to set. Dust the work surface with more icing sugar and cornflour. Loosen the marshmallow around the sides of the tray with a palette knife, then turn it out on to the dusted surface. Cut into squares and roll in the sugar and cornflour. Leave to dry a little on a wire rack, then pack into an airtight box.

Makes just over 455g/1lb.

GLACE FRUITS

I find the best places to buy perfect glacé fruits are the food halls of department stores in London and Paris. Places such as Fortnum & Mason and Harrods in London, and Hédiard and Fauchon in Paris are usually beyond my budget, but they have a fast turnover in such confections and offer the best choice. However, the crispest and juiciest glacé fruits I have ever come across were piled high in the market in Marrakech.

● Look for fruit that is not sticky. It should have an opaque, crisp, sugar coating and be soft and moist inside.
● Put a dish of fruits on the table after dinner and serve with coffee. Choose one or two fruits – say, pears and chestnuts or apricots and greengages – rather than one of several different kinds, and offer nuts too, as they make good partners.
● If you have some fruits left over, chop them coarsely and sprinkle over dark chocolate mousse or vanilla ice cream for a dessert.
● Cut glacé mandarins into slices and spread on a plate, then drizzle each slice with melted plain chocolate and serve them as petit fours.
● Look out for marrons glacés – whole chestnuts soaked in sugar syrup – in delicatessens around Christmas. Eat them whole or crumble them into double cream that has been whipped until it just holds its shape, and serve with homemade mince pies.

Glacé Fruits

Sun Tea

CARDAMOM COFFEE

Hot and spicily fragrant, this is particularly good after dinner. Save a little of the ground cardamom to sprinkle over each cup of coffee, if you wish.

Make 1 litre/1¾ pints of strong coffee with medium or high-roast beans. Remove the husks from 6 cardamom pods and crush the black seeds thoroughly. Sprinkle the cardamom on the coffee and stir in. Keep warm for 3-4 minutes, then strain into cups.
Serves 4-6.

SPARKLING STRAWBERRY DRINK

A refreshing summer drink can be made with strawberry liqueur, just as you would make a kir. Allow a tablespoon of strawberry liqueur for each glass of chilled sparkling white wine or champagne. Use chilled white wine if you prefer.

SUN TEA

To make sun tea, drop a couple of leaf or herbal teabags into a jug of cold water. Put it in the sun and leave for several hours until the water is a deep golden colour.

Pour the tea over ice and serve with a few cucumber-scented borage flowers or some fresh mint.

MANGO WITH ORANGE AND CHAMPAGNE

1 large ripe mango
2 oranges
1 bottle of champagne, thoroughly chilled

Peel the mango, remove all the flesh and liquidize in a blender or food processor. Squeeze the oranges and mix the juice with the purée. Chill thoroughly.

Place 4tbsp of purée in each of 4 tall glasses, then top up with champagne. Makes plenty for 4.

TRADITIONAL HOT CHRISTMAS PUNCH

2 75cl bottles of medium- to full-bodied red wine (Bulgarian Cabernet Sauvignon is ideal)
150cl water (i.e. two empty wine bottles full)
1 orange stuck with cloves
2 oranges and 2 lemons, sliced
6tbsp sugar or honey
5cm/2 inch piece cinnamon stick
2tsp finely grated fresh ginger or powdered ginger
2tbsp of a favourite fruit liqueur, such as Cointreau, Grand Marnier or cherry brandy (optional)

Put all the ingredients in a saucepan, then heat to simmering point, stirring until the sugar has dissolved. Keep the punch at simmering point for at least 20 minutes, but do not boil or all the alcohol will evaporate.
Makes 12 half-pint glass mugs or 24 wine glasses.

BANANA RUM PUNCH

570ml/1 pint milk
2 large ripe bananas
1tsp lemon juice
4tbsp double cream
rum to taste

Pour the milk into a blender, peel and add the bananas, the lemon juice and the cream. Liquidize until very smooth.

Fill 4 tall glasses with ice cubes and add a measure of rum; top up with the banana mixture and stir.
Serves 4.

Traditional Hot Christmas Punch

INDEX

ACKNOWLEDGEMENTS

The photographs in this book are the work of the following photographers:

Jean-Louis Bloch-Laine: 35, 54, 55, 57, 67, 68, 75, 82, 83, 84, 87, 129, 131, 132, 133, 134, 140, 142, 148, 149, 155, 161, 167, 170, 173, 179, 180, 183.
Keith Hewitt: 73, 92, 96.
James Merrell: 1, 12, 13, 14, 27, 32, 33, 45, 61, 109, 110, 111, 112, 119, 122, 125, 139, 147, 153, 157, 186.
Charlie Stebbings: 24, 26, 53, 62, 64, 65, 76, 104, 124, 126, 156, 159, 165.
Roger Stowell: 11, 16, 22, 23, 38, 99, 103.

Kevin Summers: 19, 20, 28, 31, 36, 41, 42, 43, 46, 51, 78, 81, 86, 89, 91, 94, 100, 113, 114, 115, 136, 145, 146, 150, 158, 162, 163, 166, 174, 176, 177, 184, 185, 187.
Simon Wheeler: 9, 34, 37, 49, 70, 105, 106, 121, 127, 169, 181.

NOTE The author has referred to numerous cookery books in his text and has quoted, with permission, from recipes in them. The copyright in these recipes is retained by the authors and publishers named in the text and no part of them may be reproduced without written permission.